CRUSH! CRUSH! CRUSH!

Heads, I win. Tails, you die!

Jean Sarantos

Jean Sarantos
PO Box 2824
Midland, MI 48641-2824

ISBN 13: 978-0692537039
ISBN 10: 0692537031

QUANTITY PURCHASES
Companies, professional groups, clubs, and other organizations may qualify for special terms when ordering quantities of this title. For information, write to:

Jean Sarantos
PO Box 2824
Midland, MI 48641-2824

http://www.JeanSarantos.com

CONTENTS

INTRODUCTION
Part One: Prequel / 1
Part Two: Parameters Defined / 6

CHAPTER ONE
Profits! Profits! Profits! / 11

CHAPTER TWO
Gird the Herd / 24

CHAPTER THREE
The Baleful Bailiwicks / 30

CHAPTER FOUR
Muted Mutalatah / 39

CHAPTER FIVE
The Fixxed Media / 49

CHAPTER SIX
The Swipers / 63

CHAPTER SEVEN
The Disposables / 74

CHAPTER EIGHT
Let the Crushing Games Begin / 85

CHAPTER NINE
Roundup: Weeding Out Dissidents / 117

CHAPTER TEN
Meet the Fixxers / 142

CHAPTER ELEVEN
Kryptocracy vs Democracy / 150

CHAPTER TWELVE
Battle to Take Back Our Democracy / 156

BIBLIOGRAPHY / 161

INTRODUCTION: PART ONE
Prequel

We all live somewhere. Call us citizens, inhabitants, natives, subjects, peasants, peons. We have several things in common. We live in a country. Each country has rulers. They make decisions that affect all of us. Unfortunately, they do not always act in our best interests. Why is this? I believe their actions are based on the following selfish motivation:

> *It's not, what's best.*
> *It's, what's best for me.*

Thus, they always want more power, more wealth, more prestige. As a result of their self-centered actions, things happen to us that we don't like. But, we have no real way to resist their authority.

It doesn't matter what political system we live under: democracy or dictatorship. It doesn't make a difference what kind of economic structure we work in: capitalism, socialism, fascism, or communism. Whoever is in charge makes decisions and we have to follow their dictates. There are definite patterns of behavior that occur universally because,

> *...the essential structure of society has never altered. Even after enormous upheavals and seemingly irreversible changes, the same pattern has always asserted itself, just as a gyroscope will always return to equilibrium...* —George Orwell, 1984

No citizen wants to believe that his or her country engages in behavior that is willfully negligent and/or cruel and not in the best interests of its citizenry. Unfortunately, the chapters in this book illustrate that this is indeed the case. Throughout history our leaders <u>have</u> engaged in behavior detrimental to citizens both domestic and foreign. This book reveals such behavior and explains why events happen. I wish there were different explanations to very jarring revelations and conclusions.

All the inhabitants of the world have played a role throughout history. All have been affected by a government of some sort. Most have not fared well. Overpowering governmental and military forces have inflicted harm and made them endure many cruel hardships including horrendous deaths. My book discusses some of their travails and explains why they happen. It looks at the historical records. Hopefully, I have correctly "connected the dots" from my observations and offered some revealing conclusions. The observations are rather jarring, but I think they can help explain today's current events and some rather disturbing history.

Throughout this book there are two protagonists that offer their interpretations and slants on the events of history. Each has an opening statement in the Prologues: One and Two. Each proffers an analysis of events from their own different perspective. Hopefully, the interactions between the two help clarify conflicting viewpoints.

1

<u>Before reading the book, I suggest taking this Pretest</u>:
Check-off each of the following that describes the actions of the past and present leaders of the country you live in if you think they have:

___ 1. dispossessed owners/natives of their land
___ 2. kidnapped millions and/or enslaved them
___ 3. forced conversion to conqueror's religion
___ 4. starved rebelling citizens/natives
___ 5. drafted citizens to fight in wars of conquest and/or colonization
___ 6. burdened their subjects with oppressive taxes and fees
___ 7. indoctrinated citizens to maintain their approval
___ 8. spied on all dissident elements considered disloyal or a threat
___ 9. conducted experiments that endangered their citizens.

Take a Post Test after reading the book and see if there is any difference in your checklist.

Acknowledgements

For me a traditionally written analysis of events no matter how well written can be challenging to read. With that in mind, I have attempted to liven things up to illustrate my points of view. I've borrowed and inserted excerpts from authors, literary works and song; used popular media such as the movies and TV. I've made-up limericks and composed short vignettes to drive home points. I've begun chapters with borrowed quotations from well-known figures of history and literature to help set-up different slants on their content. I've put in questions [Q], to help stimulate some interactive analysis. Some are serious, some "tongue in cheek."

Obviously, the drawings by a friend help to visually capture the essence of a particular chapter. Another associate helped tremendously with setting up the layout of the book with useful editing skills. Hands-on mentoring was essential to shaping up this book. A young accomplished specialist provided another set of eyes and assisted with proofreading. Also, I'd like to thank the close relative who kept me on task with <u>daily</u> gentle monitoring and kind words of encouragement.

I appreciate the unfathomable time and effort of those men and women I have quoted. Their hardscrabble digging for the facts and stories behind the scenes helped to piece together my conclusions and insights. With access to the Internet, I have been able to search a massive amount of their sources, which have been especially helpful. They include secret government documents and recordings recently released through the Freedom of Information Act. They have helped "rip" off the cloak of secrecy and have shown the hidden secrets that were made behind closed doors by top governmental leaders.

Their well-written articles, writings, and research provided "gold nuggets" of information. This is especially true of those who have spent countless hours slogging through government records to help in their own writings that have revealed the actions of governmental leaders. I have over 150 citations of their writings and observations. I offer a limerick to show my appreciation:

Citation to the Cited

Seekers prowl like a dogged sleuth.
Thinking, "Somewhere is the truth!"
Lies they will not buy
Real facts they do ply
"Eureka!" They'll shout, "Forsooth!"

PROLOGUES

Yachta's Memoirs: <u>Prologue One</u>
Written on the Mediterranean Sea

As I began to eat a freshly caught and cooked catch, I thought of the old adage:

> *You're invited to the table or you're on it!*

You're served filet (mignon) or you're filleted! Best to be the filleter! Everyone I associate with is in the latter category! We decide who is invited. We determine your, (the reader's) destiny. If we choose, we decide how you are filleted! We don't care how you or your loved ones succumb to our every wish. We wouldn't even notice if your carcass, like fish remains, is dumped unceremoniously into the Mediterranean Sea.

As I was lazying on my yacht for six months in the sunshine, during my yearly escape from Florida's unpredictable hurricane season, I had plenty of time to observe and to think. I wondered, "Why <u>is</u> it that I am safely on a yacht escaping the inclement weather while disaster strikes others?"

I observed that in these waters were teeming lifeforms in the food chain struggling 24/7 to beat back predators. But their skills of camouflage and speed and avoidance in the seas can fail. Anything (tuna, dolphins, fish) can be "scooped" up no matter how skillful at any time in the oceans by the ultimate predator—man! Billions of fish in the seas but few filleters!

There are billions of humans on land but few filleters!" I thought, " My friends and I are on top of *that* food chain. How did we get there?" I am pretty sure I have it all figured out. I am relaying my thoughts in this book. To help make sure anyone can understand my observations and conclusions, I am writing an interactive analysis. My protagonist, "Z" responds to my observations in shaded commentary. Occasionally, we offer questions [Q] for readers to ponder. They're designed to provoke thought. I narrate this book from Chapters One through Ten.

Yachta Yachta Yachta, 2015

Q: To escape the U.S. hurricane season I transship my yacht to the Mediterranean every year. It costs $1,000 per foot. My yacht is 250 feet long. I have done this for 10 years. How much have I spent in total to ensure the safety of my yacht and me? Show your work. Don't forget round-trip.

    A. $250,000
    B. $2,500,000
    C. $5,000,000

Costs for crew salaries, maintenance and food, etc. are not included

---

Z's Commentaries: <u>Prologue Two</u>

Z: I am worth Zero. I don't count anymore. Citizens, neither do you.
I can be "conflated" and classified as Zitizen! I thought I counted. But I now
know all those "pledges of allegiance," all that voting, all that taxation was
for <u>naught</u>—at least <u>not</u> for us! Zero! Zip! In this book I make observational
asides and comments and back-fill some historical information. My
comments are shaded. I react to Yachta's interpretation of history. He
represents the dark side of "Dark Money." He and his like-minded friends
and ancestors have reigned supreme for millennia. However, in the last two
hundred years in some democracies there were efforts to reform and
alleviate the harsher elements of life. Unfortunately, as is shown in this
book, citizens' efforts to have more control of their lives have been quashed.
Their efforts to enact reforms through political action have been defeated.
Yachta and his allies control all avenues of government and corridors of
power. They act in secret to hide and suppress their selfish actions. Their
sole aim is to enrich themselves at the expense of others.

Years ago I went to Liberty Island. I traveled through that hallowed Statue
of Liberty's inner structure. Now, I recall its inside, hollowed-out frame—a
symbol of things to come? I think a tear should be added, the torch
diminished to a flicker, and the aging "Colossus" given a new descriptive
moniker: not as a "mighty woman with a torch," not even "Atlas Shrugged."
Perhaps, "Atlas Shriveled!" is more appropriate.

At the end of the book, I ask, "Can we take back our democracy?" I don't
know, but prospects are dimming. Is democracy headed for a "flat line" and
nearing life support status?
I offer some plausible solutions in Chapter Twelve, "*Battle to Take Back Our
Democracy.*" I fervently hope, "It ain't over 'til it's over!"

Spring   2015

INTRODUCTION: PART TWO
Parameters Defined

I am a predator.
You are my prey.
I take whatever I want.
I route the flow of wealth from you to me.
I suppress all efforts to challenge me.
If you resist, I will crush you.
—Yachta Yachta Yachta

The (fixed) Wheel of Fortune

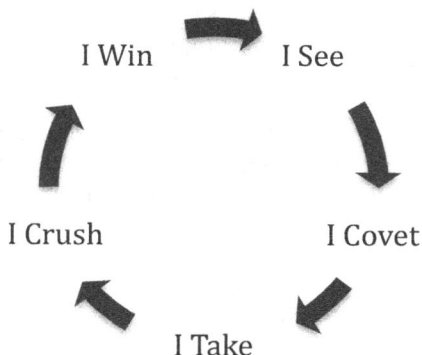

I Win   I See

I Crush   I Covet

I Take

Yachta's Narration Begins

The above interaction has been the dynamic of human history from the beginning of the human race. Events in history can be explained in the following summary:

I am the strongest, therefore
I-Take (more than you)
I am the strongest, therefore
I-Keep (more than you)
I am the strongest, therefore
I-Crush (you) — Resistance is Futile

These words with filled-in facts make up all the history of mankind with bloody, revealing, and deceiving details. This tell-all book reveals my past achievements using the above action model. It also relates those of my like-minded colleagues. It especially shows the rationale and methods used to attain what my "kindred" associates and I have pursued and achieved.

So why have I decided to write my autobiography? Actually, it's a "pan-autobiography" for I am writing for all those like-minded associates that have helped create and write the chronicles of history. First, I'm sick and tired of being picked on through negative public discourse and by some snickering news commentators. Recently, there have been all sorts of ill-conceived flak because of the way we do things. We're doing business the same way we always have. But now that the economies of the world are beginning to crumble or collapse, we're being blamed. The way I see it, if it hadn't been for us, humans would still be clobbering each other with clubs and doing so while "dressed" in real, non-artificial skin pelts!

Second, for various reasons, there is a world shifting toward heightened political instability within many countries. My analysis will help put the coming events in historical perspective. After any civil war, war or depression, we're always there to pick up the pieces and get things going again. We adjust the economic ills, and we help reset the economies of the world. We're indispensable—we always have been! You may not like our methods exposed in this book, but we get the job done!

Normally I would "muddy the waters" so you couldn't see the truth; I would obfuscate with a lot of specious, nonsensical blather to be dutifully transmitted through media outlets as "the news!" Oh, my! That's confusing!

Z: It's not clear what was just said! I know that no reporter/commentator asks any "really" tough questions nowadays that would reveal the REAL reality. OLD: "Ask me no [real] questions, I'll tell you no lies. NEW: "Ask me any question I'll tell you no lies." As Sgt. Friday would say, "Just the facts, ma'am. Nothing but the facts." Reporters no longer engage in, in-depth thoughtful analysis. [See: Chapter Five, *Fixxed Media*.]

So, let me proclaim loud and clear, "I'm 'coming out!'" I'm exposing myself to tell you the Real Truth. It will not set you free, but at least you'll know what's happening in the Age of the Great Hollowing Out and Decline of the Middle Class (especially in long established democracies). Actually, the best selling book of all time has detailed the obvious when it comes to historical narratives and revelations of what has been wrought and what will come.

> *What has been is what will be,*
> *and what has been done is what will be done,*
> *and there is nothing new under the sun.*
> —Ecclesiastics 1:9-11.

In the modern era my like-minded colleagues and I have worked without the exposure of the glare from sunshine and stayed secretly in the shadows to keep our shenanigans hidden. Politicians, corporate media and assorted shills are in our hip pocket and/or support our efforts. So I am not worried about my public disclosures in this book creating any real long-term damage or threats, if any. Of course, I put my own "spin" on things! Those individuals afflicted and affected can whine and whimper all they want, but all their lamentations can't stop the unyielding events from unfolding daily. The bottom line is that throughout history,

We rule. You rue.

We are not used to being challenged or dictated to by citizens who want governmental restraints and regulations. An illustrative metaphor can help show how we've traditionally ruled free of any restraint.

> *A wild, untamed bronco can gallop unhindered. He can run free in any direction. He is used to free ranging and free grazing. He will rebel against all efforts to be lassoed, bridled and corralled. He will buck against efforts to be broken and saddled and confined.*

Since the 1930s, there has been enhanced, concerted attempts by citizens to "rein-in" our freewheeling ways. We are beginning to "buck" the trend of ever-imposing governmental regulations and efforts to delimit our "free-range" of actions. We're not used to being "broken!" We don't like it and we're not taking it anymore! Fortunately, our consciences are not bound by any societal artifices such as the mantra, "I'm my brother's keeper!"

Oh, Brother! Keep such drivel to yourself!

Currently, in the United States, the country's political and economic landscape is gradually returning to its original, natural state (before the meddling enforced reforms of the New Deal, which began in 1930s). Those were the times before many misguided governmental efforts were enacted into law. These imposed confiscatory "taxes" to pay for social programs such as Medicare, Social Security and drug subsidies. These were foolish efforts to try to "soften" the harsh exigencies of a tough life. My associates and I say no government should have tampered with the natural order of history of the past 10,000 years. We fundamentally believe society should not mitigate the harsh circumstances of life—at least not with my dime or "on my dime!" The following quote succinctly expresses our sentiments and how to deal with the real world:

> *"Man cannot live by bread alone, but the man who cannot live on bread and water is not fit to live... [If] you are being reduced* [in wages], *go down boldly into poverty."*
> —Rev Henry Ward Beecher (PBS, n.d.)

The quotation is from the "Bread and Water," sermon during the Great Railroad Strike of 1877. Beecher was berating discontented workers complaining about a 10% slash in wages.

Thankfully, in the United States, the inexorable march back to a more *laissez-faire* time has passed the tipping point and is a man-made tsunami that cannot be repelled! In our coming New Age my friends and I will proudly proclaim, "The New Deal, the Welfare State, Social Security, pensions, etc. are null and void!" Softening life's challenges with government assistance is an anomaly, a wrinkle and a tear in the millennia-old fabric of "rough and tumble" existence. Human history has been woven though countless wars, aggrandizements, exterminations and so on.

With the current flow of campaign donations and Dark Money, we are reshaping the political agenda and placing our people in power. We have gradually "seized" the Presidency, the Congress and the Supreme Court to carry out these changes. In time we'll proudly proclaim: The Age of Aquarius is dead! Good riddance! Long live the ....

AGE OF RESTORATION!
And lower taxes, if any!

The preeminence and reign of dictators, monarchs and assorted autocrats have ruled and been challenged by opposition with little success until the mid-eighteenth century. Then Democracy reared its ugly head, and we had to tame the grand delusions of people "yearning to breathe free" and wanting to tax my hard earned profits! As I relate in the book, most history is that of ruler(s) suppressing would-be usurpers challenging our power and right to rule. This is especially true in countries where the democratic process of voting has expanded.

So now, let me show you how events in history have unfolded, and are still unfolding. As you read, you will see that only names of individuals, countries, tribes, political factions, etc. are changed to "fill-in the blanks" of historical activity. The reader can learn the practical and realistic "lay-of-the-land" and actually profit from my analysis. At least you can figure out what is really happening, and why, in your everyday life.

Z: The Kochroaches, with their hidden Dark Money, have secretly infiltrated (infested) and taken control of national, state, and local levels of government. They have purchased political loyalty through massive donations and advertising campaigns. Pro-corporation appointees on the Supreme Court have Bushwhacked us, citizens and small donors, and provided political cover to buttress the process of the "Selling and Buying of Democracy." [See: Chapter Eleven and Chapter Twelve.]

As we spread our influence and control over the inhabitants of the world, we have sucked in riches and profits from every aspect of human endeavor. We pursued and "gobbled up" the wealth of the world. We have had a voracious appetite. It is never sated! In the past we have "trawled" the earth for the following targets of wealth creation:

    Surface Soil — crops, cereals, olives, spices, salt
    Land — gold, silver, coal, oil, timber
    Cash "crops" — tobacco, cotton, furs, timber, tea
    Unpaid labor — slaves, serfs, indentured servants
    Taxes & fees — banking fees, tolls, rents, licenses, income taxes
    Loans & Usury — payday loans; student loans; credit card debt

We're still on the prowl for more and more profits and wealth! Chapter One helps to illustrate a modern concept for creating wealth—Privatization. It is a new method for redirecting wealth. The following chapter explains in detail how we "target" and redirect taxes. We have influenced state legislators to "churn" tax dollars into lucrative contracts for:

9

—for-profit charter schools
—for-profit private colleges
—for-profit prisons,
—for-profit parking meters
—for-profit garbage collection
                    —for-profit <u>anything</u>!

We have sought and won the riches of the earth from the beginning of recorded history. We want to continue to have the power to impose our right to profit in any feasible way. To continue, we must suppress all opposition to our way of doing things.

As Chapter One shows, we don't worry about suppressing any <u>compassion</u> in our quest for more wealth. We don't have any.

We do have an ardent <u>passion</u> for our one guiding principle:

Whoever has the most gold, rules. <u>THAT</u> is our Golden Rule!

Keep Your Eyes on the Prize

PROFITS! PROFITS! PROFITS!

For the love of money is a root of all kinds of evil...
—Timothy 6:10

*"It's so unfair to target people [with loss of a tax loophole]
who want to use their boat as a second home."* — Owner of
a $2.6 million yacht (McCormick, 2014)

More is never enough. —Yachta Yachta Yachta

PROFITS: RAISON D'ÊTRE?*

*Reason for Existence

No matter how we rulers gain power or how we rule, we all have the same objectives for governing. What is our underlying purpose of existence in our daily life? What is our worldview for our way of doing things? Why strive to seize wealth through conquest or corporate mergers or ever-increasing fees or sweetheart deals? What is our raison *d' être*? [f. Fr = "Show Me the Money"]. We are all about making profits and the pursuit of that biblical nemesis— filthy lucre!

Our "patron saint," St. Milton (Friedman), wrote in <u>Capitalism and Freedom</u> *"there is one and only one social responsibility of business—to use its resources and engage in activities designed to increase its profits..."*

Z: [the rest of the quote adds] *"so long as it stays within the rules of the game, which is to say, engages in open and free competition without deception or fraud."* Quoted from, **Why Conservatives Should Reread Milton Friedman,** by Gary Gutting (2013).

I completely accept the **first** part of that quote.
I completely reject the **last** part of that quote.

At our discretion and command, we change or discard rules or completely change the name of the game! Thus, our corollary to St. Milton: "Never mind, if you can get away with it!"

We love this "gung-ho" attitude of one of the richest men in the world:

> *"Life is business, and I approach life the way sharks approach life—they must keep moving or else they will drown. I'll never stop hunting more money; I'll never have enough."* —Gene [the Demon] Simmons (Smale, 2015)

Of course, unlike us, Mr. Simmons doesn't force anyone to purchase his products and says to his music critics that he's laughing all the way to... several banks! Historically, forcibly taking what others have is just the way anybody who wants to get ahead has done things. For innumerable millennia it's been the true natural order of the universe. We've been chastised, quite viciously and unfairly for our outlook and behavior but the actual truth is: We're predators and serial stealers.

We steal the world while you sing, "We Are the World." How cute and delusional! The following limerick succinctly summarizes our dispassionate concern for anyone who objects to our methods <u>or</u> is in our way:

<u>What Is Thine Will Be Mine</u>
Swine, what is thine shall be mine.
While your starved dead, you pine.
To those who cry, "Shame!"
I refuse any blame
For I dine with good food and wine!

Z: See: Chapter Six, *Swipers* and Chapter Eight, *Let the Crushing Games Begin!* These chapters vividly relate the harsh "tactics" used in pursuing the goals of world colonization and outright theft of entire continents. They relate the brutal suppression of their populations.

PRIVATIZATION: VULTURES FOR PROFIT

I am a predator and you [and your taxes] are my prey

We figure every angle to suck as much money out of each citizen through taxation, chicanery, gouging fees, etc. The latest gimmick (con) is, PRIVITIZATION. It is a painless, bloodless new *modus operandi*! It's so easy and a no-brainer to get taxpayers to pay for our grand profiteering schemes. And they aren't even told upfront what's happening! We simply donate to "bribe" state legislators and governors with cash contributions to pass favorable legislation. Then, the State governments' representatives can sign contracts to legally transfer taxpayers' cash to our enterprises.

The quiet process of back-room deals converting state prisons and support facilities [see: chart below] is a super example of how we can now legally "squeeze" citizens' taxes and transfer public taxpayer revenue into our "coffers." Is this a great country or not—at least for us!

We love crime. It produces for-profit criminals!

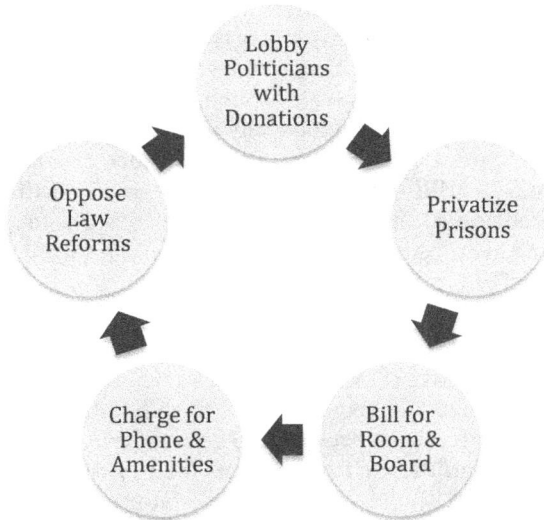

Lobby Politicians with Donations

Privatize Prisons

Bill for Room & Board

Charge for Phone & Amenities

Oppose Law Reforms

Our profits are skyrocketing with the privatization of public state-owned prisons. We convert taxpayer revenue into profit-generating machines. How do we accomplish this? Paul Egan's exposé, **Maggots found at 2ⁿᵈ Michigan Prison**, (2014) reveals our activities behind the scenes. We lobby [bribe?] legislators to pass laws converting public prisons into private ones. We promise to save taxpayers a lot of money *viz.* $12 to $16 million in Michigan. Then we:

1. Procure and sign a $145 million three-year contract with an out-of-state Philadelphia based Aramark Correctional Services Corporation
2. Eliminate 370 career state jobs with salaries and benefits
3. Hire poorly trained and low paid staff
4. Provide sub-par food
5. Set-up inexpensive and poor sanitation standards.
6. Overcharge on services for phone cards and Commissary items.

Jennifer Long's, **My Journey with Securus: Prison Phone Monopoly Punishes Loved Ones** (2015) and Timothy Williams', **Steep Costs of Inmate Phone Calls Are Under Scrutiny** (2015) provide detailed descriptions of how we profit from charges on every service provided to inmates. For example, a 15-minute call is $12.95 with a system charge of $6.95. Williams reports that, "the prison phone system is now a $1.2 billion-a-year industry...totaling more than six billion minutes in 2014..."

We just sit back on our yachts and rake in taxpayers' hard earned tax dollars for our lucrative business. *¡Ustedes son schmuckitos!*

We aren't accountable to anyone. Governors who pushed through privatization legislation have our back! Why? We've donated to the lawmakers' campaign coffers. Prisoners are always complaining and having protests about sub-par standards in the prisons. We say: If you don't like conditions—stay out of prisons. You do the crime; you do the time in my lucrative for-profit establishments! [heh, heh, heh!]

We also make great profits with federally detained immigrants. Aviva Shen reveals this in the article, **Private Prisons** [Corrections Corporation of America] **Spend $45 Million on Lobbying, Rake in $5.1 Billion For Immigrant Detention Alone** (2012). With charges to U.S. taxpayers, we make a whopping average cost of up to $166 per night. Again we are making out like "Banditos!"

¡Otra vez, ustedes son schmuckitos!

Our donations to state and national legislators have secured support for us to reap billions! We love crime! It produces criminals! They are "housed" in our for-profit prisons. The taxpayer foots the bill for our lucrative contracts with the state. The more criminals the merrier—for us!

States Guarantee High Prison Populations for Private Prison Industry's Profits (Berkowitz, 2013). We lobby state legislators to vote against any law that will reduce the prison inmate population. This objective is outlined in a for-profit public report:

> *The demand for our facilities and services could be adversely affected by the relaxation of enforcement efforts, leniency in conviction or parole standards and sentencing practices or through the decriminalization of certain activities that are currently proscribed by our criminal laws.*
>
> — Corrections Corp. of America Annual Report, 2010

In other words we encourage any efforts that will increase arrests and therefore increase our profits. So, we're for harsher criminal sentences.

And taxpayers, here's the kicker: we are guaranteed a definite "inmate lockup quota" (Berkowitz, 2013). If incarceration rates go down, we are still paid for empty beds! Our contracts guarantee payment no matter the number of prisoners actually in prison. If there were to be a massive breakout from prison with all prisoners escaping, we would still be paid! Our political donations to state legislators and our lobbying have really, really, really paid off! The continued residuals just keep pouring in!

Z: National politicians and governors have received donations from CCA. Corrections Corp of America has contributed $2,500,000 to lobbyists and politicians in two election cycles (Center for Responsive Politics). See also: **Jan Brewer, Arizona Governor, Has Ties to Private Prisons,** *HuffingtonPost Politics* (KPHO TV, 2010).

Of course any state representative voting for any for-profit prisons would have a "heads-up" inside track about such a lucrative opportunity. It would be interesting to see how many supportive legislators and their friends purchased stock in such new for-profit companies!

NOTE: Another group of "captives" is school children (K-12). School children are a great source of residual income. State testing materials are a built-in source of income. Millions of test pamphlets are non-renewable. Every year millions of hours are spent prepping students for tests. Why? The testing industry is a $2 billion a year business and heavily lobbies politicians. Nikolina Lazic's article points out that lobbying "gives the main corporations getting the test contracts a huge return for their lobbying..." (Pearson, ETS, Houghton Mifflin, and McGraw-Hill Lobby Big and Profit Bigger from School Tests, 2015). Kids hate the tests. Parents hate the tests. Teachers hate the tests. School officials hate the tests! Kelly Wallace reveals this in her article, **Parents all over U.S. 'opting out' of standardized student testing** (2015). But, politicians and the for-profit testing industry <u>love</u> them! They have built-in residuals for perpetuity!

NOTE: In April 2015, Corinthian Colleges, Inc. was shut down by the Education Department. At one time it had 120 colleges with 110,000 students. The "company annually received some $1.4 billion [not million] in financial aid for its students..." **Troubled For-Profit Corinthian Colleges Shutting Down As Education Department Faces Bill** (Nasiripour, 2015). The taxpayer will pay the bill. Allegations of fraud are being pursued.

THE UNBRIDLED "GOOD OLD DAYS" CONTINUE

"I think the enemy is here before us. I think the enemy is simple selfishness and compulsive greed ... I think the enemy is old as Time, and evil as Hell, and that he has been here with us from the beginning. I think he stole our earth from us, destroyed our wealth, and ravaged and despoiled our land. I think he took our people and enslaved them, that he polluted the fountains of our life, took unto himself the rarest treasures of our life, took our bread and left us with a crust, and, not content, for the nature of the enemy is insatiate— tried finally to take from us the crust."

—Thomas Wolfe, <u>You Can't Go Home Again</u> (Seldes, 1967)

[He] *would never get it that the raptors of the world understand only one language.*
—<u>The Girl with the Dragon Tattoo</u> (Larsson)

Wow! The above quotes are quite an indictment indicative of our typical behavior. But, they are absolutely true! We make money the old-fashioned way; rig the system to set the rules and get privileges for us. We make money without concern for the uncaring "Raptor's Way." Callous disregard for the rights of citizens and workers is standard operating procedure! It's the only way to maximize profits and enrich those with the talent and *chutzpah* to get what they can. Unfortunately, there is a dichotomy in the way people have historically viewed the events of history. Some don't like what they see and write out their objections with simple phrases or long essays. The above Wolfe quotation scathingly rejects our methods of aggrandizement! We don't put pen to paper. We're too busy figuring out how to put gold coin into our pockets! And we could not care less about concepts of injustice.

We don't worry about who gets hurt!

The following four examples illustrate what some regard as our callous indifference to "our fellow man." We say, "So what!"

#1 The Downton Abbey Way—privilege rules
#2 Enron—skullduggery and (anti)-empathy
#3 Continental Can—can "can" you
#4 Wal-Mart—discriminating tastes

#1 Downton Abbey: Lord Wellington "Schools" Whalers

Historically, we are used to taking what we have wanted and keeping it too! We never had to explain our actions. We've established our rights and don't want to give them up! A great example of our "sovereign" right to take what we can through centuries old privilege is related in an English episode of whalers' rights versus the Duke of Wellington's privileges. In <u>Moby Dick</u>, the whalers had harpooned and grounded a whale on the shores of England. The mariners claimed the carcass as "Loose Fish" for they had harpooned the unclaimed whale in open waters. The whalers had brought it ashore at great risk and cost of the voyage. The Duke sent his agent who claimed it to

say it was a "Fast-Fish" on his property and in the Duke's possession. Therefore, he stated with great authority:
"It is his."
But the Duke had nothing to do with taking this fish.
"It is his."
Is he so desperate he needs it for his livelihood?
"It is his."
How about giving us half?
"It is his."
A local clergyman through a letter begged His Grace to offer some recompense and to "take the case of those unfortunate mariners into full consideration." To which the Duke replied, "[t]*he reverend gentleman...should decline meddling with other people's business*" (Melville, 1851).

Moral of story? (We) Claim it and (We) Take It [loose fish]! Compassion and justice are irrelevant. The "harpooners" got harpooned! Touché!

#2 The Enronites Taketh: Traders Caught on Tape

Contrition and sympathy are not good traits. California paid out millions after huge utility price hikes in the market were manipulated by Enron. An Enron's West coast trading desk made secret deals to deliberately drive up energy prices by ordering power plants to shut down. Utilities were suing to get their money back. The following is the response from Enron traders in secret conversations:

> "They're f-----g taking all the money back from you guys? All the money you guys stole from those poor grandmothers in California?"
> "Yeah, Grandma Millie, man."
> "Yeah, now she wants her f-----g money back for all the power you've charged right up, jammed right up her a---for f-----g $250 a megawatt hour." **Enron Traders Caught on Tape, CBS Reports** (Roberts, 2004).

They also mused about a Bush re-election win because they predicted he would not "play this price-cap b------t." They predicted right. On May 29, 2001, Mr. Bush said, "We will not take any action that makes California's problems worse and that's why I oppose price caps." It is wise and highly profitable to have friends in high places!

#3 Continental Can Tries to "Can" Pensioners' Rights

I love the names used to disguise legal theft. As revealed in the court case *Gavalik v. Continental Can, 1981*, the company instigated the "Liability Avoidance" Program called the Bell System. It was used "to identify Continental's unfunded pension liabilities so as to avoid triggering future vesting." It placed employees who had not yet become eligible for break-in-service on layoff, and retained those employees whose benefits were already vested (OpenJurist.org, 2015).

17

Z: So if a loyal employee was nearing retirement, after years of faithful service, the company was trying to eliminate a worker's right to a pension by laying him/her off. This sleight of hand maneuver was caught by their union, which took the company to court. The cheated workers won!

#4 Wal-Mart, The Discrimination Champion

Z: There are numerous examples of discrimination against workers involving Wal-Mart. Examples can be found by researching, "Wal-Mart Discrimination." My favorite is age discrimination. Wal-Mart's Company Headquarters wanted to cut future medical costs, and e-mailed a plan of action. Store officials could not fire workers when they got older and would have more medical expenses. So, they wanted the elder workers to quit, because they could not be fired. It was suggested that they be given more strenuous, physical jobs that were challenging. They suggested older employees be required to stock higher shelves. It was hoped that such arduous assignments would encourage older workers to quit and thus lessen medical costs!

THE GOODERITES VERSUS US

Our methods for achieving greater profits have been opposed throughout history. Some see us as unfair or criminal. The way I see things, there are only two options or choices in conducting everyday life:

Option A: Gooderites: "What is best?" [Serial Healers]
Option B: Thuggees: "What is best for me?" [Serial Stealers]

Unfortunately, some Gooderites called philosophers or prophets or theologians or do-gooders have disagreed with our methods. They came up with a lot of crappy concepts to challenge how we get things done. Their ideas such as those below may gain wide sympathy or approval, but fortunately, they seldom are widely implemented by rulers or by us.

Socrates: *I would rather harm myself than harm another* [*Dialogues*]
Jesus: *Love thy neighbor as thyself; Do unto others as you would have them do unto you* [*Sermon on the Mount*]
Locke: *Government should exist that protects life, liberty, health, and property* [*Treatise on Government*]
Diwali Hindu Festival of Lights: Light over Dark; Good over Evil Knowledge over Darkness

Even popular culture torment people through song and literature to question self-centered, selfish choices:

Are we meant to take more than we give?
Or are we meant to be kind?
And if, if only fools are kind, Alfie
Then I guess it is wise to be cruel
And if life belongs only to the strong, Alfie
What will you lend on an old golden rule?
—"Alfie" originally by Cilia Black; Dionne Warwick lyrics.

I almost "dropped my plate" when I read that the new pope supports a totally bizarre challenge to the world's reality—and my profits! My associates and I vehemently disagree with the following:

> "*As long as the problems of the poor are not radically resolved by rejecting the absolute autonomy of markets and financial speculation and by attacking the structural causes of inequality, no solution will be found for the world's problems or, for that matter, to any problems...Just as the commandment 'Thou shall not kill' sets a clear limit in order to safeguard the value of human life, today we also have to say 'thou shalt not' to an economy of exclusion and inequality. Such an economy kills.*" Reported by Paul Brandeis Raushenbush (Don't Call Us Marxist Because We Critique Capitalism -- Call Us Christian, 2013).

Another do-gooder wrote a stinging challenge to my right to profit:

> "*The profit motive, when it is the sole basis of an economic system, encourages a cutthroat competition and selfish ambition that inspires men to be more concerned about making a living than making a life.*" — Rev. Martin Luther King (Braxton, 2011)

Commentary: What Would King Do?

Q: Write a paragraph comparing the two philosophical views.
Title: Thuggees Rule! You Rue!
1. Compassion for the suffering: Love thy Neighbor
2. Callous indifference for the suffering: Screw thy neighbor
Which do you ascribe to and is your way of thinking? (Cite examples.)

I've noticed that even though the Ten Commandments outlaw certain perceived reprehensible behavior, governments and societies don't (or can't) stop us from achieving our goals of maximizing our income and/or profits. The most fundamental religious tenets or laws are ignored or circumscribed by my friends and me.

Q: Match the correct letter with the event that violates the Ten Commandments regarding "re-allocation" of land:
A. Thou shall not kill
B. Thou shall not covet
C. Thou shall not steal
___First we surveyed the world [visually looked at the vast span of Earth and saw that it was good—for the taking!]
___In the morning, we drove off the native landowners
___In the afternoon we surveyed their land [set new property boundaries.]

If we adhered to those commandments, we wouldn't have been able to steal away [our way] at will. Laws and courts are set up for you, "small" people, not us! We do not fear any challenge to us based on such abstract moral grounds. I wonder who came up with the concept, "I am my brother's keeper." All these abstract ideas of love are so-called "noble" ideas that pollute and obfuscate reality. They are illusions conjured up by writers and theologians and sellers of self-help books!

Z: Recently, in the past few decades, Yachta and his friends have been trying to restore the natural order. They harken back to a time before the 1930's. They condemn what they consider the mishmash about "Love thy neighbor!" In the article, **Filthy Rich CEOs Are Lobbying to Cut Medicare, Social Security**... Sarah Anderson states that one group, "Fix the Debt" has 135 chief executives as spokespeople. Another group of 200 CEOs, the "Business Roundtable" wants everyone to work until 70. NOTE: The average monthly retirement for each member is $86,000; the average monthly Social Security check is, $1,237 (2013).

I guess average retirees should have worked a little harder! We have never believed in tampering with the historically natural order of human endeavor. Nor do we believe in tempering the harshness of daily life with ill-advised social reforms such as those listed here:

  Unemployment compensation
  Minimum wages
  Food stamps
  Medicaid
  Aid to dependent children
  Social Security

The truth is we never have believed in Social Security. We are working to eventually eliminate this imposed socialistic governmental program. President Ronald Reagan was our favorite champion to publicly oppose Social Security and Medicare in campaigns before being elected president. He labeled them as socialistic. President Bush has stated that not privatizing Social Security was his biggest failure. If his reforms had succeeded we would have made a ton of money in management fees!

The Real World run by us, usually trumps by defeating the Ideal World conjured up by the Gooderites. We have been organizing our money and efforts to counter the recent democratic onslaught on our absolute right to sow and reap all the profits and "filthy lucre" that we can. [See Chapter Eleven, *Kryptocracy vs Democracy*]

COMPASSION: STINKIN' THINKIN'

I owe my mother nine months rent!

As is apparent from the discussion so far, there are no moral guidelines for our actions. We know that our behavior has always been designed to benefit us. We do not divert our efforts even if our actions bring starvation and death. We ignore the plight of the poor and the starving. There's no profit in helping the poor!

We're not selfish—we're businessmen, not callous men—we love *our* kids, but we're in business to make money. So far my discussions should have left no doubt in the reader's mind what this following limerick professes:

> We Don't Do Compassion
> If it is food your kids lack
> We will cut you no slack,
>   We say to the starving
>   While meat we are carving
> Our profits must stay in the black! —Yachta Yachta Yachta

The notion of feeling sorry for the less fortunate is an artificial artifice. A canard set-up by the Gooderites to play on the heart strings of those who have swallowed that _line_ of thinking, "hook, _line_ and sinker!" As was related to you earlier, I'm going to "lay my cards on the table" and tell you exactly how my friends and I have "ruled the roost" since the beginning of time. Compassion plays no role in profit seeking.

Mission Statement: The Greed Creed

The following "Mission Statement" encapsulates our guidelines for carrying out our daily business actions without any emotional concerns for our "fellow man." I call it the Greed Creed by a prominent Robber Baron.

> _And while the law (of competition) may be sometimes hard for the individual, it is best for the race, because it insures the_ **survival of the fittest** [emphasis added] _in every department. We accept and welcome, therefore, as conditions to which we must accommodate ourselves, great inequality of environment the concentration of business, industrial and commercial, in the hands of a few, and the law of competition between these, as being not only beneficial, but essential for the future progress of the race._
>
> — Andrew Carnegie, The Gospel of Wealth, 1889

Popular literature in the last couple hundred years has encouraged the concept of helping others who are less fortunate. Every Christmas we must suffer through different renditions of Charles Dickens' A Christmas Carol. Poor Ebenezer Scrooge is beset by some Gooderites looking for charitable contributions: for those in "want of common necessaries."

They: Hundreds of thousands are in want of common comforts.
He: Are there no prisons?
They: Plenty of prisons...
He: And the Union workhouses...are they still in operation?
They: Both very busy, sir...
He: Those who are badly off must go there.
They: Many can't go there; and many would rather die.
He: If they would rather die...they had better do it, and
     decrease the surplus population.

Poor Scrooge is badgered into accepting a different set of guidelines for functioning in life! Do you really think a couple of bad nightmares such as those experienced by Scrooge will deter us in our quest for greater wealth? In reality, we don't do charity—not real charity. We don't even "flinch" when we rule for greater profits over starving masses. How we responded to the Great Famine of Ireland in the eighteenth century is a great example.

Starving babies, children, parents and seniors were no concern of ours. It wasn't our fault intensive farming methods produced blights and disease in the farmlands.

Case Study: Irish Expendables

It's easy to halve the potato if there is love.
May misfortune follow you the rest of your life... and never catch up.
[In Ireland there wasn't enough love; and misfortune caught up.]

We don't even let the starving of millions deter our quest for profits. Compassion gets in the way. Our heartfelt concern is for making money. We make money when we make profit. We don't make any "ifs, ands, or buts" to this fundamental principle. No saccharine sweet sentimentality! We weren't responsible for the fickle fate inflicted by Mother Nature that ravished the potato farms of Ireland and starved the population. Some say we were heartless. Maybe so, but, I say above all, we were profitable!

Z: I always heard that a potato disease caused the Irish potato famine. It is estimated that between 1,000,000 and 1,500,000 died. The starved dead were found with green-stained mouths from trying to survive eating grass and leaves. So, surely if there were something that could have been done, someone or some government would have done *something* to prevent one of the greatest human tragedies in modern times. I thought there was no food. I thought wrong! There was starvation but no famine. Food existed but was exported. (University of College, Cork, n.d.)

OK! The truth! There was food and there were food exports, too. Supply and demand set the price and if someone could supply the money, we would supply the food! The Duke of Wellington observed, "It is starvation, ...although there is an abundance of provisions in the country...[the starving] do not possess even the small sum of money necessary to buy a supply of food." Wellington condemned us for not providing free food! He said we were too busy "amusing [ourselves] in the Clubs in London.... or on the Continent" and the government wouldn't find remedy because it would affect "the pockets of Irish Gentleman." Those would be some of my rich ancestors. We made a "pretty penny" *exporting* foodstuffs to the hungry ...on the Continent as long as they could pay!

Z: The Rev. Dr. McEvoy, a parish priest of Kells observed,

> *With starvation at our doors, grimly staring us, vessels laden with our sole hopes of existence, our provisions are hourly wafted* [moved] *from our every port. From one milling establishment I have last night seen not less than fifty dray* [loads] *of meal moving on to Drogheda, thence to go to feed the foreigner,* [food was being exported] *leaving starvation and death the sure and certain fate of the toil and sweat that raised this food.* (University of College, Cork, n.d.)

Well, we had contracts to maintain. We got a lot of verbal flack and were accused of "unnaturally keeping up the price of provisions, and doing this for the benefit of a selfish class who derive at the present awful crisis pecuniary advantages to themselves," and for maintaining laws that kept the prices up. Fortunately for us, the Irish didn't have weapons to fight for their food and could not commandeer the exports! Even in tough economic times and high unemployment, we're opposed to food stamps. No food stamps (bridge cards) should be paid for by me or by my friends or any taxpayer. The hungry, like the Irish, should be weaned off the public government tit and face the <u>grave</u> consequences!

C'est la vie! C'est vol de mort!

Hopefully, I've succeeded in showing our self-centered singular intent—making oodles and oodles of money. We have no regard to pathetic protestations of those concerned with the downtrodden and their supporters. When there is adversity, you should just suck it in or die!

Why do we triumph so often? How can a handful of us rule so easily and command loyalty (or at least submission) to our way of doing business? The ensuing chapters show how we maintain control and suppress efforts to chip away at our traditional rights, especially when it comes to a lot of moneymaking. It shows why history has unfolded the way it has. There are patterns of behavior we rulers and leaders use that help us maintain control. It shows how dominant forces, political and military, have usually won out and subdued rebelling populations. We "call the shots" and rule over a hapless, defenseless world of humanity.

The following chapters relate how we few succeed in dominating and ruling over the bulk of humanity. We have to secure the tacit approval by citizens as to our way of doing things. At least we must make them acquiesce in our rule over them. In democracies we must "woo" the citizens. Our best methods in garnering support are to appeal to unbridled patriotism and to create fear of "the enemy," both internal and external!

CHAPTER TWO

Gird the
HERD HERD HERD

"We are great. We are free. We are wonderful. We are the most wonderful
people in all the jungle! We all say so, and so it must be true!"
—Bander-log monkey chant, The Jungle Book by Rudyard Kipling

"We will cleave you from the herd and watch you die in the wilderness!"
—Warning to TV president, "House of Cards"

"Our ancestors were not paralyzed by guilt. Confident in their culture and
civilization, they believed in their superiority over what Kipling had called the
'lesser breeds without the law.' This idea of America as a creedal nation bound
together not by 'blood or birth or soil' but by 'ideals' that must be taught and
learned...is demonstrably false." —Patrick Buchanan, State of Emergency

Z: (regarding above Buchanan quote) "We are all omnibuses in which our
ancestors ride, and every now and then one of them sticks his head out and
embarrasses us." — Oliver Wendell Holmes (Sr.) 1867

HERDING

Robbing a bank is easy.
Keeping the money— and staying out of jail is harder.
Conquering and grabbing land is easy.
Keeping control of it (and its people) is harder.
We rely on herd instincts and/or loyalties to help manipulate and keep
control of our subjects. I mean, loyal citizens. I can't explain the real or
psychological reasons as to why people choose "to herd" and identify with a
group—but thank goodness they do! Of course we make sure that what they
are made aware of in the real world is shaped by our well-paid
spokespeople! [See: Chapter Five, *Fixxed Media* for an exposé of all media].
Consider the following: Why do ants herd? Why do different kinds (of
animals) "flock together" and attack other flocks? Why do humans
viscerally attack others who have different characteristics, traits or national
loyalties? Read the following two scenarios and then answer the question.

Scenario #1   Ants *vs.* Ants

Henry David Thoreau at Walden Pond observed a "Battle Royale" between
two armies of ants, one all-red, and one all-black. He observed the onslaught
and slaughter, the gnawing away of tentacles and limbs. The attacking
warriors were relentless and unforgiving. None considered retreat and
none showed any mercy. (Perhaps they were fighting, as armies often do, to
capture a prime piece of real estate or terrain.) Even though hundreds of
dead bodies littered the field, no victorious ant pondered to lament, "Oh, the
hum**ant**ity!" They just gnawed away!

24

Scenario #2   Herd of Welcomers

The buoyant Partisans had flocked from all over the territory to await the magical moment of greeting the returning heroes. Despite wintry bitter cold and snow-covered roads, they had amassed: men, women, and children. They were bedecked with colors matching their heroes' uniforms. There were victory shouts and banners waving as they breathlessly waited. They had never seen them up close before. They would catch a short glimpse of their *"conquistadores!"* They would holler with unmitigated, exhilarating joy as the heroes marched by. They would probably never see them again and remember few names. They were welcoming home the conquering heroes. The foot (ball) soldiers had won the long-awaited, long-coveted bowl game title and had brought back the trophy! A TV viewer of the victorious battle had proclaimed, "This is the best day of my life!" **Chilly MSU fans swarm returning Spartans with green gratitude**, (Seidel, 2014).

> **Q: What do you think the author's (Yachta's) purpose is in including these two stories?**
> A. Show individuals identifying with a group based on perceived loyalties.
> B. Show a commonality of "herding" individuals
> C. Show an instinct for loyalty to like "packs"
> D. All of the above

Z: Incidentally, an extraordinarily loyal fan, can purchase a coffin (pre-paid, of course) of a college team's motif as an interior decoration... and I do mean *interior!* Go_ _ _ _ _ _ _ _ s [fill-in favorite team]!

BREAKING B[RE]AD

"It's wrong for us to eat at the same table and "break" bread with those who killed our Lord." — Follower of oldest Christian religion

A ruler looks for any means to maintain loyalty from the tribe/nation/ herd and supporters. Recognizing one's enemy used to be a lot easier. You could physically tell the difference between an enemy and you. There were literally *concrete* characteristics you could touch or see or hear before you lopped off his/her head or enslaved its owner.

Scrolling back into history, we see loyalty to the Herd was based on certain common factors: clan, tribe, religion, and location. But such uniformity and homogeneity were gradually diversified and now in a democracy such as the United States we have to contend with wedge politics. We must cobble together coalitions to maintain power. If you play your "cadres" right [heh, heh, heh!, not very funny], you can stay on top with a "winning hand!" [groan!] Thank goodness for focus groups!

Somehow all of the following individual characteristics have had to be melded under the collectivist concept of "nation" or "country," for at least a major portion of any nation's population. These categories are universal. Some are concrete and visible.

Language dialects: you say bag, I say sack, *nes pas?*

Skin hue: only the invisible man is not "colored"
Hair texture: wigs, Afros, curly, straight
Physique: Height: Watusi, pygmy;
> Weight: Thin is in! Fat's where it's at!
Religion: transubstantiation, consubstantiation, love all
Attire: Chain Store vs. Rodeo Drive
Symbols: tall hat, cape, cane, mascot, flag, robe, collar, cigar
Music—You call that music? Arias vs Rap
Taboos—Who do voo doo?
Rites: cross left to right; right to left; or bow down
Grooming: So much hair (everywhere), so little time
Caste: the other caste is always inferior to yours
Income: Poverty sucks!
Status: tutor for 3 year-old tracking for Harvard
Family: "You can't touch that:" single, married, divorced, co-hab, gay,
> transgender, miscegenation, et. al, whatever
Origin: country [See: below Quota Immigration]
Parent: test tube, adopted, natural, cesarean, alien (foreign and space)

The world's nations are replete with internal factions or separate "herds" that can't seem to integrate and get it together. The splintering of the Ukraine into warring factions and a disintegrating Iraq are the latest vivid failures that show the "fracking" of countries in 2015.

Serving-up Patriotic Testosteroni

We have realized that ruling citizens is so much easier when they respond enthusiastically to a leader's military actions and show of force. "Rallying the troops" consolidates emotional support and buttresses the legitimacy of the ruler(s). For example, President Ronald Reagan unilaterally launched a bombing mission of U.S. combat planes against Libya. Ten year olds in an elementary school yelled instantaneously and whooped-it-up when they heard of the attack. They were in the eighth poorest school system in the country. None knew where Libya was. A large number of them would not graduate from high school, let alone go to college. The students were jubilant and cheering upon hearing of the attacks! [Think Jerry Springer!] The resolute President announced to the citizens:

> "Gadaffi counted on America to be passive.
> He counted wrong!"

Z: Wow! That's throwing red meat! National media headlines cheered the result. No act of war was declared by Congress. Few politicians opposed the action. The national polls showed an 80% approval rating. But, how to get a knee-jerk, "Gung-ho" style consensus like that? It is paramount that the rulers have a cohesive belief narrative that garners absolute unquestioning loyalty to the tribe or country or citizens of a nation. The "purer" the racial/ethnic make-up is, the easier it is to manipulate and to rule.

QUOTAS: KEEPING OUT "WRONG" IMMIGRANTS

"The one absolutely certain way of bringing this nation to ruin, of preventing all possibility of its continuing to be a nation at all, would be to permit it to become a tangle of squabbling nationalities."
— Theodore Roosevelt   Speech October 12, 1915.

Z: He was warning against not truly loyal "hyphenated" Americans clinging to Old World loyalties and referring mainly to <u>northern</u> European immigrants (not the "scourge" from South America or southern Europe). The above quote was mis-interpreted by Patrick Buchanan. Roosevelt **was** proposing one creedal belief system. He was not referring to race.

During the 19th century in the U.S., my business friends had succeeded in passing laws allowing millions of immigrants into the country. Their labor was needed to help with rapid industrialization in our steel mills, mines and factories. Unfortunately, fear of being inundated with the "wrong kinds of people" through continued unfettered immigration, frightened citizens. Their fears spurred the anti-immigration acts of American voters at the beginning of the twentieth century.

By then, a large working labor force for continued mass industrialization had been built up with millions of immigrants. Americans wanted to halt those coming to the United States that didn't fit in. Also, the American citizens wanted their citizens to be loyal, unquestioning followers of the "American Way" of life. Many immigrants arrived with beliefs contrary to what we wanted: loyal employees with unquestioning loyalty. That's what we always insist on. Some brought their socialistic ideologies to American shores and were causing labor unrest and work stoppages.

Some refugees emigrated from countries having violent upheavals. They brought their socialist ideas to American shores. Revolutionaries in Mexico (*Vivá* Zapata) and Russia (Czars—Nyet) were violently overthrowing and killing my kind of people and taking back the lands we had swiped legitimately centuries ago! We worked hard to get all the lands into our hands! In Russia and Mexico, serfs and illiterate *compesinos* were being liberated and we were being liberated of our property—and life! President Wilson tried to stop this and ordered in American troops into Mexico and Russia. General Pershing crossed the Mexican border in a fruitless attempt to try and capture the popular Pancho Villa.

Failed Interventions: Mexico, Russia, Iraq

Z: [How'd that Iraqi intervention work out, Tomacito?*] After the Bolshevik Revolution in Russia in 1917, Wilson organized and sent U.S. troops in the "Polar Bear" Unit to Archangel in northern Russia to intervene and to crush the Bolsheviks after WWI. American soldiers died in Russia.
[Note: A Polar Bear Monument can be seen in Troy, Michigan, from the road. Several Americans are interred—killed by Russians in Russia <u>after</u> WWI had ended! [How'd that Iraqi intervention work out, Tomaski?*
*See: History of the Friedman Unit (Mitchell G. , 2014).]

27

At the same time, the American people, I mean the really true-blue Americans <u>and</u> us, were in panic mode. There were many strikes that were often violently broken up by police. Labor leaders with funny ideas and/or names led workers with funny ideas and names. We feared violent revolution within the shores of the United States. Fortunately, we had friends in high places. The government responded to this internal threat in three ways: limit immigration (the gateway to America); set-up tax-supported police forces and a secret police force to ferret out the *enemy!* [Read about the Attorney General Palmer Raids in the book, <u>The Red Scare</u> by Robert K. Murray. Also see Chapter Nine, *Roundup.*]

The "Tweeners" for Quotas

Roosevelt was concerned that not all immigrants would follow the same American ideals and beliefs that he felt made America great. In the earlier quotation, he was not condemning the ongoing unfettered limits on immigration of "inferior" races, but riled up voters were! Cartoons in the newspapers depicted a bedraggled, swarthy [Why are they always swarthy?] bomb-in-hand-knife-holding villain sneaking up behind the Statue of Liberty. We were no longer desperate for a massive influx of immigrants. Americans felt besieged, so we joined in and allowed for restrictive immigration! We tried to maintain a proper looking herd.

It's always a good idea to promote the homogeneity of the herd. Look-alikes tend more to act-alike. Political leaders can see the advantages. Immigrants from southern and eastern Europe and the Middle East didn't look like natives (not the old, old natives—the Tweeners—after Indian removal and before new immigrants). At times, you could actually *smell* them—at least when they used garlic in their cooking!

Z: "You donna eata the meat? We serve you the lamb!" See movie: "My Big Fat Greek Wedding!" which shows virulent ethnocentrisms in a humorous way. [ethnic: f. Gk. εθνικός = you don't look like me]

To achieve a more homogenous citizenry, quotas were set-up with the *Immigration Act of 1924* limiting unfettered entrance to the U.S. "Look-alikes" were favored in a yearly quota system to look like earlier citizens:

>Germany (51,227); UK & N. Ireland (60,007); Ireland (8,567);
>Italy (3,845) before: 200,000 admitted each year 1900-1910;
>Spain (131); Albania (100); Bulgaria (100); Greece (100);
>Armenia (100) first nation to recognize Christianity;
>Palestine (100) home to three major religions.

Z: The following individuals would have failed the Quota System. Basically anyone that looked "different" or had funny names—especially ending in "ski" or "i", "o." The following would have been excluded:
Marconi, Toscanini, Armani, Plato, Aristotle, Socrates, Euripides, Sophocles Archimedes, Herodotus, Thales, Thucydides, Prometheus, Pythagoras, Stassinopoulos (shortened name to Huffington), <u>Papa</u>nikolaou (developed <u>Pap</u> smear test), and muscle-guy, Leonidas (See: movie "300")
First family of Christianity: Mary, Joseph and anchor baby

Biblical Authors: Markos, Matthaios, Giannis, Loukas
Movie director: Elia Kazanjoglous [Kazan] b. Constantinople
Basketball geniuses: Krzyzewski, Calipari, Izzo.

Creating uniformity and demanding obedience are the best methods for maintaining a compliant citizenry. Civil unrest and violent revolutions disrupt profit making. Therefore, it is necessary to force citizens/subjects of varying ethnic, religious backgrounds to coalesce into a country of loyal, unquestioning followers. In the U.S. it's called the "Melting Pot."

Z: The recent [2013] World cup victory by Germany unleashed spasms of out-pouring of elation and cheering by "native" Germans for their "German" team. Eleven of twenty-three team members had foreign-born parents including: Khedira of Tunisia, Boateng of Ghana, Podolski of Poland, Mastafi of Albania, and Shkodran of Albania. They are all considered part of the German herd (melting pot)! I'm sure German racial purist Adolf Hitler is rolling over in his grave—wherever that is!

It's best to gain compliance and loyalty by not cracking heads—or cracking bones! However, we can't simply rely on the loyalty of the Herd. Tribal and herdal allegiances are often based on emotion and can change. Money (bribes) can also be a great influencer! How do we maintain loyalty? History has shown that the best system to get citizens to accept and to obey their leaders as legitimate rulers is one that bestows rewards for loyal behavior. It requires obeying the dictates of one's superiors—or else! Chapter Three, *Bailiwicks,* explains this process.

The Baleful
BAILIWICKS BAILIWICKS BAILIWICKS

It's not, what's best. It's what's best for me!
— Apparatchik

*It's organization, which gives birth to the domination of the
elected over the electors...Who says organization says oligarchy.*
—Robert Michels

Omertà: *You do our bidding, and we support you*
carte blanche! Capiche?
— Yachta Yachta Yachta

Citizens need to carve out a niche in society to a make a living.

Whistleblowing and pursuing "truth, justice and the American way" are not recommended for job longevity!

Every government is structured to maintain control through various governmental and societal institutions. They are designed to enforce our laws and suppress any troublemaker. We must put our loyal subordinates in positions to carry out our wishes and our orders. Different countries use various methods to achieve this. Democracies provide some voting system, which allows for a more peaceful transfer of political power between political parties vying for control. However, like dictatorships, democracies and various institutions are also structured to suppress any opposition. Each has a basic framework to help us instill beliefs and maintain control. In modern times many countries use some form of a "democratic" voting system to select leaders in non-violent ways. But, barring major economic collapse, civil war or invasion, the same basic structural institutions continue unchallenged in all countries. Through these controlling structures, we continue to reap the benefits as we suck up the wealth from the powerless "little" guy.

We stay entrenched and are rarely challenged. Many prominent politicians and citizens in the United States, through speeches and books, have revealed the truth time and time again about my friends and me.

> [...political parties] *have become the tools of corrupt
> interests, which use them impartially to serve their selfish
> purposes. Behind the ostensible government sits enthroned
> an **invisible government** [emphasis added] owing no
> allegiance and acknowledging no responsibility to the
> people. To destroy this invisible government, to dissolve the
> unholy alliance between corrupt business and corrupt
> politics, is the first task of the statesmanship of the day.*
> — Theodore Roosevelt, 1912

Well, it's been a hundred years since <u>that</u> revelation—a whole century since that speech let the "cat out of the bag!" Nothing really has changed for us. We're not the least bit threatened by the citizens! We're more entrenched than ever! Talk about slow learners!

Occasionally, citizens have challenged us and tried to reform things. They've demanded more regulation of segments of their society that they perceive as harming their interests. Their demands are opposed to our interests and our desires. Thus, for example, safety belts and pollution controls were dictated by demanding citizens at great costs to us. (We didn't want to expend money in safety research and retooling our factories). However, nothing has changed fundamentally. We keep getting our way in our constant quest for profits and gain. [See: Chapter Ten, *Meet the Fixxers*].

All hierarchies of various institutions within a country exhibit the same imperceptible see-through "NanoVeil." It camouflages reality. It's like a reverse "the Emperor has no clothes" syndrome. What citizens see and what they hear does not reflect reality. There is deliberate subterfuge and overt cover-up. Such NanoVeils are carefully constructed around each bailiwick of authority, *viz*. politicians, governors, chairpersons, bishops, mayors, Boards of Trustees, etc. The positions of all their subordinates within these bailiwicks are also "draped" by an imperceptible NanoVeil. They hire spokespersons and press secretaries to obfuscate and hide any negative truth. A true "Mission Statement" for all individuals within a bailiwick is the same: Hold on to the position you occupy at all costs. They adhere to the adage:

It's not, what's best.
It's what's best for me!

Self-interest is paramount! How is this accomplished? The individual leading at the top must suppress <u>any</u> <u>adverse</u> <u>attacks</u> that challenge that person's position. Telling or exposing the truth is not the *modus operandi*. We "can't stand [to tell] the truth"—or have it exposed!

Opacity of Nope: The NanoVeil

Z: The idea for the NanoVeil came from reading a passage in <u>The Souls of Black Folk</u> by W.E.B. DuBois, 1903. The author exposed the oppressive Jim Crow system and wrote of the "poor Southern Negroes" and their hopeless predicament, "… in which they live, their souls are bitter at the fate **which drops the Veil between them and opportunity** [emphasis added] of the millions of Negroes, North and South…"

The Bluffers' Performance

Let's take a peek behind the NanoVeil and see in one instance how individuals "cover their tail" while looking like legitimate government bank regulators. They try to bluff their way through intensive questioning about their failure to take any Wall Street banker to trial. [View YouTube: **Elizabeth Warren Embarrasses Bank Regulators**.]

The video shows an inquiry by the U.S. Senate banking committee's investigation of regulatory oversight. Bank regulators are being queried about banking regulation enforcement [and lack, thereof]. A perception exists of openness and an effort to get at the truth with lights and cameras; congressional hearings, and expert testimony; media commentator and news analysis. The regulators receive a salary, medical coverage and retirement benefits. So let's see what they do, rather, what they <u>don't</u> do to earn those benefits.

> <u>Senator</u>: *I want to ask a question about supervising Big Banks.....
> about how tough you are* [on them]. *Tell me a little bit about the last
> few times you've taken the financial institutions on Wall Street all the
> way to trial?*
> <u>Chairman</u>: [Dodge #1] *...we "correct deficiencies...through
> settlements."*
> <u>Senator</u>: interrupts and repeats question
> <u>Chairman</u>: [Dodge #2]...We've had a fair number of consent orders
> and don't have to bring them to trial.
> <u>Senator</u>: *...No, my question is, "When did you bring them to trial?"*
> <u>Chairman</u>: [Dodge #3] We have not had to do it to achieve
> supervisory goals...
> <u>Regulator</u>: [Dodge #4 attempts to answer]
> <u>Senator</u>: (interrupts) Can you identify when you last took the Wall
> Street Banks to trial?
> <u>Regulator</u>: I'll have to get back to you with specific information.
> [Dodge #5]

The Senator has to repeat and repeat the question as each regulator tries to bluff his/her way with mumble-jumble about meeting "performance goals." The Senator simply wanted to know when was the last time any banker had been taken to trial. None of the regulators knew. The "YouTube" presentation, if completely viewed, will reveal to the American citizen how the existence of public institutions [such as a regulatory agency] does not translate into doing the job and correcting bad behavior. Public Hearings are "dog and pony" shows to give the appearance that those oversight regulators are doing their job.

The book, <u>This Town</u> by Mark Leibovich (Blue Rider Press, 2014) is a scathing indictment of how "Washington D. C." functions. It provides a detailed view of various lobbyists, regulators and politicians at work—and at play! The political parties have plenty of parties! One editorial title sums it up: (2013) **Something Rotten; The hustlers and parasites who make up Washington's political establishment.** The book vividly reveals various politicians and political interests interacting to achieve self-centered behind the scene goals and legislation. Another title could have been, <u>Our Town of Bluffers</u>. It's not a pretty sight! *The Economist* referred to the book as "the most pitiless examination of America's permanent political class....or 'the Beltway establishment'—that has ever been conducted." [See Chapter Ten, *Meet the Fixxers.*]

We rely on "bluffers." There are bluffers in all niches, bailiwicks, and positions of society: public, private, and religious. They must <u>appear</u> "to have their ducks in order" and make sure their actions adhere to and please their immediate supervisors. We rely on their behavior to protect our Supervisors up the Chain of Command (Control). We expect their acquiescence and see no strenuous opposition from any segment of society. Metaphorically speaking, they're in our "chain gang" and we can yank their chain link at any time!

NanoVeil Cloaked

Teddy Roosevelt referred to an invisible government. That's us! We're camouflaged with what I call the NanoVeil: invisible, imperceptible, but always present, always there. This imperceptible NanoVeil permeates governmental structures <u>and</u> private institutions. It does not matter what form of organization or government is analyzed—they all have the same common patterns whether it be a committee, a democracy, an autocracy or dictatorship [<u>democracy</u> (δημος (people)-crat or <u>autocracy</u> αυτο (self)-crat (f. Gk. κρατϖ = I hold power]. Holding one's position is paramount. Rulers and heads of any organization or segments of society want to <u>hold</u> on and even <u>expand</u> their power. We want to eliminate any challenge or threat or nuisance by a subordinate or even worse, and outsider such as a reporter! It doesn't even matter what form of government rules or what the institution is. The pattern is universal.

How do we build such an "invisible" control? Collusion and Fear!

FEAR: of demotion on the job

FEAR: of exposure/criticism/loss of prestige

FEAR: of loss of income (job/position)

FEAR: of losing an election

FEAR: of loss of life, imprisonment

<u>Wink! Wink! Wink! Why Collude?</u>

"Those members within a bailiwick coalesce into an interlocking tapestry to form a shield against any challenge. It's woven with the golden threads of greed and self-survival. Any challenge will be met with a crushing blow to terminate a malcontent's employment." —Aegis

"Collusion (f. Gk: κολλϖ = I glue, attach) is the "glue" that holds the whole political /economic/social fabric together". —Aegis

Is Dilbert fact or fiction?   Just asking!

Employees must follow the dictates of their supervisors, and they of their supervisors, all the way up the chain of command. We know this. We rely on each employee to do what he/she is told to do. Each must carry out all our wishes. We know they have two choices: Comply or die! In a democracy you just get fired and/or blacklisted!

33

Bailiwick Oligarchy Chain of Command

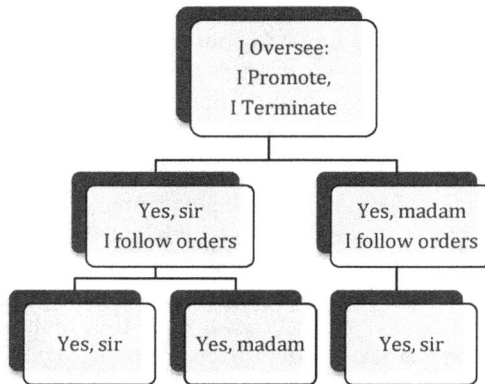

Bluffers in each bailiwick must meet performance goals and/or cover-up to please their supervisors. These include college presidents, police chiefs, bishops, superintendents, commanders, etc. They in turn must support "underlings" to receive support in return for their allegiance. If underlings "screw-up," everyone helps "cover-up." [Omertà (f. Latin=Deny! Deny! Deny!) is the *modus operandi*]. The Bluffers always support us. Why? We're the "hand that feeds them!" They don't want to lose their station in life. They're always "looking over their shoulder" to see what we want them to do. It's informally called the "Wink! Wink! Wink! System." They cover for us, we cover for them! Everyone covers his or her ~~ass~~ —derrière.

Thomas Jefferson, with great disdain, succinctly summarized his narrow assessment of each "cog" in every bailiwick:

> *It is impossible to calculate the moral mischief...that mental lying has produced in society. When a man has so corrupted and prostituted the chastity of his mind as to subscribe his professional belief to things he does not believe, he has prepared himself for the commission of every other crime.*
> (Seldes, 1967)

What he writes is true! But we count on everyone in our pay to follow <u>our</u> directives "for the commission...of every other crime!" Those who object or become whistleblowers end up like rounded-up, non-loyal Christians facing the lions in the Roman Coliseum: Gulp! Gulp! G..... [heh, heh, heh!].

Underlings Self-Think: "I must comply or I will die!"

We must control and dictate to all strata of society in order for us to maintain our power and authority. We set the parameters of behavior. We select the gatekeepers that watch over our varied domains. These are purchased echelons of supporters. They are our own handpicked coterie of followers who help to enforce detailed rules of inclusion. They block the entryway to upward mobility and monetary privilege. Most importantly, they help eliminate troublemakers who challenge us. Everything we decide to do is designed to hold on to power and grab more—all for our own personal benefit and/or profit!

Z: Friendly warning: Avoid friendly fire! Avoid the "Spiral of Death!" Do not overtly express your outrage at wrongdoing within your bailiwick or at your place of employment, especially within the government or the military. To preserve your position, carry out unquestioningly the wishes of your superiors. Do not become a "whistle blower!" [I suggest you read some Dilbert for "enlightenment!"] However, if you are moved to act due to your beliefs of maintaining fundamental ethical standards of decency, wait until retirement or until you receive a very large inheritance!

Botched Bailiwick: Wounded Warriors

Failure is an option! Nobody's held accountable!
— Sign on every government building

"It was like my best friend betrayed me.
I had given the Army everything, and they took everything
away." — Kash Alvaro

"I feel very sorry for the people who work at the Phoenix VA.
They're all frustrated. They're upset. They all wish they could leave
'cause they know what they're doing is wrong..." —Dr. Sam Foote, ret

It appears to be particularly heartless to neglect and/or abandon our wounded warriors. That is true! Our goal is more and more profits, not sentimental concerns for troops sent into harm's way and suffering combat fall-out. [See Chapter Eight to see why we deploy troops "from the Halls of Montezuma to the shores of Tripoli."]

Recall the discussion on Bailiwicks? The number one goal of those at the top running each bailiwick is survival by looking competent. Secure the job, get promotions and/or bonuses. Don't look incompetent even if you have to "cook the books" to cover incompetence. This is what happened recently (2013) throughout many offices of regional Veterans Administrations. Unfortunately, citizens get particularly visceral when veterans suffer neglect by their own government officials. Now, thanks to some citizens' outcry, we must expend many more millions (billions?) to fix the broken system that's been malfunctioning for years and years and years. I detest more unnecessary taxes! I have better use for my money.

Z: The Veterans' Administration is the quintessential dysfunctional bailiwick. It failed to meet goals for solving ever-demanding problems caused by an influx of new veterans. Supervisors ordered schedulers to falsify data and hide the true time it took patients to be seen by a doctor after making an appointment. [They were directed] *"...to manipulate information so [supervisors] could meet performance goals, which would help top officials get bonuses..."*

CNN reported many instances of malfeasance. **More VA employees said they were told to falsify data** (Curt Devine, 2014). There are complaints that veterans died after long waits. **A fatal wait: Veterans languish and die on a VA hospital's secret list, CNN Investigations** (Bronstein, Griffin, & Turk, 2014).

No head of any agency [IRS, SEC, etc.] is going to complain out loud that they can't do a good job. It would mean failure. It would mean job loss. So everyone lies or covers-up! Underlings remain silent, too. Why? It would mean job loss As Dr. Sam Foote, ret. revealed:

> *"but they have families, they have mortgages and if they speak out or say anything to anybody about it, they will be fired and they know that."* —Dr. Sam Foote, ret.

No one will admit to the following: veterans on disability are being "culled" from disability lists. They are being "pushed-out" of the ranks of the disabled. Why? It's really, really expensive to provide so many billions of dollars for their care. Military reviewers get the message from their superiors: "Cull the herd!" [Wink! Wink! Wink! Such directives are never specifically stated in writing]. Veterans can have their discharge status downgraded to less than honorable and charged with "trumped-up" misconduct discharges. Then their disability allowance will be cut off. Since 2006, 76,000 have been kicked out of the army and denied disability benefits. Kash Alvaro, quietly weeping, remarked about his mistreatment: "It was like my best friend betrayed me. I had given the Army everything, and they took everything away" (Phillips D. , 2013). The article, **Disposable: Surge in Discharges,** relates "strong-armed" methods used to terminate veterans' benefits. It is truly heartless and despicable. And cold-blooded! This seems heartless but those in a bailiwick chain must comply with the unwritten desires of their superiors and "kick-out" the costly disabled veteran. Any trivial excuse is used to "dump" the wounded recovering veteran. The online video, "Body of War" tells the intimate struggles of those whose bodies have been maimed and whose lives have been destroyed.

UPDATE: Only 3 of 280,000 VA employees lost their job regarding the VA scandal in the Spring of 2014. Only one was actually fired! **Few People Lost Jobs With V.A. in Scandal** (Phillips D. , 2015). Omertà pays off!

Recent wars have cost plenty. It is necessary to "downsize" post war costs that have ballooned with so many long-term veterans' benefits. These add-on costs of war's aftermath are ridiculously high. How can the budget be balanced and taxes kept low? Everyone must sacrifice. My suggestion: "Never volunteer!" We never do! And neither do our children!

OMERTÀ: PASSING THE TRASH

It's not what's best; it's what's best for me —Loyal Employee

We abhor the sexual assault on children by adults. After all, we have children too! It's not the crime that's scandalous; it's the deliberate cover-up by those in authority! Why is there cover-up? As I have explained before, those in charge of any bailiwick have to protect their position. Leaders of universities and religious institutions are often complicit. It's obvious that scandal can ruin individuals serving at the top echelons. They must rely on good public relations and avoidance of scandal. (Everyone knows about the recent molestation scandals at the University of Pennsylvania and efforts to cover-up shameful wrongdoing. The winningest college football coach in history and the university president were fired!) It is a rarity that anyone suffers any consequences for covering-up sex scandals! Why? The answer is simple: Bailiwicks close ranks!

All leaders of institutions handle sexual criminal offenses by suppressing the truth. They fear that public exposure will bring bad publicity. They help the perpetrator avoid public prosecution and scandal. Thus, their position and reputation remain unblemished. Why do they cover-up potential scandals? The flow of money is dependent on others to provide the funds for their existence or to keep their jobs! They must maintain "goodwill" to keep the money flowing. They don't have the luxury of being honest and being scrutinized by the public, especially when innocent children are involved! They have allowed despicable felons to go free. How do they do this? They sweep allegations "under the rug."

Cover-ups by religious institutions are particularly galling! All major religions have engaged in cover-up. Explore online: "sex scandal" (NAME OF ANY MAJOR RELIGION)] and there will be a listing of coverer-ups of sex scandals. The scandal isn't that there is a sex scandal involving children. The scandal is that every effort was made by respectable top individuals in each institution, each bailiwick, to ignore the problem and to suppress the truth! Predators were let off scott free! Their protectors covered their own derrière!

Cardinal Timothy F. Dolan has ridden the ladder of success up his religious bailiwick. He has gone from archbishop of Milwaukee to archbishop of New York to Cardinal Dolan. He has been judged and selected each step upward in the chain of command by his superiors. Years ago as bishop, he was more concerned about protecting his religious institution <u>and</u> his reputation from expensive libel suits filed by sexually molested children.

As bishop in Milwaukee he wrote in a letter to Cardinal Joseph Ratzinger that, as "victims organize and become more public, the potential for true scandal is very real." He tried to protect church assets. According to records as reported by Laurie Goodstein, **Dolan Sought to Protect Church Assets, Files Show** (2013), he wanted permission from the Vatican to move "$57 million into a cemetery trust fund to protect the assets from victims of clergy sexual abuse who were demanding compensation." Goodstein also reported that Dolan made payments to abusive priests of up to $20,000 "to encourage them to seek dismissal" so they could be "removed quietly from the payroll" **In Milwaukee Post, Cardinal Authorized Paying Abusers** (Goodstein, 2012). Exposure and scandal would have blocked his advancement and besmirched his religious institution. Today, he is a cardinal! He followed the advice: It's not, what's best! It's what's best for me! Omertà pays off, again!

Universities have a clever way of quashing any sex scandal such as rape involving their enrolled students. Tyler Klingkade exposes college officials in her article, **How Colleges Let Sexual Predators Slip Away To Other Schools** (2014). She writes,

> *[If] a college student is disciplined by a school for sexual assault, the rapist can skip the punishment by transferring to a new university without anyone ever knowing.*

Repeat offenders can continue to get way with crimes using this "attack-and-escape" mechanism that colleges have set-up. There is no trace and no law to require tracking or alerting the new college. Poof! The offenders' records don't exist! They're free to reoffend! Thus, university officials quash any possibility of bad publicity! They can keep their sterling reputations— and their jobs! Their careers are not tarnished! Their reputations remain intact! College Bailiwicks closed ranks! Omertà pays off, again!

¡Vergüenza!

Z: When a teacher was hurriedly transferred from one school to another, everyone knew the rumors. The "trash" was being passed! In the new school, incidents were observed by teachers and reported to the principal. Nothing was done...until the predator molested again but in another school after having been hurriedly transferred again! The local newspaper reported his conviction (finally!) as follows in <u>very</u> <u>tiny</u> print: it did not mention the culprit was a teacher, only his name. It only gave an address but not the name of the school. All the adult administrators involved with super degrees from super universities had "passed the trash" three times. Their careers were not tarnished! Their reputations were intact!

Omertà pays off, again!

Until the twentieth century, women have not occupied <u>any</u> real position in any major bailiwick of authority. Historically, we suppress <u>any</u> constituency that could organize and be a threat to us. We have used, and still use, world-wide governmental and religious bailiwicks to suppress efforts by women who want to gain more power and rights. They want the right to tax us more to pay for socials services and benefits for their families. Rebellious, demanding women are such a nuisance to deal with!

Cheez! Nowadays, they want to become the "Big Cheese" in all areas of society! I say stay home and make a soufflé or lasagna or quesadilla, or pastitsio! Macaroni & Cheese is good too!

Chapter Four, *Mutalatah,* shows all our valiant efforts to suppress the "little lady" and keep her where she belongs: "under our thumb!"

MUTED MUTED MUTED
Mutalatah*
SUPPRESSION OF WOMEN

*f. Sanskrit: your dog has more rights

*Women are never given any equal rights.
They must always fight for them.* — Aegis

Porphyry Chair: It was rumored that a woman had disguised herself and was elected Pope. So terrified that a future pope would be another female, the male prelates made a chair with a round opening on the bottom. Before a person could become pope, he would have to raise his gown, sit on the chair, and be inspected from below to make sure he had the "balls" to be pope!

Virginity is a valuable non-renewable commodity. —Aegis

"THE WAY WE [WOMEN] WERE" MEANT TO BE.
Bodies, Babies & Boobs

Women have been effectively controlled and relegated to their domain that revolves around family matters. Traditionally, women have been put in their place AND they have known their place. Only recently have we had to blunt their incessant demands. For us who traditionally rule, it's been a long, arduous task trying to keep them in check! They have fought and challenged our authority, especially when they are allowed to vote. The "fairer" sex has become quite a thorn for us. It's so unfair!

We oppose all efforts that challenge the stability of the *status quo.* We oppose all efforts to expand the rights of any new group of individuals. The first and most important domain we have had complete control over was the family unit. Let's focus on half the population of civilization, the women. We have used varied means to control this element. Taboos, rituals, and rites reinforce traditions. They have succeeded for thousands of years in keeping a woman in her place where she belongs.

Z: It's not until the 20th century that women actually began to develop any individual "stand-alone" rights, at least in western democracies. Up until then men, the other (better) half, had an "Invisible Hand" that metaphorically could reach up inside a woman, grab hold of her uterine tubes, and yank them at any time forcing women to painfully comply to the demands of family. That "Hand" held the pen that wrote the religious laws that established behavioral patterns for women in their society. A strict set of punishments befell any woman who crossed the parameters established by those laws. Strict taboos and established rites were promulgated and written in stone in Holy Texts. Compliance was demanded and adhered to often under penalty of death by stoning, especially for a <u>female</u> adulterer (unlike the lyrics in a song, not everyone got stoned!).

Through enforcement of adherence to Holy Religious Texts (see below), we have always been able to suppress women's rights. Historically, we have only allowed religious institutions to exist that support our views and right to rule. Religious leaders with religious councils, and their laws have supported us when we govern. They help us to maintain control by establishing strict guidelines for female behavior that curb their "friskiness!" We only support and allow those religious leaders who support our way of thinking. They know how to figure out who "butters their toast" and holds the "sword over their head!" [heh, heh, heh!]

Z: In a democracy, women tend to vote for politicians that want more public financing for family services. That means more taxation or distribution of taxes for social services. Women challenge the control and dictation of rules in regard to all aspects of their lives. However, women's rights have been traditionally opposed for thousands of years. Vested religious interests have developed dogmas that have opposed their expansion of rights. For example, opposing birth control for their female followers ensures more babies to help replenish the number in future congregations. It also helps maintain the amount of future monetary donations!

We have had absolute control in regard to all aspects of a woman's life until.......... the Pill! Of course we opposed it and fought it until birth control was made legal, only 50 years ago in 1965 with the Supreme Court decision, *Griswald v. Connecticut.* We wanted to keep women in their place and to prevent them from getting any political power. Male dominated hierarchies, especially in religious institutions, are our allies. Opposing birth control is a no brainer! We tried to keep a woman "barefoot and pregnant!" —and in her traditional subservient place! Traditional songs used to tout women's proper *"life choices"* which were clearly delineated.

Deaf Women's Courtship Song
Old woman, old woman will you do my washing?
Old woman, old woman, will you do my ironing?
Old woman, old woman will you do my darning?
Old woman, old woman, can I come acourtin'?

Q: What is the meaning of the word *darning*?
   A. Trashing old clothing
   B. Going to the mall and buying a replacement
   C. Mending (repairing) torn clothing

Z: For millennia a woman's position in society had been determined by the dictates of the male. Pulitzer-prize winning, <u>The Age of Innocence</u> by Edith Wharton portrays the late 19th century daily life in America. She shows in vivid detail the stultifying female world of male dominance and the contrived behavior by women and their "snap-to-it" acquiescence. Although the book was about the upper echelons of society in New York City, it illustrates how, clothing, speech, mannerisms, and marriage and (non) careers were determined by everyday society. Wealthier non-working creative women were relegated to the soft arts: piano, singing, and literature—while plopping out kids!

Now they want to "have it all!" Through their vote in Western democracies, they have demanded that politicians pass laws so I have to pay more taxes. Why? It's to feed their brats, educate their children and provide them free lunches! No wonder we dodge taxes worth billions in offshore banking! They plop kids on shore; we plop money off shore!

For centuries, we have been able to withstand the ridiculous, unrelenting onslaught against the accepted natural customs that defined proper roles for men and women. We (men) have dominated and ruled since the beginning—and I *do* mean, *'In the Beginning' viz.*...God was ticked off at Eve's sinful disobedience for eating the forbidden Fruit, And for her "rebellion" [viz. sin] in *Genesis 3:16 "To the woman he said, 'I will greatly multiply your pain in childbirth, in pain you shall bring forth children. And* [your husband] *he will rule over you.'"*

We used such religious texts and institutions that supported them to blunt any effort by women to alter the *status quo*. But, we constantly have had to fight against some namby-pamby writer or "thinker" who infects the thinking of some female discontents with cockamamie ideas. For example, read the following quote and then answer the question:

> *That the principle which regulates the existing social relations between the two sexes—the legal subordination* [inequality] *of one sex to the other—is wrong in itself, and now one of the chief hindrances to human improvement.*

— John Stuart Mill, On Liberty, 1870

Q: This radical idea of equality has encouraged:
A. Female activism
B. Rebellious, back talking wives
C. Equality in pay, jobs-hiring, etc.
D. All the above

We have made the suppression of women (and their sexuality) and denigration of women a non-stop effort around the world for millennia. Why? To keep ruling we must always suppress, and protect our vested interests. These efforts against women have worked until recent challenges involving the spread of voting rights. Listed below are some historical perspectives and efforts to support our dominance, demean women, and suppress a woman's demands for legal rights, equality and protection.

- Religious Holy Texts support the idea of woman's subservience to man: 1 Cor. 11:7-10, "For man ought not to have his head covered, since he is the image and glory of God; but woman is the glory of man. For man does not originate from woman, but woman from man; for indeed man was not created for the woman's sake, but woman for the man's sake. Therefore, the woman ought to have a symbol of authority on her head." [This is an example of convoluted Yooism logic. See p. 53]

- Ephesians 5:22-24: "Wives, submit yourselves to your own husbands as you do to the Lord. For the husband is the head of the wife as Christ is the head of the Church, his body, of which he is the Savior. Now as the Church submits to Christ, so also wives should submit to their husbands in everything." [Another Yooism]

Z: The book by Pearl S. Buck and the movie, The Good Earth provide an excellent portrayal of Chinese women's traditional submissiveness and obedience to a husband. It was late in the 20th century before a Japanese woman did not have to trail behind her husband.

- Rape captive women: Homer's Hellenic book, the Iliad depicts the famous feud between Agamemnon and Achilles while Briseis, a female captive awaits in a tent to see which one will win the argument and the right to rape her.

Z: Achilles "wrath" was not against rape but the right to rape a captured defenseless victim! Such actions are war crimes today. The admirers and professors of Homer followed the "heroics" of those ancient Warriors as they ascended out of their Man-Cave. Oh, the 'Humanity Classes' missed that factoid! Some of their descendants are in today's Greek fraternities.

- Rape: Military—protection for women in the military is blocked by Senator McCaskill who demanded a *super majority* of 60 votes [not 51 majority] to bring the bill to the floor of the Senate for a vote, thus filibustering the bill. Vote was 55 for passage but 60 votes were needed to move the bill to a floor vote.
- **Why rapists in the military get away with it.** (Speier, 2012) Rapists have 92% chance of avoiding a court martial. Also refer to, *The Invisible War* documentary that shows the story of a female's struggle for justice as an ex-Marine.
- Rape: civilian—**Untested rape kits in police storage**: Hollywood FL (WSVN TV, 2014), 100; Robbins Il, 176; Detroit, 11,303. Also, refer to *Huffington Post Miami*, **Hollywood police discover untested rape kits dating back to 2005: Report**
- "Abortion Insurance Opt-out Act" requires women to purchase a "separate abortion rider if they would like the procedure covered, even in cases of rape and incest." Laura Bassett, (Michigan 'Rape Insurance' Bill Passes Into Law, 2013).
- Rep. Lawrence Lockman of Maine: "If a woman has [the right to an abortion], why shouldn't a man be free to use his superior strength to force himself on a woman? At least the rapist's pursuit of sexual freedom doesn't [in most cases] result in anyone's death."

(Republican Lawmaker Apologizes For Saying Men Should Be Able To Rape Women If Abortion Is Legal, 2014)

Other historical examples:

- *droit du seignew*: Right of First Night by a medieval Lord of the manor to ravish the new bride. For a fee, the Lord would forgo the pleasure! (No Dip=Ultimate Fee)
- Lacking legal person standing: In Ken Follet's <u>Pillars of the Earth</u>, a single woman could not sell her sheep's raw wool at an open market. No male merchant would even *talk* to her because she was unattached to a male.
- Women denied "personhood" by Canadian Supreme Court. The case, *Edwards vs Canada* answering the question, "Does the word 'person' ....include females...?" The Court said, "No." But, the Privy Council of England on October 18, 1929, ruled the word person "includes members of either sex..." Until that decision no Canadian woman could be politically appointed above a certain political level. Why? She wasn't a person!
- "Passing" for male: female authors disguise gender. Mary Ann Evans [George Eliot, <u>Silas Marner</u>]; J. K. Rowling used initials].
- No right to vote: Until the 20th Century women could not vote. Wyoming was the first place on Earth to allow women to vote.
- Dowry paid by woman's family or else she won't get a husband. (Pay to Dump—arranged marriage).
- **Indian woman and baby burned alive for dowry...** Harmeet Shah Singh, CNN News (2014).
- Male birth preference: When Michael Corleone in *The Godfather* is told his wife had a miscarriage, he angrily demanded to know, "Was it a boy?" He didn't ask about his wife. Today, many mothers are relieved when their first-born is a boy. (Boy—Smile; Girl—Frown)
- Termination of female embryo: Villages in India are being de-populated without females and potential brides due to imaging scans showing a female fetus. Husbands demanding abortion ensures a projected imbalance. No Dowry=Motivation
- Unwanted females: abandoned female babies had been placed on bridges in China to be picked-up in pre-communist China.
- Married women in India have a Tikka Dot on their face to show they are claimed by marriage.
- Damaged ovaries! Stop driving! **Top Saudi cleric says women who drive risk damaging ovaries.** "If a woman drives a car, not out of pure necessity, that could have negative physiological impacts as functional and physiological medical studies show that it automatically affects the ovaries and pushes the pelvis upwards." (McDowell, 2013)
- Women cannot get drivers' licenses and are forbidden to drive in many countries.

Also, we have dictated how we want our women to look and behave. Today, we earn billions profiting in various ways by promoting female body alterations to meet our envisioned ideal female.

We make a pretty profit, prettifying the female body! Read on.

DEXTERous ALTERATIONS

(altered) CHINS UP— (fixed) SMILES ON (f. Hunger Games)

Trophy Wife: a woman bolstering man's __inflated__ ego and/or __deflated__ anatomy. — Aegis

Décolletage: f. Fr = Hanging Boobs

The best way to keep women "in their place" and keep them subservient is to determine what their role is and how they should look to please us. We need to divert them so they don't get too rambunctious. Women in western nations have gradually been freer to express their sexuality and alter their natural body to fit our desires. It amazes me to what extreme some females will go to obtain and maintain our approval.

Idealized, contrived beauty by men, instantly labels a woman as a "good" catch and keeps her in a constant "tizzy" to "please her man," lover etc. Of course we **object**ify women. If we object to how they look and behave—We Object—(heh, heh, heh!) We judge women by three adjectives: booby, boobier, boobiest! Consider the following stories that buttress my views.

- Women as sirens. *Detroit Free Press:* **Cleavage** [décolletage] **Rules! Enduring allure of women's figures gives them some measure of control over their lives.** (Kovanis, 2014)
  "Sliced and diced" bodies: females have used a varied list of methods to alter their: weight, boobs, [enlarge or shrink], face: crow's feet, eyelids, teeth [straighten and whiten], chin tuck, sanding, Botox, etc.
- Venezuelan teenage beauty contestant sews a patch on her tongue to make it painful to swallow solids in order to lose weight. Good Girl! Thin, but not too thin! (Murphy, 2014).
- Retouched dangerously thin magazine models as seen on the Internet: [View: **You'd Be Shocked at What These Fashion Editors Are Editing Out of their Photos,** *HuffingtonPost,* (Wade, 2014)]; View Images: Leah Hardy, former editor of *Cosmopolitan's* exposé telling how she retouched "frighteningly thin" models. [Click on pictures]
- Foot fetish and torture—High heels [oh, my aching feet]. Painful binding of feet of Chinese girls to make "three-inch golden lotuses" shape [Research: Chinese foot binding]. Toes are broken and bound underneath with bandages. A woman was not marriage eligible without dictated deformity. Now that is a foot fetish! Also, the difficulty in walking increased dependency and restrictions.

- Beauty Pageants for 3-year-olds and on up! One mother had a make-up consultant, hair stylist, music coach, dance coach, and costume maker for a six year old!
- Trophy wives! If all the above efforts fail to meet our specifications we can jettison the old wife for a new jet setter! Because we have the money and the option, we dump our wives for someone 25-35 years younger. (Research Family Values advocates: Clint Eastwood, Donald Trump, Newt Gingrich, Rush Limbaugh.)

Q: Make a graph: Total-up the number of wives each of the above persons has had and make a BAR GRAPH. Also, Research and make a LINE GRAPH showing the age differentiation between each with his latest wife. Title: TROPHY WIVES

Best Snagged Trophy Wife

My good friend and fellow yachtsman, Ari, snagged the #1 best trophy wife of all time: Jackie-O-oh-oh! Imagine! She threw away her citizenship, (or at least put it in dry dock), tossed out one ancient religion for another ancient religion (learned a reversal in hand cross-making), and maintained respectability! The paparazzi had a field day at their wedding! I always wondered how he had rekindled their old friendship. Years ago she had visited him on his private yacht, away from prying eyes, on the Mediterranean while vacationing away from the White House.

Ari, you old dog, you!

Another good friend of mine had hoped his son's pursuit of the British icon, Diana, would result in marriage, and respectability and citizenship for him. It's tragic he didn't achieve his goals—and lost his son and a hoped-for ticket purchase to British citizenship and respectability.

LIBIDO HAS TO GO-GO! SHUT IT DOWN!

We have tried several ways to suppress a female's libido that we believe will help stabilize traditions and the family and keep the little lady "under our thumb!"

- Virginity (hymen intact) must be assured for marriage. (This is also a good "bargaining chip.")
- Clitoris mutilation cutting usually done by a female relative. This unsanitary procedure seals off a girl and just leaves a hole for urinating and menstruation. It is reopened for marriage and sex!
- Women's body parts covered to forestall or eliminate temptation that might corrupt a man by a shameless seductress.
  - Ancient Persian stonewall reliefs show women being hanged by their hair for failure to cover it!
  - In modern Iran, (21st century) Morality Police forced a clothing storeowner to saw off the "breasts" of shapely mannequins displaying the latest Parisian fashions!
- Chastity Belts installed by soldiers during the Crusades.

- Of course the usual efforts to control "promiscuous" women:
  - no divorce
  - no birth control
  - no abortion
  - no sex education
  - no pre-marital s_x
  - husband's right to sole custody
  - widows can't remarry
  - public shaming and stoning of sinful women
- Identity through husband: Mrs. John Smith *nee* Jones
- Control freaks on steroids! There are veils and then there is a mesh veil! A mesh veil cuts off any peripheral vision so a woman must look directly at an object to see it. [Refer to Internet Images to see mesh veil]. Thus a husband, or her escort, can see <u>exactly</u> what she is looking at. At least such control freaks are honest in their intent!
- The line, "Her Eyes are just kept to herself," is from the lyrics of the Rolling Stones song, "She's under my Thumb." The lyrics perfectly encapsulate our view of the ideal submissive women and our efforts to control them. [View Internet for song lyrics]
  Z: Do theses iconic singers really think of women this way?!
- In many countries women must be escorted and monitored 24/7 by a male escort outside the home.
- The "sins of the father" and other men is discouraged through admonition of bad behavior. <u>The Scarlet Letter</u> by Nathaniel Hawthorne tells of colonial life that shames the woman, Hester, for adultery. "A" for adultery is sewed on her clothing. Her lover, the minister, allows her to go unwed and her child fatherless!
- A Hobby Lobby lawsuit against the Affordable Care Act argues in a brief to the court: "Thus, it has come to pass that **the widespread use of contraceptives has indeed harmed women physically, emotionally, and spiritually...**" [emphasis added]. Thus, the suit argued birth control should not be covered. The plaintiffs won!
- Birth control was illegal until the Supreme Court decision *Griswold v. Connecticut*, 1965—protected right to privacy, 7-2. [View on Internet: <u>The Margaret Sanger Story</u> by Peter Bagge—first birth control clinic in Brooklyn]. In the past it was against the law, and therefore illegal to speak in public about birth control. Public speakers were arrested!
- "Philomena" movie portrays attitude toward unwed mothers not being allowed to keep babies. The mother stayed with nuns for one year and then was forced to give-up her child.

WARNING to Single Women: "The grandmotherly message of yesterday is still true today: Men won't buy the cow if the milk is free." Susan Patton, *The Wall Street Journal* (A Little Valentine's Day Straight Talk, 2014).

Stieve's List
Shut that thing down

It amazes me that so many learned, educated men are "scientifically" driven to examine and theorize about women's functioning body parts and reproductive organs. To my way of thinking, it's a big waste of time. Even the Greek philosopher Aristotle thought only women got *hysterical* due to their physical reproductive organs. Thus the word (Gk, *υστερία)* hysteria was coined. (It's true the Greeks have a word for *everything!*) I wonder if a *hysterectomy* has stopped a woman from "freaking out!"

Senate candidate Todd Akin blew his chances to win a Senate seat due to his remarks about women not getting pregnant during rape. Supposedly extreme stress would "shut that thing down." Where did he get such whacko ideas? [**Aiken rape theory rooted in Nazi death camp experiment,** *Raw Story.* (Edwards).]

Just because someone like me opposes women's rights doesn't mean I support every whacko's theory. The Gestapo (secret police) of Nazi Germany rounded up resisters as spies who were condemned to death for treason. Female prisoners were turned over to medical doctors such as Dr. Hermann Stieve for experimentation while alive to see what effect stress would have on them. When women were tracked and ready to menstruate, they were told ahead of time what date they were scheduled to be executed in order to create extreme stress and anxiety in the condemned. "Upon the woman's execution, her pelvic organs were removed for examination." Herr Doktor wanted to determine whether a woman's menstrual cycle could be interrupted due to extreme stress! Shades of Aiken!

Other female bodies were sent to prestigious university anatomy labs. "The University of Vienna had a special streetcar hearse that delivered female cadavers direct from the execution chamber…" A researcher, Dr. Sabine Hildebrandt, has identified 31 anatomical departments at universities under German Nazi control that "received bodies of the executed from the execution chambers." He read the letters of the condemned. An article by Victoria Gill revealed the ghastly experiments. **Victims of Nazi anatomist named** (2013).

One letter to a mother reads,

> *As a last wish I have asked that my 'material' substance be left to you. If possible, bury me in a beautiful place amidst sunny nature.* —Libertas Schulze-Boyse.

Her cremated ashes were "dumped" and she became soot from the smokestacks. No doubt her captors had a good guffaw over the letter to her mother and her request.

I really see it as a waste of time and energy pursuing such experiments. Scarce resources were wasted during wartime. Surely there was a better use of such female captives and all rounded up innocent civilians. We could have generated very lucrative profits as we have always done with captive slaves!

A lot of the European Nazi leaders enriched themselves by confiscating the riches of those they rounded up and exterminated. The movie, "Woman in Gold," graphically illustrates how this was done. The SS Troops had a lucrative enterprise sending captive men to industrial hubs. They made good profit with dozens of businesses. Of course with slave labor, it is easy to make money. And of course, no slaves had to be purchased.

Those Nazi nuts really screwed up the world by launching a devastating war (1939-1945). A lot of our property and assets (billions and billions) were destroyed. And, of course, a lot of people died; let's not forget that!

Unfortunately, there was a lot of political instability around the world after the war ended. We had to organize our "propaganda machine" to help shape the citizens' opinions and support our efforts to crush opposition to our continued rule. We have used all media venues to deliver our point of views to citizens. And it's a fact that we have always needed to "shape" citizens' opinions in a democracy. We have advanced from controlling and suppressing women's rights to doing the same to all citizens—everywhere!

Chapter Five, *The Fixxed Media*, discusses how we have created a vast network of manipulated and invented "truth." We fear the adage: "The truth will set you free" [John 8:32]. That's why we determine our "truth" that we want you to hear and to believe. We get "a little help" from our Fixxed Media friends. Actually, we get a ton of help! Their messaging delivers what we want you, the citizens to know. In Russia the truth is called Правда [*Pravda*]. We call it propaganda.

CHAPTER FIVE

The
FIXXED FIXXED FIXXED
MEDIA
Manufacture and Engineering of Consent

"Elite media features elite power."
— Phil Donahue

The
FiXXED FiXXED FiXXED
MEDIA

"Look out Kid, they keep it all hid!"
— Bob Dylan, Subterranean Homesick Blues

He who tells the truth is chased from many villages! — Old World proverb

*During the times of universal deceit, telling the truth
becomes a revolutionary act* —George Orwell, 1984

*Humpty Dumpty smiled contemptuously, "When I use a word...it means just
what I choose it to mean—neither more nor less."*
*"The question is," said Alice, "whether you CAN make words mean so many
different things."*
*"The question is," said Humpty Dumpty, "which is to be **master** [emphasis
added]—that's all."*   — Through the Looking Glass by Lewis Carol

MASTERS OF THE [MEDIA] UNIVERSE

Dictatorships: the State controls everything.
The State owns all media, press, TV, etc.
The published "truth" is the slanted truth.
   Of course, dictators can close down any news outlet and imprison media
personnel and editors who don't comply with their dictates.
   Democracies: private ownership dominates.
Private owners own all media, press, TV, etc.
The published "truth" is their slanted truth.
   Of course, owners can fire and dismiss any editors or reporters who don't
comply with their dictates.
   Corporations run major news outlets in democracies. What is their
number one goal? It's not enlightening the citizens with some version of
press freedom. It's profitability! Each has a legal fiduciary duty to show a
profit for their stockholders. Making money is their primary obligation.
That makes a lot of sense to me. My friends need to make money. But, their
number two goal is using their power to shape the news content of their
media outlets. They decide what reporters can report to the reading public.
Each media outlet constructs its own "bailiwick" of hired personnel. They
must support the dictates of the owners. Freedom of the Press does not
mean Honesty of the Press. Let me explain. The following analogy helps to
explain the limits of "press freedom."
   If you play in a band the Band Director selects the songs. Then you play
your part according to the music. If you deviate from the established notes,
you are ostracized, banned from performing. It's like Lisa in her school band
on "The Simpsons" when she played an independent musical interpretation.
The band leader "showed her the door!" Gone! Fired! There was no room
for improvisation.

Of course the real world isn't a band. But, it's run like one in the media outlets. It is <u>we</u>, my friends and I, who own and/or control media outlets. We dictate and tell our hired employees:

- what to "play"
- how to "play"
- how long to "play"

Likewise, we determine what truth is and how it is to be reported. We are the media world. We own the media.

Who do we own? *Anyone* we give a paycheck to:

- Reporters
- Commentators
- Performers
- Sunday morning panelists.

There's a short (not long) string attached to any news broadcaster or reporter! Actually, it's a chain. We own every link! We say to our paid hires, "You have 'forged it in life' submitting to our guidelines, our parameters, for your pay. No one forced you to! You have learned…if you're still employed, but especially if you've been fired, that, 'It's *our way or the highway!*'"

MEDIA BLACKOUT: ENGINEERED TRUTH

Most people in western democracies have been inculcated with a fundamental concept that there is a free press that always reports the truth to its citizens. Do you believe in Freedom of the Press? We don't. Read the following quote. It should end the delusional belief that America's media owners always search for the truth and then inform their readers. Consider the following quote "straight from the horse's mouth!"

Secrecy and the Press

"We live in a dirty and dangerous world. There are some things the general public does not need to know and shouldn't. I believe democracy flourishes when the government can take legitimate steps to keep its secrets and ***when the press can decide whether to print what it knows."*** [emphasis added]

— Martha Graham, Editor, *The Washington Post,* 1988 Speech to CIA recruits (WantToKnow) **Owner Katharine Graham Advocates Secrecy in Press and Government**.

Friends of mine, media owners and their hired editors, decide what to print. They publish in our best interests and you, the public, by design do not even know what's going on!

Journalism 101   "Getting Schooled"

Z: The Interview

<u>Who</u>? Martha Graham the owner of the influential and oft-quoted *Washington Post.*

<u>When</u>? 1988

<u>Where</u>? CIA Headquarters

<u>What</u>? Gave "Secrecy and the Press" speech
<u>Why</u>? Profess loyalty to truthful obfuscation

Dialogue gleaned from the Cloud. Thank you, NSA
      Reporter: As citizens don't we have a right to know?
      CIA spokesperson: You can't stand the truth!
      Ms Graham: Ditto that!
      Reporter: But, but.....
      Graham and CIA chorused: It's called "protecting America! Ask
        Senator Feinstein."
      Reporter: What are you protecting?
      Graham: Freedom
      Interviewer: Freedom for whom? Define freedom.
[Voice off camera: "Never mind his fingerprints! We have his coordinates! And NSA will help out!"]

We're the true <u>Masters of Deceit</u>. Our guidelines for the media are simple. Support all efforts to suppress all challenges, domestic or foreign, to our right way of thinking. Then, you will be accepted and well-paid and lauded as Peter Hart points out in his article, **Media Millionaires: Journalism by and for the 0.01 Percent** (2013). Those invited to the annual Correspondent's Club dinner are headed in the lucrative right direction! Everyone laugh: Ha! Ha! Ha! Obviously we can't let the truth out unless we're cracking jokes—no one takes it seriously when everyone is laughing. Our approved media "mouthpieces" don't let facts and reality curtail the "truth." They correctly deliver our message and points of view with a straight face!

Z: Let's have a little levity
      DickHead* and Karl (never-ending news commentators)
* dickhead: a stupid, irritating, or ridiculous person [not to be confused with "dicky bird" (a little bird)]

Karl: Who are you?
Dick: Yes! Yes! Yes! I'm the "yes man!"
Karl: No! No! No! I ask, "Who are you?
Dick: I am the "Yes Man"
Karl: Where do you come from?
Dick: I come from Poll Land
Karl: What did you do there?
Dick: I "yessed" for Bill & Hillary, Inc.
Karl: Will it work here?
Dick: Yes! Yes! Yes!
          After several bad polling fiascos, 2012
Karl: You must Go! Go! Go!
Dick: Why? Why? Why? Just because lately I have had extraordinarily inaccurate poll results and make the wrong calls?
Karl: Yes! Yes! Yes!

Dick: Will you Go! Go! Go! too?

Karl: No! No! No! Someone has to stay and say Yes! Yes! Yes!

Dick: But, you keep getting it all wrong, too (esp. Election Night) and still manage to keep being interviewed and quoted as an expert!

Karl: I study Friedman * and Kristol. Those experts get it all wrong too.

Dick: Whom can I work for? I need a new gig.

Karl: <u>Anyone</u> running for president. Just don't say, "Nein Nein Nein!"

* See: "A History of "Friedman Unit" (Mitchell G. , 2014)

I say don't bite the hand that (controls and) feeds you! We want the media tame, not lame. Many critics complain about bad reporting, or lack of it. Reporters know who is "buttering" their toast, and they follow their proscribed script to make sure that **they** aren't "toast!" The public should quit blaming reporters and news commentators! They do what we pay them to do. They must follow our dictates or suffer the consequences! See friendly warning below:

z: Don't get yourself Donahued!

donahue v. 1. to terminate a non-complying political commentator: Martin was donahued for honest, but acerbic analysis of political and current events. 2. v. to be schooled

A leaked MSNBC Memo suggested that Phil Donahue be terminated from his talk show because he broadcasted his opposition to the then imminent Gulf War. He would "be a difficult public face for NBC in a time of war." (Kluger, 2005). A more detailed account is provided by Chris Hedges, **The Day That TV News Died**, *Truthdig* (2013).

Q: Read the following two poems. Discuss which "reporter" you think made the best life choice.

#1 (Ex) Reporter's Lament
> One day I thought to write the truth.
> But my editor did yell, "Forsooth!"
>> While I so insisted,
>> Soon I was blacklisted.
> Now I report from freezing Duluth!

#2 The Chiseller
> The paid epitaph inscriber chiseled "for them **whatever they wished**" [emphasis added]... upon the tombstone even after realizing the truth of those that died.
>> "But still I chiseled whatever they paid me to chisel
>> And made myself party to the false chronicles
>> Of the stones,
>> Even as the historian does who writes
>> Without knowing the truth,
>> Or because he is influenced to hide it."
>>> <u>Spoon River Anthology</u> "Richard Bone" by Edgar Lee Masters

Establishment Choristers

Z: Reporters make "Faustian" pacts with owners that cover-up and/or minimize the truth about world occurrences that their governments engage in. John Pilger quotes a former British government spokesman: "*We would control access to the foreign secretary as a form of reward to journalists. If they were critical, we would not give them the goodies of trips around the world. We would feed them factoids of **sanitized intelligence** [emphasis added] or we'd freeze them out.*" (Pilger, The accessories to war crimes are those paid to keep the record straight, 2014) [Sourced through *Truth-out*].

We couldn't have the truth about military "excesses" in the Iraq War. We did not want the citizens to turn against our war efforts. Our news outlets for almost a decade have used the term "enhanced interrogation" [not saying the word which cannot be spoken...T_ _ _ _ _ _ _] by reporters/commentators.

The Elephant in the Dungeon
None dare call it torture!
Who knew?
Yoo* knew!
Media too!

Z: More levity: "It only hurts if you laugh!"
Prisoner: Ouch, that hurts! Please, sir, no more!
Guard: O. K. No more torture.
Prisoner: Really? Thank you.
Guard: Now, only <u>enhanced</u> <u>interrogation</u> techniques.
Prisoner: What does that mean?
Guard: Yoo* [Yooism p. 53] tell me! Beats me! —I mean you! It only
       hurts if you laugh with that cracked rib!
  It's ludicrous that no one in the media will call it:
t _ _ _ _ _ Huh! What's turtle got to do with it? Is that a benign euphemism? "He was turtled!" That doesn't sound right! It sounds kind of cute! Better than tortured.

YOOISM* par excellence!
YOOISM: a legalese-convoluted logic creating a non-existent reality and transforming it into a plausible logical fact or action to justify an illegal and/or immoral course of action.
Professor John Yoo is teaching law at the University of Berkeley Law School. He provided written legal position papers for the Bush administration to give the CIA personnel legal coverage to "turtle" terrorist suspects without calling it torture. Professor Yoo:

"There is always someone around to make any crazy claim you want, and if you are the ruling party, intellectuals will crawl out of the woodwork to say what you want them to say." Llewellyn H. Rockwell Jr. [founder of Ludwig

von Mises Institute] **Sic Semper Tyrannis,** <u>The American Conservative</u> (Rockwell Jr, 2007).

Jack Mirkinson discusses the reluctance of the Fixxed Media to use the word torture (2014). **The Media Is Still Dancing Around The Word 'Torture.'** Finally, in August 2014, President Obama spoke the word that could not be spoken, "We tortured some folks." Wow! Chalk one up for the constitutional law, professor for that bold statement!

Note: "Enhanced interrogation" is a new word in the OED.

HEADLINE WARRIORS
Wars are generated by those above.
Wars are fought by those below. — Aegis

No citizen laboring many hours a week to earn a living, pauses from his/her daily routine and ponders, "Why don't we go to war against_____ (fill-in)?" It's obvious we have to use the media to "whip-up" the working populace into a state of acceptance for our manufactured reasons for going to war. The media must be complicit in our efforts and deliver the reasons for war and "drag the people along…"

> *"Naturally, the common people don't want war. But after all, it is the leaders of a country who determine the policy, and it is always a simple matter to drag the people along whether it is a democracy or a fascist dictatorship, or a parliament or a communist dictatorship. **The people can always be brought to the bidding of the leaders** [emphasis added]. That is easy. All you have to do is tell them they are being attacked and denounce the pacifists for lack of patriotism and exposing the country to danger. It works the same in every country."* —Hermann Goering, president of Reichstag, Nazi Parliament, 1934. (ThinkExist.com, n.d.)

In 1917, England's Prime Minister Lloyd George unabashedly revealed that the horrors of war had to be kept from the public:

> *If people really knew the* [truth], *the war* [World War I, 1914-1918] *would be stopped tomorrow. But of course they don't know and can't know. The correspondents don't write and the censorship wouldn't pass the truth. What they do send is not the war, but just a pretty picture of the war with everybody doing gallant deeds.* (West Mick, n.d.)

We manipulate public opinion through the media. We scare the bejesus out of fellow countrymen! We can change the names of the "eternal enemies" at will as we constantly form and reform alliances.

<u>Kill the (temporary) "Eternal" Enemy</u>
Woooooooooooooooo! Wooooooooooo! Create panic!

We have to make a great propaganda effort using the Fixxed Media to portray our enemy as Horrible Horrendous Marauding Huns. It is easier to slaughter an enemy with negative attributes! Fortunately, an army with full citizen support goes forth to kill the enemy we have chosen for them to kill. The tribal herd instincts mentioned earlier "kick-in." This assures a frightened, submissive population that will adhere to our war efforts no matter who the current enemy is. Of course we don't tell them the truth. Senator Jim McDermott ratified this observation when noting the "drums of war" beaten again by politicians calling for bombing Iran.

> *"There is a principle of communication, which is very well known, and has been documented in a variety of different ways. But it comes down to, if you can make people afraid, you can make them do anything. And these warmongers are fear mongers, and they are creating as much fear in the American people as possible."*

Lawmakers Who Seem To Have Forgotten Iraq Insist They're Right About Iran (McAuliff, 2015).

It's obvious we want a unified, loyal citizenry if we determine we must go to war. We can easily whip people up into war frenzy; raise taxes and ship out their unquestioning sons (and daughters) off to war at "the drop of a hat!" In 1914 British socialists picketing army recruiting stations to oppose an impending war [WWI] threw down their picket signs and went inside to enlist upon hearing England had entered WWI. Pavlovian dogs couldn't have responded quicker!

We decide who the enemy is and whom you should kill. Choosing an enemy sometimes depends on exigent circumstances. We also decide whom we want to be eliminated and arrange for *altered states* in foreign governments by fostering civil wars. [See Chapter Eight, *Let the Crushing Games Begin.*]

Sometimes in the past, my friends in different countries have engaged in foolish rivalry. Warring nations will expend billions and deploy millions of foot soldiers in an effort to procure billions in profits and/or boost the ego of the victors. Different herds of citizens will be brought together to make alliances to fight against other different herds. The citizenry of each country must be driven by the "drums of war" pushed by the headline makers in the Fixxed Media. The news media drive the populace of opposing nations to war. Governments determine the enemy, and the people rally!

During World War II, Germany and Japan were the enemies of the United States, China, and Russia (Soviet Union). The United States mobilized millions of men and women and spent billions of dollars to defeat their enemies. Military deaths for the U.S. were 420,000; Soviet Union, 20-28,000,000; China, 10-20,000,000. For four years Germany and Japan were portrayed as evil monstrous, marauding conquerors. Madison Square Garden bond rallies were held in the U.S. to raise money for besieged Russia. Huge Russian flags with the hammer and sickle were draped alongside the U.S. flag. Throughout the U.S. there were posters showing heroic Russian soldiers and Chinese families "fighting for freedom!" These posters can be found for sale on the Internet.

All efforts were made to destroy their common enemy. Americans planted "Victory Gardens" to grow food for the war effort. War deaths for Germany were 7-9,000,000. Japan suffered 3,000,000 deaths. We used the Fixxed Media to shape public opinion and spur the citizens on to victory! We bombed dozens of cities in Germany and dropped two atomic bombs on Japan to decisively crush and defeat the common enemy!

Within an instant of historical time, former enemies have become friends and former friends have become enemies. Within two years after the end of WWII, after tens of millions died slaughtering their enemies, governments "flip-flopped" and changed the names of the "bad guys." This happens all the time to fit our objectives. We have to use the compliant/supportive media in dictatorships or democracies to convince citizens to hate a newly "minted" enemy. Within 1,000 days after WWII, enemies and adversaries switched sides. Japan and Germany became allies of the U.S., and Russia and China became enemies.

Woooooooooooooooo!

Z: 20,000,000 people died in WWI and the media enthusiastically cheered on each country's war efforts. Trench warfare and poison gas did not deter the media from printing screaming headlines in reporting the "Chronicles of Death & Glory."

The corporate owned media won't publish the truth, but many books (largely unread) have relayed the horrors and follies of war. The Guns of August by Barbara Tuchman chronicles the lead-up to and war preparations by the soon-to-be warring nations in WWI, including France, Germany and England. They had spent decades and billions of taxpayer dollars developing war machines to attack and defend against the other. After four years of slaughter and 20,000,000 military and civilian deaths, the war ended on the eleventh hour of the eleventh day of the eleventh month, Armistice Day. Today it is called Veteran's Day.

Those former warring enemies who shelled and gassed each other's troops in the trenches are current friendly allied member states of NATO. The Fixxed Media has successfully promoted and established new friends' and enemies' lists! Anti-war books relate in graphic detail the reality of war that the mass media misses and/or chooses not to print. The book, All Quiet on the Western Front by Erich Maria Remarque also shows how society expects its citizens not to shirk one's duty. Students' teachers exhorted them to enlist for the glory of the Fatherland. The teachers, of course, stayed behind to cheer them on. The book shows that the "Eternal Enemy" is a human being, not a marauding Hun! A surviving veteran realizes the folly of his war:

"But now for the first time, I see you are a man like me...now I see your wife and your face and our fellowship. Forgive me, comrade. We always see it too late. Why do they never tell us that you are poor devils like us, that your mothers are just as anxious as ours, and that we have the same fear of death, and the same dying and the same agony—Forgive me comrade; how could you be my enemy?"

—Remarque, <u>All Quiet on the Western Front</u> depicts trench warfare, WWI

THE PRINCETON RADIO PROJECT

"You had nothing to guide you except your knowledge of the principles of [Insoc] *and your estimate of what* the [fill-in the blank: owner, party, government] *wanted you to say."*

— George Orwell, <u>1984</u>

Clamoring for war using jingoistic headlines is an easy way to herd the masses towards war. But that's short-term manipulation for short-term goals. We have had to systematically stunt the constant threat of the spread of more democratic demands by citizens. It was obvious we had to construct a pro-propaganda system to "head-off" the growing demands of the democratic voting public. Voters were organizing (especially in the twentieth century) and challenging our absolute right to have our own way to run things. Organized labor was gaining in their efforts to confront and chip away at our absolute right to dictate our wishes. That "giant right-wing conspiracy" thing began a long time ago. We've been busy!

The discussion that follows is based on the writings from Andrew Gavin Marshall's article, **"The Propaganda System That Has Helped Create a Permanent Overclass Is Over a Century in the Making"** (2013).

The "Project" began in the 1930s funded by the Rockefeller Foundation. It was founded by one of us, billionaire John D. Rockefeller. It was sort of a prototype to the dozens of Think Tanks that have sprouted up after the 1970's and funded by millionaires and billionaires. They have secretly funded our efforts to spread our message through the media to help blunt leftist pro-worker, pro-welfare, and pro-regulation philosophies. The Project was to help start a program fostered between the private corporations (which own the media, advertising, marketing, and public relations industries), and the state itself.

We felt threatened by the organizing "masses" against our economic interests. We sought out like-minded professionals to collaborate with. During WWII John Marshall wrote,

> *in a period of emergency...the manipulation of public opinion to meet emergency needs is to be taken for granted...**those in control must shape public opinion** to meet emergency needs* [emphasis added].

The same concept of "shaping public opinion" is also required during peacetime. We have spent a ton of money and energy getting control of the Fixxed Media. Today, we influence and shape the news. In 2015, most news outlets are controlled by owners who agree with us! Ashley Lutz points out there is little competition in the Fixxed Media. **These 6 Corporations control 90% of the Media in America** (Lutz, 2012).

"that the public was 'a bewildered herd' of ignorant meddlesome outsiders."
Walter Lippmann

Walter Lippmann was the foremost leader of creating government propaganda to blunt the threats to us. In his book The Phantom Public, he wrote, "that the public was 'a bewildered herd' of ignorant meddlesome outsiders." That was kosher "music to our ears." It played well at the many lavish parties we invited him to.

Z: He's writing, dear reader, about the citizens and voters of American democracy! A complete reading of the article, **The Propaganda System that has helped create a Permanent Overclass**... is very revealing. It names all the top names in the media, especially television, that adhere to this way of thinking (Marshall, 2013). A new bailiwick of sophisticated supporters was developed to ensure development of a widespread propaganda system. They were armed not with lethal weapons, but college degrees! They have collaborated to suppress the goals of democratically organized groups and their ideas. The article offers a mind-blowing exposé of the depth and reach of corporate controlled media. It shows 100% support for anti-democratic views and the disdain and fear of its citizens. A reading of **"Outsider" Stone vs "Insider" Lippmann** on the website of IF Stone (Stone) will dispel any illusions you may have of a "free" press. Stone's article provides a complete exposé of one of America's preeminent and influential columnist who disdainfully "ran political interference" for the expanded manipulation of public opinion. He sure "suckered" me in with his newspaper columns that I used to read!

PLAUSIBLE DENIABILITY

"I didn't do it!
Nobody saw me do it.
There's no way you can prove anything!"
— Bart Simpson, You Tube, "I didn't do it!"

*The rulers of the State are the only ones who should have the privilege of lying, either at home or abroad; **they may be allowed to lie for the good of the State** [emphasis added].*—Plato, The Republic (2,500 years ago)

Shhh! It's not torture. It does not exist. — Professor Who?

After World War II there was a massive concerted effort by my colleagues and our allies in the U.S. government and its allies to contain and defeat any form of left-leaning foreign government. We strenuously opposed any political movements that did not support our private pro-profit philosophy. [See Chapter Eight, *Let the Crushing Games Begin* for a complete discussion].

After WWII it was the clean-cut Good Guys, (United States) versus the very, very bad guys (Communist Russia a.k.a. Soviet Union). Russia was portrayed quite accurately as a barbaric totalitarian menace to the non-communist world. Russia imposed a cruel dictatorial system wherever it could throughout Europe. Millions were imprisoned and murdered. After WWII, Eastern Europe fell under Russia's imposed brutal dictatorships. This time frame after WWII is known as the Cold War. It was necessary for us to eliminate this threat. The United States had to step-up and suppress all opposition to the Free World's way of life. We wanted our efforts to be in secret. We wanted to be able to act undetected. We wanted to be able to take extraordinary means to "knock-off" our enemies and anyone who resisted our worldly objectives. The operative word is "knock-off" as in, "Bang! Bang! You're dead!"

But, we couldn't have the "Guys in the White Hats" who were out saving the world from Evil Doers being hindered in their efforts. [Some of these secretive and violent efforts are detailed in Chapter Eight]. On June 18, 1948, President Harry S. Truman signed a national Security Council paper (NSC 5412) now located at the National Archives, RG 273, which defined all covert operations as,

> *all activities conducted pursuant to this directive which so planned and executed that any U.S. Government responsibility for them is not evident to unauthorized persons and that **if uncovered the U.S. Government can plausibly disclaim any responsibility for them** [emphasis added].*

NSC 5412 broadly defined "covert operations" as,

> *all activities conducted pursuant to this directive which are so planned and executed that any U.S. Government responsibility for them is not evident to unauthorized persons and that if uncovered the U.S. Government can plausibly disclaim any responsibility for them. Specifically, such operations shall include any covert activities related to: propaganda, political action; economic warfare; preventive direct action, including sabotage, anti-sabotage, demolition; escape and evasion and evacuation measures; subversion against hostile states or groups including assistance to underground resistance movements, guerrillas and refugee liberation groups; support of indigenous and anti-communist elements in threatened countries of the free world; deceptive plans and operations; **and all activities***

compatible with this directive necessary to accomplish the foregoing [emphasis added]. (NSC 5412, National Security Council Directive on Covert Operations).

Thus, the all-encompassing, "all-cover-upping" rationale was conceived and hatched behind closed doors by America's top political leaders. The term "plausible deniability" was a policy developed for the CIA to allow more senior members of the newly created government bailiwick's spy agency to "cover their a_ _ _ es" if the truth were uncovered. The hundreds of billions of dollars in costs to carry out such secret activities around the world outlined above were paid for by you, dear taxpayer! And you didn't even know it! Thanks!

We like working in secret. This isn't a problem within dictatorships. We can do anything we like. But in democracies we must carefully enlist the media and owners to help by not examining too closely what we do. Media people are our friends! Even if a reporter insistently probed for the truth of some event from the government, the truth could be legally lied about and the facts kept hidden! If a reporter asked about government involvement, there could be legal protection for those higher up in the chain of command.

A close relationship was revealed in the Carl Bernstein's article, **The CIA and the Media, How America's Most Powerful News Media Worked Hand in Glove with the Central Intelligence Agency** (1977). Owners of news organizations allowed their overseas reporters to secretly funnel information about a country's internal situation to CIA operatives. The media were not unbiased pursuers of the truth. First and foremost Bernstein writes,

> *There is ample evidence that America's leading publishers and news executives allowed themselves and their organizations to become handmaidens to the intelligence services...In all, about twenty-five news organizations... provided cover for the Agency* (1977).

This media assistance was occurring during the Cold War with Russia. We needed to keep track of our former Russian allies to see what were the internal strengths and weaknesses of the eastern Soviet communist bloc of countries. Reporters were a good source.

History: (De) Constructing the Truth

Z: From some movies viewed in childhood I learned about:

Conquistadores—Handsome Tyrone Power waded ashore and planted the flag for Spain and claimed Mexico. It did not show him whacking off the heads of native landowners.

Crusaders—heroically reclaiming former Christian Lands. It did not show them whacking off the heads of "heathen" landowners.

Knights—in shining armor professing chivalry and love. It did not show Sir Lancelot whacking off the heads of restive serfs.

Book publishers sell two versions of U.S. History textbooks—one for the North and one for the South. A publisher of U.S. history must print two versions of the Civil War: one to be sold in the North and another version to be sold in the South. I doubt either version is accurate!

The Northern soldiers waged a courageous war against the South to free the slaves. But there's no mention of the New York City riots against the draft by those who said, "Hell, no! We won't go!"

Southern soldiers waged a courageous war against the "War of Northern Aggression." But, most Southerners didn't even own one slave.

Before the Discovery Channel or books, or chronicles of glory and conquest were written, the conquests of foreign lands had to be made. Conquest is not a pretty sight—but hey, everyone was grabbing land anyway they could! The "world was our oyster" for the taking! With sword we conquered! With money we hired the historians to say how wonderful such thievery was! Artists painted famous Battles of Conquest. Sculptors carved our noble features. Monuments were built to honor our conquests. Castles, mansions and cathedrals were built with the wealth we gleaned from the world we carved up. Swiping land from weak adversaries was easy. The world was easy "pickings!" As we see in the next chapter, not all could be winners. No hired historian writes about the billions of earth's inhabitants who lost all to us. ¡Qué lástima!

CHAPTER SIX

SWIPERS SWIPERS SWIPERS
The Great Land Robbery: A Fixxed History

I will not lend thee a penny, Pistol: Why, then, the world's mine oyster, which I with sword will open. —Shakespeare's "Falstaff"

This land Is Your Land...and I'm seizing it! —Yachta Yachta Yachta

Buy land. They aren't making any more. —Will Rogers

Where property rights aren't secure, neither is freedom… and without freedom, there is nothing the government can't destroy.
—Jeff Jacoby, *The Boston Globe* (2014)

SWIPING THE WORLD
Yesterday: I covet
Today: I steal
Tomorrow: I survey

Funny thing about history books, those who write them are in the employ of the rulers and winners or like Pharaoh's scribes, hired inscribers. We won't let the true version of history "out of the bag!" We never ask, "Do you want to be a slave?" or "Do you want to give us your land?" or "How many hours do you want to work in our gold mines?" No one recorded your pathetic "Oliver Twist" requests for leniency or compassion: "Please, sir........." The gory, bloody events are "sanitized" for textbooks and citizens' consumption. We build glorified monuments and statues that illustrate the "accomplishments" of our conquests. The Fixxed Media offers up praises to our victorious, conquering feats. Tourists visit our edifices and museums.

Most history is about the struggle to transfer wealth from one set of landowners to another. The Great Land Robbery (1492-1900) was never written down in detail so that today's citizens could learn of the brutal, but necessary, methods used to conquer and steal at will. It is the true story of the massive real estate transfers that occurred in the New World.

Z: Historians writing for textbooks and mass consumption have been hired to bleach out the blood and smooth down the sharp edges of conquest. Screams and wailings were not recorded. Fear and terror were not pictured. [You can see some of this in news footage of terrorized refugees from countries such as Iraq and Syria]. New bailiwicks of supporters were developed after the Carnage of Defeat of the original owners of the land. Administrators of the land, parchments, deeds, physical control of the subjugated—all required loyal supporters recording the deeds and property rights of the new owners.

Writers of history, although called historians, must "toe the line" if they want their textbooks accepted and sold in public and private schools and universities. College and university professors must "toe the line" if they wish to secure tenure and become a valued "family" member. Citizens don't read about the really, real truth. Going to war and conquering land and people traditionally has not been a problem for dictatorships. Dictators just do their thing! But in democracies, citizens aren't told how their taxes are used to further the goals of profit making and aggrandizement. This is especially true when conquering and colonizing inhabitants around the world. The narrative is shaped to allow a historical record that justifies conquests of weaker populations. Historians provide the rationale.

We figured out how to steal the land right out from under the owners and make it look legitimate and relatively bloodless! We hired some historians and preachers to cleanse out the messy parts. School textbooks reflect the very, very abridged version. Let me tell you of the unabridged history.

Land has been the source of wealth for thousands of years. Whoever owned land decided who could pass through it or use it. In high school you needed a hall pass to "travel" around the school to the bathroom or library. "Woe be unto ye" who failed to have one! It's been the same story since Pharaoh's time—you needed a "pass" or permission to be on the land. Whoever dispensed the "passes" sought remuneration through taxes and fees. My ancestors became wealthy! The successful land grabbers, that is!

You're familiar with some famous marauders and land grabbers: Attila the Hun, Xerxes of Persia (as seen in the "300" movie), Pharaoh Ramses, Ashurbanipal, Alexander the Great, William the Conqueror, Hernando Cortez. The days of yesteryear with derring-do "free-wheeling" rulers and out-and-out conquerors have gone. This is especially true in the five hundred years after the discovery of the "New World." But before the "dust settled," the *conquistadores*, pious colonialists and other land grabbers would have circumnavigated the world and carved it up. The ancestors of my friends and I were the predators. We continue that tradition. We continue to prey upon the hapless. Nothing has ever stopped us!

GETTING LEGAL AUTHORIZATION

Explorers, businesses and settlers needed a "pass," or an acceptable authority from some governmental entity such as a monarch or legislature to O. K. taking possession of newly discovered lands. Explorers planted the flag of their monarch as they waded ashore to claim the new land in central and southern America. In the north, one ship of English businessmen and religious travellers missed their destination of Virginia for which they had an authorized written charter (a pass) from the British monarchy. They were way off course and in cold, wintry November landed in Plymouth.

They had no "pass" or authorization from their monarchy for that unsettled territory. This is why the *Mayflower Compact* was signed. It was a charter for a legitimate government drawn-up by the travellers before they left the ship so there would be some kind of <u>legal</u> <u>authority</u> to refer to for that uncharted territory. The compact was a legal basis for a government.

Once European explorers began discovering new lands in the Western Hemisphere, countries such as Spain and Portugal began to quarrel about land rights and their legitimacy of ownership. They needed a charter or a "pass" to get legitimate authorization for the conquest of any new lands. Also, they needed to know what to do with the natives (original owners) that they subdued.

On May 4, 1493, Pope Alexander VI issued a papal bull *inter caeterar* which drew a "Line of Demarcation" allowing Spain to take newly discovered lands. The *Treaty of Tordesillas* was signed on June 17, 1494, at the urging of the pope. Essentially, this granted Brazil to Portugal. Thus, the fate of all who lived in those lands of Central and South America were divvied-up. The English and French would divvy up North America later on. No one asked the original native owners. It never occurred to us!

Let the conquering games begin!

Whoever Controls the Eviction Process, Wins!

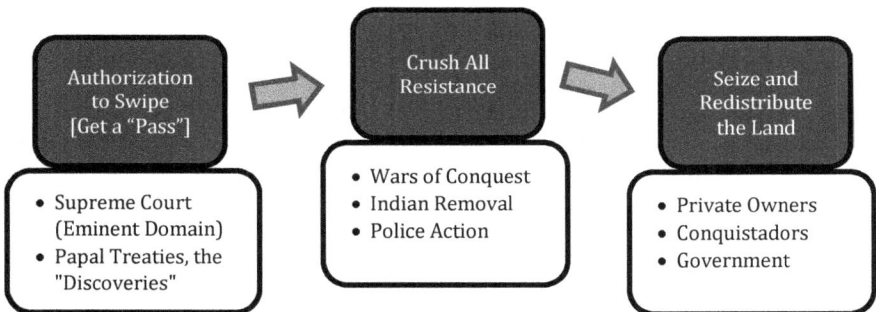

Authorization to Swipe [Get a "Pass"]	Crush All Resistance	Seize and Redistribute the Land
• Supreme Court (Eminent Domain) • Papal Treaties, the "Discoveries"	• Wars of Conquest • Indian Removal • Police Action	• Private Owners • Conquistadors • Government

I salivate at the thought of all the wealth that was about to be created and transferred. It would be the greatest land redistribution—and land heist in history! And all the thieves were blessed and given a free "Pass" through governments and religious sanctioning! It was *eminent domain* on super-sized steroids! If it were a video game, it'd be called <u>Grand Theft World</u>!

> **Q:** Estimate the total area of involuntary "land transfer" from the populations of the New World to the conquerors of the Old World.
> Round off to nearest 100,000.
> North America   9,540,000 sq. mi.
> South America   6,890,000 sq. mi.
> Answer: _____

And there's more! A Bull is a special kind of patent or charter (pass) issued by a pope. The *Doctrine of Discovery* (as several treaties and Papal

Bulls became to be known) sanctified and granted *carte blanche* rights to the conquerors with complete freedom to act as they wished.

An excerpt referring to the conquerors states, *"we make, appoint, and depute you and your said heirs and successors lords of them with full and free power, authority, and jurisdiction of every kind...*[and the church authorities] *trust in Him from whom empires and governments and all good things proceed."*

THE JIHADIST CREED: SUBMIT OR DIE

One Bull, *dum diversas, 1452*, instructed countries to invade the Near East,

> *to invade, capture, vanquish, and subdue all Saracens, pagans, and other enemies of Christ,* **to put them into perpetual slavery, and to take away all their possessions and property** [emphasis added].

The "Mother of all Bulls" regarding the lands in the New World was:

El Requerimiento, 1513

The YOOISM [definition p. 53] to justify the seizing of the land in the new world was laid out by Palacios Rubios, a papal lawyer. The document *El Requerimiento* was written to justify all conquests and transfer of all land to the new owners. The logic went something like this: God sent his son, Jesus. He had disciples to help spread the word of God. One of them was Peter. He was crucified in Rome where St. Peters and the Papacy were later located. The Papacy is charged with spreading God's word. It would be blasphemous to deny God's emissaries, the Conquistadores. Therefore, the heathen natives should suffer the consequences if they resisted these "Holy Men" and rejected God!

The Conquistadores read the *Requerimiento* out loud to all villagers throughout the New World. It was read in Latin and was a mere formality to unleash military might to quash all resistance. It decreed:

> [If you do not recognize our jurisdiction]
> *I certify to you that, with the help of God, we shall powerfully enter into your country, and shall make war against you in all ways and manners that we can, and shall subject you to the yoke and obedience of the Church and of their highnesses; we shall take, you, and your wives, and your children, and shall make slaves of them, and as such shall sell and dispose of them as their highnesses may command; and we shall take away your goods, and shall do you all the mischief and damage that we can, as to vassals who do not obey, and refuse to receive their lord, and resist and contradict him: and we protest that **the deaths and losses which shall accrue from this are your fault,** [emphasis added] and not that of their highnesses, or ours...*

Such honest, open, and frank admission of intent should have been a public relations disaster if the natives could have understood the words!

Imagine revealing to the conquered what would happen if they resisted in any way! The threats worked after a few beheadings! First, the executed were baptized to save their souls. All Indian nations in the New World eventually succumbed to conquest. The natives were to be ruled by the conquistadores and subdued and converted by their missionaries. All European countries that could were in on the swiping of land in the New World. We were the predators and the subdued were our prey!

> Q: Write an essay comparing the above *Requerimiento* "manifesto" with that of speeches made in recently conquered cities by ISIS in Iraq where citizens were gathered in each village and forced to listen to:
> *"I swear to god we will see a caliphate based on the prophecy. This state is a state fueled with the blood of the martyrs. Be with this state or I swear you will be the ones to be killed because they fought with god and the Prophet. I swear you will be killed like a sheep, a chicken, a cow. I swear to god if you do not accept the religion of god...."*
> **Heads line streets of ISIS capital,** *CNN* **(Walsh, 2014).**

Z: God gets blamed a lot for such skullduggeries! What would Jesus do? Look out newly conquered owners; it's eviction notices and slavery for you! [ORIGINAL SIN: To harken back to something as an origin or source.] The ideas of the *Doctrine of Discovery* were legal cover for the theft of Indian lands in North America. The doctrine is another type of YOOISM. It was cited by U.S. Supreme Court Chief Justice Marshall to give legal basis for swiping Indian lands in the United States. *Johnson v. McIntosh 1823* upheld "that the principle of discovery gave European nations **an absolute right** [emphasis added] to New World lands." Add Judicial Bailiwick to Yachta's "legal" power grab! The concept of "eminent domain" in the Constitution continues legalized swiping! (See "Dissenting Opinion," p. 70)

> Missionaries Accomplished: A Helping Hand
> *To the Victors belong the Spoils*
> *Hired historians laud our laurels,*
> *Convert them we will*
> *Or else we could kill*
> *As we did swipe all their soils.*
> *(And precious metals, etc.)* — *Yachta, Yachta, Yachta*

The conquistadores were also to baptize and convert the savages. *"...you purpose also, as is your duty, to lead the peoples dwelling in those islands and countries to embrace the Christian religion."* We needed help doing this. We brought in the missionaries once we swiped the land. The missionaries we supported were on a mission (heh, heh, heh!)—they worked for God <u>and</u> us. Their job was to convert the heathen. From the converted and conquered inhabitants, a loyal coterie of religious supporters would emerge. It was a New World bailiwick from the Old World. It was easy to see that loyalty paid off with better food and clothing. Plus, loyal clerics and their entourage didn't have to work the gold mines or toil in the fields! We took good care of them. In return the missionaries helped to control the newly subjugated. It was Win (for us) Win (for them) Lose (for the subjugated)!

Each conquered territory was converted to the "one true faith" of the conquering army. This necessitated a religious hierarchy to "rule" over the religious conversions of the conquered. Thus, new, highly structured bailiwicks of religious hierarchies were developed. Old religious structures and religious beliefs were dismantled and eliminated. Throughout the Americas, massive cathedrals were built to replace the temples of old gods. Some of these can be seen by searching: Cathedral Mexico City; Cathedral Lima, Peru. These became massive symbols of wealth and superiority of the new religions over the old gods.

Z: Regarding conquered natives: it is an axiom that subjugated and conquered inhabitants anywhere in the world have always converted to the religion of the conquering army. "Might" earns the right to be right—and convert. One's life literally depended upon conversion. Similar acts of forced conversion have occurred in the recent [2014] brutal ISIS religious attacks in Syria and Iraq.

Up-Sell: Promises, Promises, Promises

"Your money or your life?" If a musket or a machete is pointed at your head, you will bobble it up-and-down (capitulate) or lose it (decapitate)! We lined up the citizens of the New World and gave them a choice: "accept our religion [and our absolute rule] or else!" Those who resisted were baptized (we had to save their souls from eternal damnation) and then beheaded! There's a lot of that going on around the world today!

The missionaries provided the rationale for conquest: "Have we got a deal for you!" Work hard, obey your masters and (eventually) your soul is saved and you get to heaven. Promises for the Promised Land were taught through song and/or prayerful beseeching of God:
"Swing lo, sweet chariot, com'n for to carry me home...[to Heaven];"
"Thy will be done on earth as it is in Heaven."

Z: The conquerors of Middle America, Hernando Cortes and his soldiers could not believe the city (Mexico City) of the Aztecs with its beautifully laid out avenues and abundance of food. [View Internet Images " Tenochtitlan, pictures" to see city and pyramids.] Modern historians have estimated that it was the largest city in the world at that time, larger than London or Paris. My history books and Hollywood movies always depicted Indians as primitive, living in tipis; scalping, and kidnapping white women!

My Spanish and Portuguese compatriots subjugated their conquered populations, kept them on the land, and used them to create wealth from their farming and the mining of silver and gold. They and their ancestors did pretty well and have lived an amazingly great lifestyle—they still do! It is true that *los patrones* were a little abusive to the conquered. They branded their faces on the cheeks so they could keep track of "ownership." Some of the vanquished bore several scars because the patrones would bet them in poker games and if they lost...the captives had to be rebranded!

Así es la vida! Así es la cara!

WHAT IS THINE WILL BE MINE

For some, a mule and forty acres is not enough — Aegis

"They [the White man] made us many promises, more than I can remember, but they never kept but one.
They promised to take our land and they took it." — Chief Joseph

"Kill the buffalo and you kill the Indian." — General Philip H. Sheridan, 1866.

Things were done differently in the English colonies. We engaged in an "Indian Removal" policy. We wanted to sell and settle Indian land with white settlers. Land speculation was our ticket to wealth! We had no need of Indian labor. By the Bicentennial celebration of U.S. independence, most Indian nations (about 500) had been depopulated of their inhabitants, moved or corralled into restricted, clearly defined territory. Yes, some of my conquering ancestors could be pretty brutal! It's too bad those heathens resisted! They should have just "thrown-up their hands," obeyed, lined up quietly, and been removed to their new reservations from their ancestral lands and centuries-old way of life. We had them outgunned!

Z: Hollywood could have turned the whole removal process into an action packed movie series with many sequels—*"Invasion of the Indian Snatchers!"* Blood! Gore! Massacres! Pillage! Butchery!

Rigged treaties and forced removals by U.S. troops drove the natives onto reservations (a euphemism for concentration camps); [but they were not allowed to cancel their reservations. As in *"Hotel California"* they could never check out ...without getting shot!]

The Nez Perce of Wallowa Valley Oregon was one Indian tribe ordered to be removed. Chief Joseph fled with 800 tribesmen and tried to reach Canada. The U.S. army pursued them for 1,100 miles through Idaho and Montana. Just 40 miles shy of the border a battle ensued for five days. Reduced to 431 tribesmen, Chief Joseph surrendered October 5, 1877.

Excerpts: Surrender Speech

"I am tired of fighting...It is cold and we have no blankets. The little children are freezing to death. My people, some of them, have run away to the hills and have no blankets, no food. I want to have time to look for my children and see how many I can find. Maybe I shall find them among the dead...My heart is sick and sad...

I shall fight no more forever."

Of course we took the land—and look what great things we have done! It was primitive totem pole and teepees versus modern Space Needle! No comparison. What kind of ridiculous name is Nez Perce? [Pierced nose!] They should have surrendered right off! All those tribes weren't nations.

Z: Grade school children are taught that George Washington was a surveyor. The history books never wrote exactly whose land he was surveying. Figuratively speaking, he and other land speculators drove off the Native Indians in the morning and surveyed their land in the afternoon! Ten years before the American Revolution Washington wrote a letter to William Crawford, September 1767, seeking his help in making land claims. England had issued the *Proclamation of 1763* making it illegal for Washington and the colonists to continue westward encroachment onto land of the Indian nations. The Crown could not afford the expenses of defending British subjects against Indians protecting their lands and attacking them. Washington asked Crawford to "look me out a Tract of about 1500, 2000, or more Acres" within the Pennsylvania Line. He wanted him to secure land as soon as possible to prevent others from claiming land "as nothing is more certain than that the Lands cannot remain long ungranted when once it is known the Rights are to be had for them." (Congress, n.d.) Washington was disdainful of the "law of the land," the Proclamation of 1763. The British government would no longer grant a "pass" for continued white man's intrusion and encroachment upon the Indian nations' lands. He wrote, "For I can never look upon that Proclamation in any other light (but this I say between ourselves) than as a temporary expedient to quiet the Minds of the Indians and must fall of course in a few years especially when those Indians are consenting to our Occupying the Lands."

In June 1683, Governor William Penn, a Quaker, had purchased land directly from chief Tamanend with the *Treaty of Shachamaxon*, June 1683. He proclaimed his attitude of purchasing land: "*We meet on the broad pathway of good faith and good-will; no advantage shall be taken on either side, but all shall be openness and love. We are the same as if one man's* body was to be divided into two parts; we are of one flesh and one blood." (Penn Treaty , n.d.).

Q: Write a research paper responding to the following questions:
1) Compare the attitude of Washington with that of Penn towards native land ownership. Which do you agree with? Why?
2) How did 500 Indian nations lose the most productive land in America and end up on the most unproductive land?

Research the following and include in your paper:
U.S. Indian Removal Act 1820 and President Jackson clearing out Indians on Eastern lands. Also view PBS.org Indian Removal, Part Four. Use as a source, John Ehle's <u>Trail of Tears: The Rise and Fall of the Cherokee Nation</u>, that relates the forcible removal by troops. Thousands died on the forced marches away from their homeland. The Chickasaw, Choctaw, Muscogee Creek, and Seminole nations were depopulated and citizens removed. Also include examples about the futile efforts by Chief Pontiac and Geronimo and the Plains Indians in their resistance to U.S. encroachment.

History is swiping thy neighbor's possessions and sugar coating and white washing "events" with slogans and rationales. It may not have been God's will or Manifest Destiny but Theodore Roosevelt said it best:

> *"This continent had to be won. We need not waste our time dealing with any sentimentalist who believes that, on account of any abstract principle, it would have been right to leave this continent to the domain, the hunting ground of squalid savages. It had to be taken by the white race."* — Roosevelt ~1892 Lowell Institute Lecture

> *The truth is, the Indians never had any real title to the soil.*
> — President Theodore Roosevelt, <u>The Winning of the West</u>

Z: For over a century the U.S. government declared the Indian nations "sovereign" so they could legally negotiate to have a treaty signed by tribal representatives. The U.S. Senate ratified these treaties. I was told the Indians were gradually "pushed-out" little by little as a consequence of the unstoppable march of settlers. The truth is the U.S. government actively negotiated treaties with the nations/tribes, which called for their removal. There was systematic negotiated U.S. governmental efforts to remove them! Presidents like Andrew Jackson were directly involved.

There were always those Gooderites, always moralizing! William E. Channing wrote a letter to Henry Clay in 1837 decrying the demand for more land. He condemned the idea that the Indians and Mexicans [condemned as a degraded race] were "melting away" from American advancement.

> *"Away with this vile sophistry! There is no necessity for crime. There is no fate to justify rapacious nations, any more than to justify gamblers and robbers, in plunder"* (Blum).

"Rapacious nations!" Well, at least <u>we</u> were ravenous. But, our newspapers and the Fixxed Media headlined vicious wanton attacks by the natives upon helpless white settlers. Thank goodness the jingoistic herd instinct rallied the nation! [Jingoism: the feelings and beliefs of people who think their country is always right and who are in favor of any aggressive acts against other countries]. Of course our ancestors, land speculators, and land-hungry predators couldn't wait to legally "steal" the lands. Assault rifles, not "hot moralizing words" would have saved the Indian nations!

We're Coming to Take Your Land Away

> *"A government big enough to give you everything you want, is big enough to take away everything you have."*   —Thomas Jefferson

Boo-Hoo! Feeling sorry for "them Injuns" losing all their land through treaties imposed by the government in Washington D. C.? We land speculators along with our allies in Congress are always figuring out ways to take land from rightful owners. Look out—you and <u>your</u> property could

71

be next! Eminent domain restrictions are so "rear-view mirror." The U.S. Supreme Court has new guidelines. Our friendly justices made "theft" legal.

Z: The "Robed Ones" on the Supreme Court have joined the Robber Barons and Yachta in their pro-corporation attitude toward the rights of Americans. The really, really activist court eviscerated your constitutional right to own your land and everything on it. The *Kelo v City of New London, 2005* decision was eminent domain on steroids! It allowed politicians in a state legislature to approve any private business enterprise. This gave a legislature the right to dispossess homeowners for private commercial development of their land.

<u>Dissenting Opinion:</u>

Today, the Court abandons [the Fifth Amendment's] *long-held, basic limitation on government power. Under the banner of economic development,* **all private property** [emphasis added] *is now vulnerable to being taken and transferred to another private owner, so long as it might be upgraded, i.e. given to an owner who will use it in a way that the legislature deems more beneficial to the public...in the process"* —*(Kelo v. City of New* London: Dissenting Opinion by Justice O'Connor (2005)

The Never Ending Land Robbery

We're not through grabbing the rest of the public land that was stolen from the original Americans, the native Indian tribes. We already had converted millions of acres of land to private for-profit railroad corporations. Don Strack outlined how the government helped to bankroll and assist the railroad corporations. In the 1860's we began the process of gaining private title to the swiped land. Don Strack researched how this came about. **Federal Government Assistance for The Building Of The Union Pacific Railway** (1982). Congress passed,

> *[An] Act to aid in the Construction of a Railroad and*
> *Telegraph line from the Missouri River to the Pacific Ocean,*
> *and to secure to the Government the Use of the same for*
> *Postal, Military and Other Purposes.*

It was known as the Pacific Railroad Act of 1862. We wanted to build a national railroad transportation system. We didn't have the financial resources to build the prohibitively costly railroad tracks through the land. We made "oodles and oodles" of money selling off parcels of land adjacent to the railroad tracks to re-locating citizens. The U.S. government had sent in Expeditionary Forces (the Calvary) to defeat and to drive out the original owners, the Indians. That cost us nothing because the taxpayers footed the millions of dollars in costs for that! Oh, yeah. Some lives were lost.

Who ~~is~~ was Colonel Custer?

Today we're "licking our chops" getting ready for the next "Grand Theft" land grab. Will Rogers has written that, *hundreds of millions of acres of national forests, rangelands, wildlife refuges, wilderness areas and historic sites will revert to the states or local governments or be auctioned off. These lands constitute much of what's left of the nation's natural and historical heritage* (Our Land, Up for Grabs, 2015).

We want to transfer jurisdiction for these lands to state and local governments. Then, politicians in the legislature can parcel the land out to our friends by "giving states and localities more control over the resources within their boundaries." Sharpen those carving knives! Citizens lose again!

Z: The beat down goes on! In 1955 President Eisenhower designated thousands of acres in Arizona to be free from mining. This action protected Apache sacred religious sites and public camping grounds from commercial use. In December 2014, mining lobbyists and Senator John McCain slipped in a rider to a bill, which allows 2,000 acres to be transferred from the Forest Service to the private foreign owned Resolution Copper Mine.

As we have seen, Flyover USA is where we fly over, covet and figure out a legal way to take your land. When we want your land and resources for any reason, we'll figure out a way to get them! We even have forcibly removed citizens from their homes against their will in order to drop experimental A-bombs on their vacated residencies! [See "Bikini Exposure" below]. Take digital pictures of your home and estate so they can be remembered—and easily digitally deleted if we come after them!

All citizens of the world should also take pictures of family members, too! You are all expendable and subject to elimination and/or experimentation. In order to obtain our goals we have absolutely no qualms about sacrificing you, your family, your tribe, or your country whenever we need to. The next chapter documents how we have not hesitated to inflict the harshest of evils down upon an unsuspecting populace. When we succeed against an enemy, our supporters cheer and overlook any death and destruction. But, we keep things hidden when we have used humans as guinea pigs to test a variety of modern weapons. An unsuspecting, trusting public absolutely refuses to believe or accept the secret scientific experiments we have sanctioned. We needed to do testing and experiments in order to get ready for the next worldly challenges by any enemy. Of course we didn't announce our efforts and have never suffered public scrutiny. Chapter Seven, *Disposables* provides proof of our nefarious, hidden efforts.

DISPOSABLES DISPOSABLES DISPOSABLES
At (y)our Disposal

"Please, God, don't let us have killed John Wayne!" —Scientist, Defense Nuclear Agency [See Human "Lab Rat" below]

Operation "Project Seal".... developed a "weapon" of mass destruction based on a tsunami... to be used in WWII by the U.S. [See Wipeout below]

Savoir dissimuler est le savoir des rois: dissimulation [to hide under a false appearance] *is the art of* kings — Cardinal Richelieu finance minister to absolutist monarch King Louis XIII

DISSIMULATION IS THE OPERATIVE WORD

We lie all the time! It's our birthright! A citizen's birthright is to be lied to (by us)! Otherwise citizens would be more defiant and rebellious and resist our efforts to suppress and control. Our other operative words are evasiveness and obfuscation, not disclosure and veracity. The slogan, "Truth, Justice and The American Way" exists in a fictitious comic book world, not in reality!

As I have been explaining, governments will take any measures to suppress and defeat any perceived enemy. These measures even include human experimentation on its own citizens to test the efficacy of new weapons! Naturally, we never publicly alert anyone! All politicians and rulers must make profound, heartfelt statements of their willingness to assist and protect their citizenry and keep them from harm, domestic or foreign. We must profess that all our efforts and actions are to help the country's citizens. This is especially true in western and European democracies.

Of course people in the United States do not believe that a democratically elected government would ever <u>deliberately</u> inflict harm on any of its citizens. What a foolish delusional conviction! Actually, I hope my writings will disabuse you of that ridiculous misconception!

We are not at your disposal. You are at ours!

Unfortunately, from time to time my friends and I foolishly formed alliances to wage war against each other. We would prefer peace and stability so we can pursue our desire for profitable enterprises. However, we believe in times of war it's one hundred percent okay, in order to win, for governments to "whack" an opponent's citizenry with all military means available. When we go to war against each other as the saying goes: "All's Fair in Love and War!" Figuring out any way to "delete" an enemy is fair game. Part One below documents our various efforts to eliminate whoever we are at war with! Part Two documents the secret experiments we have subjected citizens to in order to test new weaponry.

PART ONE: Tsunami-ing People

& Other Annihilations

Even the Devil would not claim credit for the vicious acts that we humans have inflicted upon our "fellow" man. Of course the Devil was merely after souls! There is no such thing as a civilized war when an adversary is out to kill you or we're trying to swipe their land. You either win or you lose. You must do unto them before they do unto you. The following is an incomplete list of examples that illustrate the ever-increasing innovative means that have been used to crush an opponent's hapless citizens. Any citizen could easily be on the receiving end of similar extreme measures—even you!

1. Massacre! Massacre! Massacre!
   So, O. K. 500 native American nations were wiped-out (men, women, children), but those were Indians who couldn't compete. We pointed a gun to their heads and told them to move. If they resisted, Bang! [View Images on the Internet, "Wounded Knee Massacre" in which four Hotchkiss machine guns were used. See Image: pictures of dumped bodies in a massive grave. Also see: Washista Massacre by General Custer's seventh Calvary]

2. Glub! Glub! Glub!
   The start of torpedoing passenger ships causing civilian deaths. The *Lusitania* was carrying war material and sunk by the German U-Boat Campaign to block illegal U.S. war supplies from reaching England, causing 1,800 drowned civilians.

3. Splat! Splat! Splat!
   England started massive bombing of cities and civilians in Germany, WWII. Nazi Germany began massive bombing cities and civilians, WWII. Each side claimed the other side started it! Dead is dead!

4. Gasp! Gasp! Gasp!
   Using poison gas and trench warfare, all sides WWI included many democracies: millions of troops died.
   Deliberate Firestorm destruction of noncombatants in Dresden: WWII—3,300 tons of incendiary bombs consumed oxygen. [Kurt Vonnegut wrote of the attack in Slaughter House Five. Bodies in bomb shelters had turned blue from asphyxiation, 300,000 died.]

5. Whoosh! Whoosh! Whoosh!
   Only one country in the history of the planet has succeeded in "vaporizing" a civilian population. White, chalky smudges seared onto concrete sidewalks are the "remains" of many A-bombed civilians of Hiroshima and Nagasaki, 300,000 dead.

6. Wipeout! Wipeout! Wipeout!
   (View Internet to see recent destruction of a real Tsunami: You Tube, "Indian Ocean Tsunami 2004" by Joseph Friedman that killed 230,000.

Views 7,000,000.) **'Tsunami Bomb' In Development During World War II,** (Bennett-Smith, 2014). The U.S. government detonated 3,700 bombs off the coast of New Caledonia during WWII to test for creation of a man-made tsunami to use as a weapon of mass destruction against the islands of Japan and their conquered lands. According to New Zealand author, Ray Waru, tests showed that "a series of 10 large underwater blasts could have created a 33-foot tsunami wave.

7. Starve! Starve! Starve!
   - Kill the buffalo, kill the Indian! 30,000,000 buffalo were systematically slaughtered through U.S. policy to starve the Plains Indians and force them onto reservations. Civilian hunters were allowed to use military forts as bases of operation to "sally forth" and slaughter at will. [View Images on Internet of pictures of tall hills of piled buffalo skulls and hides.]
   - Famine subdues your enemy. Ukraine: Bread Basket of Europe where 7,000,000 were deliberately starved (1932-1933). The dictator Stalin seized the crops and exported the food to starve the resisting people of Ukraine into submission and collectivization (History Place, n.d.). [Pictures can be viewed on the Internet; "Stalin, Ukraine starvation" for gruesome pictures of the starved.]

8. Germs! Germs! Germs!
   Our British brethren gave "gifts" of small pox contaminated blankets to Indians to infect people and cause epidemics in Indian tribes. There are gruesome Internet Images on line: "Smallpox pictures" and gruesome descriptions of the ravages of the disease.

During the Vietnam War, the U.S. funded studies to try to develop rice diseases and defoliants to destroy Asian food supplies. Millions would have starved. The University of Pennsylvania signed contracts with the military for their researchers to try to develop "weapons of mass destruction." [See: Joel Aber, Germ Warfare Research for Vietnam: Project Spicerack on the Pennsylvania Campus.]

> **Q: Discuss:** Is it morally OK to use any means necessary to defeat an enemy nation or rebelling citizens? Include discussion of food destruction viz, slaughter of the buffalo herds; Stalin's starvation of the Ukrainians.

PART TWO: Human "Lab Rats"

It is desired that no document be released which
*refers to **experiments with humans** [emphasis added] and might have*
adverse effect on public opinion or result in legal suits.
— April 17, 1947, memo, Col. O. G. Haywood

"I said, 'Who were these people and why did this happen?' The only thing I could think of was Nazi Germany." — Energy Secretary Hazel O'Leary [upon learning of human radiation experiments, <u>Newsweek</u>, 1994]

"If the chemical was harmless, why did the government do everything in secret? Why were they so sneaky weaky with us?" — citizen comment regarding the Army's secret spraying of chemicals

Only dictators do "nasty" stuff to their own citizens.

Right?

Wrong!

Presidents and their staffs have also allowed "nasty" stuff.

It was necessary to develop all kinds of weapons to help subdue any enemy after WWII. We approve of this. Political leaders in the U.S. and Soviet Union pushed to develop nuclear weapons after WWII. We didn't know exactly how to develop and use them. Our competing ruling elites had to figure out how to use them. We didn't know the limits and ramifications of nuclear war and the aftermath of war on the citizenry. Therefore, to find out, we had to hire scientists and researchers to conduct experiments. The "guinea pigs" were human. They were citizens. They were kept in the dark, except when radiated. Then they "lit" up! [heh, heh, heh!]

The following examples illustrate that our allies and foreign governmental leaders will do <u>anything</u> to gather information and intelligence in order to be protected from enemies. We consider citizens as necessary expendables in our efforts. Once again constitutional rights are nonexistent. You are at our disposal and have been kept in the dark—even when lit up with our radiation experiments [heh, heh, heh!]

I Saw My Bones Through My Flesh

The first "lab rats" were U.S. troops who were ordered near the experimental nuclear blasts in Nevada, 1953. We wanted to see how troops would react when confronted with a nuclear blast going-off! One veteran related how troops were ordered to close their eyes and cover them with their hands. He told of seeing the bones in his hands when the radiation came. Military personnel ordered near the blasts suffered innumerable cancer afflictions. So far $138 million has been awarded according to **Atomic Vet Benefit Long Time Coming** (Hasson, 2012). The article highlights a soldier who had been exposed to 11 atmospheric nuclear tests and had battled lymphoma, colon and thyroid cancer. His descendants received compensation seven decades after the blasts!

The "Down-winders"

Of course, all above ground nuclear tests released radiation upwards. But, no one was warned. There was an increase in thyroid cancers downwind from the nuclear blasts throughout the country. No one was alerted. Taking Iodine tablets could have helped, especially for children. No one was alerted to stay indoors. No one knew. The movie "The Conqueror" was being filmed downwind. Crew and cast remember white "stuff" floating down. It burned

their fingers when they rubbed them together. They hadn't been warned. No one was. The "down-winders" who died of cancer: 91 of the 220 cast members, including Susan Hayward, Agnes Moorehead, Dick Powell and of course...John Wayne. *People Magazine*, (Jackovich & Sinnet, 1980) **The Children of John Wayne, Susan Hayward and Dick Powell Fear That Fallout Killed Their Parents.**
and see also: **Inhuman Radiation Experiments,** by John LaForge, Counterpunch (2013). The article examines public declassified documents that show the U.S. "conducted 2,000 radiation experiments on as many as 20,000 uninformed vulnerable citizens." Radiation in various methods was tested on pregnant women, children and men's testicles.

The Plutonium "Files"
In Idaho in 1985, the Energy Department deliberately released radiation in simulated meltdowns from nuclear plants. Eileen Welsome won a Pulitzer Prize for **The Plutonium Files: America's Secret Medical Experiments in the Cold War** (MacPherson, 1999).

The Secret Spray of St. Louis
According to Jim Salter, in **Secret Cold War tests in St. Louis…** secret chemical compounds were sprayed from motorized blowers on buildings and from back of station wagons. Residents have suffered high incidences of breast, thyroid, skin, and uterine cancer. "I feel betrayed. How could they do this?" asks a cancer survivor (2012).

The CIA Secretly "Drops" LSD
On November 19, 1953, the CIA spiked the drink of Frank R. Olson with LSD to determine its effects on human beings and potential adversaries. Nine days later he was dead from a fall from an apartment building. Twenty-two years later President Ford met with family survivors and apologized. (AP, 1975) They received $750,000 in compensation. (Gaines, 2013)

The Tick Cometh to Lyme
"By the pricking of my thumbs, something wicked this way comes."
Act 4 Scene 1, *Macbeth*
The Plum Island Animal Disease Center was established in 1954 by the U.S. government to do research to study methods to control animal diseases. Diseases transmitted by ticks were studied. They "escaped" and found refuge offshore! Plum Island is 38.5 miles from Lyme, NY. West Nile virus was also studied. [See Internet: "Plum Island" for discussions about migratory birds and swimming deer inadvertently spreading diseases off the island].

Bikini Exposure
You can't go home again—ever! It's not there!
The inhabitants of several Marshall Islands were forcibly removed against their will by the U.S. Government. It conducted 67 above ground nuclear tests (1946-1958) on their homeland. [View Internet images: "Bikini

nuclear tests" for aftermath pictures.] Among other targets, tests were designed to see the effects of radiation contamination on nearby warships in case of nuclear war. Of course naval personnel were not warned as they sat offshore absorbing the sun's rays—and radiation

Secret Agent [Orange] Man
*"I was introduced to Agent Orange
on my husband's deathbed."* — Widow [See below]

*Project 112 (1962-1974): classified "biological and chemical warfare
vulnerability tests"* [See below]

*"Were we marines used as guinea pigs on Okinawa?
I think so."*[See below]

We also needed to develop alternatives to nuclear weapons. (Dropping LSD solutions into an enemy's water supply was proven to be inoperable). A-bombs were rather unwieldy. We couldn't just "drop and blast" an enemy anywhere we wanted to. Besides, their explosive aftermath left flattened buildings with a horrible radiation residue. No duster for that! There's little opportunity to make a profit amidst such ruins, such detritus!

But, we had to find an alternative to nuclear weapons. Testing on civilian human subjects would be challenging. One thing advantageous about subordinate military personnel: they have to go where ordered to go. They have to do whatever they're ordered to do. If they don't, they can be court martialled. They are "caged-in" and must obey. It is the ultimate, "we gotcha" under our control! After WWII, Marines were ordered to Okinawa to conduct chemical defoliant experiments. They were like "caged rats!"

Z: Unsuspecting and unprotected Marines had to obey commands. The members of the 267 Chemical Platoon reported for duty to participate in Project 112. The following information is revealed in Jon Mitchell's well-documented article, **Were U.S. Marines Used as Guinea Pigs on Okinawa?** *Japan Times* (2012). Another article reveals Michelle Gatz's logbook evidence of SS Schuylere Otis Band transporting defoliants to Okinawa. Don Heathcote, private first class at Camp Hansen, 1962 claims he sprayed and "killed large swaths of the jungle...with chemicals from drums..." He further notes, "After I returned home, I underwent an operation to extract polyps from my nose. The doctors removed enough to fill a cup. Plus they diagnosed me with bronchitis and sinusitis connected to chemical exposure" (Mitchell J. , Agent Orange 'tested in Okinawa' Documents indicate jungle use in 1962 , 2012).

Gerald Mohler notes:
> *"We were told to erect tents at a five-acre brown spot
> devoid of vegetation and sleep there for a few days.
> We received no training during that time. We just sat
> around and did nothing. Nearby we discovered a stash of
> approximately 40 50-gallon barrels of defoliants. The odor
> was unmistakable...Were we marines used as guinea pigs*

on Okinawa? I think so" (Mitchell J. , 2012).

Mr. Mohler suffers from pulmonary fibrosis and Parkinson's disease.

   The Pentagon still has not resolved health claims to over 250 Marines suffering from toxic chemical exposure. One widow claimant has had a claim pending over 8,600 days, **Bergmann & Moore Client Testifies Before Congress** (Vetlawyers.com, 2013). Her husband, died at age 39 "as a result of exposure to the toxic herbicide Agent Orange." The Pentagon has repeatedly concealed and/or lied about defoliant experiments. The Pentagon is on record and has said such chemicals were never on Okinawa despite online pictures of lined up barrels of chemicals and testimony by victims.

> *These documents* [discovered naval log books] *are the smoking gun. Now there is no way that the Department of Defense can continue to deny defoliants were ever on Okinawa. It's time they owned up and started giving these sick veterans the justice they deserve.* —Michelle Gatz

   Actually, O ye of silly faith, there is a way to deny. The Pentagon simply won't act. It can't. It must: Delay! Delay! Delay! To admit the truth means an admission of systematic lying and cover-up by government/military officials. Citizens might get disillusioned. We can't have that! To admit the truth means to admit their leaders were lying and/or hiding the truth.

Z: The Pentagon functions with governmental approval. Defense Secretary McNamara and top politicians approved such testing. After decades of lying, and denying; lying and denying *ad nauseum* especially to citizens of Okinawa (until recently a home to U.S. military bases) there is no way the military and the U.S. government can do an "about face" and tell the truth. It would blow the cover on decades-old deliberate systematic deception and lying. Dissimulation and cover-up rule the day!

PART THREE: The Ultimate Abuses
Maimed, Neglected & Dead

> *To care for him who shall have borne the battle and for his widow* —President Lincoln, 2nd Inaugural Address

> *"It was like my best friend betrayed me. I had given the Army everything, and they took everything away."* —wounded veteran stripped of veterans' benefits [See: below]

   There are always little slip-ups and glitches when so many military personnel are involved. Governments can't be expected to operate perfectly in an imperfect world. The American people are surprised and even outraged when men and women in the military suffer abuses. We fight against any blame especially in the military. We just delay and delay and delay any public exposure of a snafu in hopes that adverse publicity will be quashed. Settlements cost money and mean more taxes to pay for "mess-ups." It's also lousy PR and would damage military careers if there were any admissions of neglect or malfeasance. A critical letter in one's file can cut-off a career. Dissimulation is inbred in every officer and his/her press release! The following examples show that the military bailiwick knows how to cover-up.

It's unfortunate that lousy water caused some little blips in the health of Marines and their families for decades at Camp Lejeune. William R. Levesque exposes deadly water contamination in his article, **Camp Lejeune vets suffer from drinking water contamination,** (2009). One widow wrote, her husband "died never knowing what poisoned him."

For years "[C]ritics fault the Marine Corps personnel with a decades-old campaign to either hide the contamination or minimize dangers and then doing too little to alert people." So far, [about] "1,500 claims have been filed against the government seeking $33.8-billion in damages." Known chemical contamination was allowed to continue for decades. Obviously, no one wanted to "blow the whistle" on his/her superiors. Omertà rules!

Sailors positioned off the coast of Japan after the nuclear plant meltdowns are suffering debilitating illness from radiation poisoning. The Fukushima radioactive fallout contaminated navy personnel when on March 17, 2011, the USS Reagan was sent to aid Japan in "Operation Tomodacci" (Friendship). CNN News reports, **Sailors Sue Japan Nuclear Plant Owner, Saying disaster Made Them Sick,** (Watkins & Mungin, 2012). Lynne Peeples writes, **U.S. Armed Forces Sickened After Fukushima Meltdown Get Help From Online Fundraising** (2014). [View Internet showing personnel in Haz-mat gear scrubbing down the decks.]

> In the midst of a snowstorm, deck hands were enveloped in a warm cloud that came with a metallic taste. Sailors testify that the Reagan's 5,500-member crew was told over the ship's intercom to avoid drinking or bathing in desalinized water drawn from a radioactive sea. The huge carrier quickly ceased its humanitarian efforts and sailed 100 miles out to sea, where newly published internal Navy communications confirm it was still taking serious doses of radioactive fallout. Quote from Wasserman (2014), **Documents Say Navy Knew Fukushima Dangerously Contaminated the USS Reagan.**

Japan, South Korea and Guam refused port facilities for the Reagan to enter for being too contaminated. Of course the Navy is refusing to recognize thousands of claims. Those would cost a ton of money and be very, very bad PR! Public testimony by debilitated sailors would be horrendous publicity! Hey, at least they are alive and didn't have to face the horrors of war!

The Artful (War) Dodger
'I am tired and sick of war. Its glory is all moonshine. It is only those who have neither fired a shot nor heard the

shrieks and groans of the wounded who cry aloud for blood,
more vengeance, more desolation. War is hell!"
— William Tecumseh Sherman
"Give 'em all the same grub and all the same pay [and no daily showers]
and the war would be over and done in a day."
—All Quiet on the Western Front

We don't do war—except for profit.
We send others to war. But, "we've got your back"—way back!
[heh, heh, heh—laugh if you're breathing!]
We have always figured out ways to "avoid" war or keep a safe distance.
During the Civil War, if drafted, we could divvy up a "commutation" fee of
$300 [$5,746 today's dollar rate] and opt out if we could find a substitute.
Obviously we had the cash to bailout before we had to "fall-in!" [heh, heh,
heh!] We freely admit we have passed laws to "rig" past drafts to help us
and/or our sons "opt out" of wars in the pre-Iraqi era. (Thank goodness for
the fearless National Guard, especially the "Texas Champagne" Guard Unit
during the Vietnam draft era! I'll drink to that!).

A Polemic: (fr. Gk: πολεμικός = We won't Go!)

Z: Since 1950 many political candidates for higher office and prominent
people never served during America's wars. In recent times, only those who
achieved the Presidency needed to learn to salute the military (as civilians)
when they came and went by helicopter.

Daddy, What did you do during the War (WWII)?

Ron: I served and I made training movies but never left the states; I only
"saw" Hollywood blank bullets.
John W.: Hey, Pilgrim, during the war I killed-off the enemy in the movies
on Hollywood war sets. The real Pilgrims faced more dangers than me
during their perilous ocean crossing, 1640! I didn't serve.
Hubert: I wanted to go but I had a hernia.
John K.: I was in the navy. [See: "PT-109" movie] My brother was killed. He
wanted to be president, if he had lived.
Constantinos Saranthopoulos: I had four dependents and was told by my
draft board because of them and my age that I would not be shipped
overseas—36 year old veteran saw action, European front. Born in the
USA. Thanks, Dad!
Note: George Bush Sr., Richard Nixon, Dwight Eisenhower, and
Robert Dole actively served.

Daddy, What did you do during in the Vietnam War?

Dick: I worked hard to get four deferments. It was a tough slog! Thank
goodness I was a Dad.
Mitt: I "stood my ground" and bravely demonstrated <u>for</u> the war. Hey,
those UCLA antiwar placards were dangerous! [View Internet: Images,
Romney, Vietnam; protest picture] I got four deferments and travelled

overseas to help the heathen French get (my) religion. I also learned to eat those disgusting French Fries! *Ces't la vie!* My father, Governor George Romney, approved. Thanks, Dad.

Dan: I "landed" in the Indiana National Guard where I played a lot of gulf and helped proofread for my Daddy's many, many loocrative newzpapers. Thanx, Dad.

George: I served in the dried-out "Champagne Unit" in the Texas National Guard and sort of *rather* disappeared until the war was over. My father approved. Thanks, Dad.

Al: I was there as a reporter but no one noticed me (as usual) as I sort of just blended (blanded) in and went where there was no live action. My father, Senator Al Gore, approved. Thanks, Dad.

John: I served on a swift boat on the Mekong Delta where real bullets whizzed by and I saw men die. I earned some real medals. I was not a casualty of real war. However, I was "shot down" and swift-boated in the political battle of my life!

Bill: I suffered an injury and this could be construed, or misconstrued, depending how one defines the word "injury," as a casualty *during* the war in England whereto fore I bit my lower lip climbing the stairs at university whilst I was attending University College, Oxford as a Rhodes scholar, (where I studied Aristotelian logic) which meant I am really, really smart and I conclude this to be true because I have my very own Presidential library. That's logical!

Ted (political activist): I have bragged how I got out of the draft. My "number was up [actually down]" but I "dodged a bullet" [literally and figuratively] through my shenanigans. Did someone take one for me? Were you a most loyal, true-blue native-born non-Kenyan American? (Actually, I am really brave shooting down unarmed animals—from a very, very safe distance!) "Rock on," Daddy-o!

Note: John McCain served and was a POW.

ODE TO THE UNSEEN FALLEN

They will send your children, grandchildren to war
> But not their own

Millions sent into Harm's Way
> But not their own

Millions of arms, legs, eyes, brains, souls
> But not their own

Millions neglected, suffering, moaning, disabled
> But never their own will suffer
> ...while contending for the honor
> of our dear and cherished flag
> [nor] suffer 'mid the wounded or die among the slain[?]

—"Was My Brother in the Battle" by C. S. Foster

Note: A programmed non-human mechanized letter-signing signature machine is used to "sign" the official, "We regret to inform you" letter.

You can't pawn *that* signature. As the British would say, "It's a bloody fake!"
[End of Z's enhanced polemic]

The dead and wounded of any war are not our primary concerns. Decades of neglect as outlined above illustrate that! [Review, "Maimed, Neglected & Dead"]. The Walter Reed Hospital scandal and exposé a few years earlier showed mold and falling ceilings. Once the TV camera lights were removed, little changed! Such bad publicity is unfortunate! Of course, nothing has really changed. Careers had to be protected. "Sweep it all under the rug!"

===

But, why did we use human "guinea pigs" to conduct experiments? Obviously, there was a "method to such madness." We needed to test new weapons capabilities. But, why were these developed? The simple answer is we were worried about the political instability in the world after WWII (1945). The political makeup of the world was extremely volatile. We needed to develop every possible weapon and defense mechanism against all possible battle contingencies. We were being challenged of our right to rule and right to our property and assets. Our way of doing "business as usual" was being threatened—as usual!

Chapter Eight details how we "collected" colonies around the world and developed spheres of influence. It details the methods used to hold on to our forcibly acquired assets. In the 20th century, billions of people worldwide were "restive!" They wanted independence from our colonial rule and domination. They wanted to get rid of people like my friends and me. This meant all our lucrative businesses and our enterprises were in jeopardy. And that meant our profits would disappear! We had to launch a massive worldwide counter offensive to stop and roll back any and all challenges to our traditional way of rule and dominance.

We spent trillions in taxpayers' money to hold on to them. Governments used taxes, resources and manpower and mobilized forces in a massive effort to win and dominate. This is what we have done throughout the world. Whatever is needed! When there was resistance by native populations, we sent in Expeditionary Forces to quell the "restive natives!" We used taxes, resources and manpower to crush our perceived enemies. That's what we have had to do throughout the world to crush the world's rebelling populations! We had to use all means to suppress rebellion to our rule and dominance. We crushed all opposition! —well, at least we tried!

CHAPTER EIGHT

Let the
CRUSHING   CRUSHING   CRUSHING
Games Begin

Now this is the law of the jungle
As old and as true as the sky,
And the wolf that shall keep it may prosper,
But the wolf that shall break it must die,
[show no mercy]   — Rudyard Kipling

Whatever happens, we have got
the Maxim gun, and they have not.
(and the Gatling gun too)

What is "(r)ight is only in question between equals in power,
while the strong do what they can and the weak suffer what they must."
—Athenian general   [See Melos below]

The three parts of this chapter drive home the major theme of our philosophy in foreign affairs. Our objective is the ever expanding and growth of our profits, possessions and wealth from around the world. We will do anything to crush any opposition that challenges our efforts. Citizens in democracies are kept in the dark and not told the truth of these secret efforts. Why? We need their taxes, resources and manpower [sons & daughters] to achieve our objectives. Therefore, all governments lie and/or cover-up their real objectives. There is no exception! They cannot reveal the true reasons for traversing the world, which is to suck in the world's wealth into our coffers. As always, "restive" natives had to be militarily suppressed.

PART ONE

WWI & WWII CALAMITY & AFTERMATH

The post-war chaos of WWI [1914-1918] led to Germany's total political and economic instability. The allies foolishly punished Germany with unrealistic demands for reparations to pay for the cost of the war. John Maynard Keynes' book, Economic Consequences of the Peace, related the devastation of the war and post-war bankrupt nation. He predicted the collapse and ruination of Germany. France's Clemenceau insisted on punishing Germany and rendering it so weakened it would not be a future threat to France. In retrospect, we should have helped Germany recover from the war and make it stable. Possibly the rise of Hitler and World War Two could have been avoided!

Depression, run-away inflation, and steep unemployment helped lead to the Nazi's Adolf Hitler and his ascendency. First, the voters elected his party members and with a majority of elected delegates, Hitler took over the country. He took over the reins of power of government, especially the military, the interior ministry and the secret police.

Rah! Rah! Rally for Hitler

In the beginning, we enthusiastically supported him with money to fund his fascist party and organize his bullying Brown Shirts who helped quash any democratic opposition. We just wanted to have him get in power and stabilize the chaos. We wanted him to get rid of all the pesky troublesome liberals, communists, unionists and socialists who threatened to destroy our way of doing business. We helped him secure his rule in the country and then...he went rogue!

He couldn't just do what ordinary run–of-the-mill dictators do: Rule with an iron fist and suppress any opposition by any means possible. We wanted him to create stability and let us return to good, profitable, normal commerce. Unfortunately, he was certifiable! [Never put a mystic or visionary in power!] He had this "vision thing" about a "Greater Germany" spreading throughout the hoped for, soon-to-be conquered Soviet Union. That Third Reich invincibility vision would lead to WWII and doubling the deaths of World War I with chaotic and world destruction! What a mess!

And that thing with the Jews and gays…What a waste of assets! And the wasted manpower and resources to round up, ship and exterminate so many, while a war was going on! I. G. Farben chemical company had the right idea. The Monowitz Labor camps, which can be viewed on the Internet, [View Drone Images of Monowitz concentration camp] produced synthetic rubber and chemicals. Twelve thousand inmates from concentration camps were leased out by the powerful SS military units. Life expectancy was four months. Mine workers lasted one month. Although I was opposed to such lunacy as the concentration camps, I did what the top Nazi officials did and invested in the chemical factories that provided a steady residual lucrative income. Hey! "Go with the flow!" (No pun intended!) I was lucky the railroad tracks and my chemical factories weren't bombed or my profits would've been immensely curtailed.

Z: Chemical companies can always get export licenses and ship their lucrative trade to any thug dictator. The BBC of England reported September 1, 2013, that chemical export licenses to Syria for potassium fluoride and sodium fluoride were granted by Business Secretary Vince Cable's Department for Business…10 months after the current Syrian uprising began against President Assad. These chemicals made the sarin gas that killed 1,500 civilians. [View Internet Image: "Syria gas attacks" for pictures.]

And the weapons, especially the bullets! Half the 6,000,000 were killed all over Europe in fields away from the camps and were executed by gunfire. There's always good profit in ammo and weapons and war! My friends in the U.S. shipped hundreds of airplane engines for the Luftwaffe before the start of WWII. Hey! Go with the flow (of arms)! We are true Merchants of Death. That book, authored by Engelbrecht and Hanighen, details our profiting of war material to all warring nations.

Hitler's "Rocket Man," Herr Wernher Von Braun, had the right idea for building his V-2 rockets: use very, very, very cheap labor. He used the Jews and other captives as slaves to help build his "Baby Blasters." It only cost about 10,000 lives of workers (due to hunger and exhaustion) to build his rockets. I would have fed them more to get a little more usage out of them. What a waste! After getting the OK from Der Fuhrer, (Sieg Heil), Von Braun fired off his V-2 rockets that indiscriminately devastated England and blew up everything and everybody.

Z: The people of England sent their children to the countryside to avoid Von Braun's devastating rockets. C. S. Lewis would give a fictional account of England's fleeing children: Lucy, Edward, Peter, and Susan in his book, The Lion the Witch and the Wardrobe. They were shipped to the Professor, out of harm's way, until war's end. Hitler ordered Herr Wernher Von Braun to develop a long-distance rocket to cross the Atlantic Ocean and attack the U.S. coast. He believed the American people, once attacked, would demand an end to the war! He was really, really certifiable!

Von Braun tried to make such a rocket, but failed. Within a couple of years after Hitler was defeated, **Herr** Von Braun became **Mr.** Von Braun and was employed making rockets for—the U.S.A! Is it a great country, or what! Go with the flow (of money)! Look out world! Once, he was heard to bitterly mutter, "Nein!" to good union wages; he was accustomed to unpaid slaves!

The war ended in 1945. We surveyed the world. It was in shambles! From the bombed-out cities and the ashes of war, we saw political instability everywhere. Countries were greatly weakened and financially exhausted. We remembered what happened to chaotic Mother Russia and Germany after WWI. Instability led to revolution and communism in Russia and chaos and Nazism in Germany, and the rise of Hitler. We didn't want a repeat of such insanities!

The Russians Are Coming! The Russians Are Coming!*
*1966 comedy movie spoof

In October 1917, a mere 30 years before in Russia, the communist Bolsheviks, led by Lenin, had seized control of the government, eliminated the Russian Czar (despite some die-hards' wishful thinking, Anastasia too!) and defeated the Mensheviks. We remember the failure of all the nations that intervened with troops to try to defeat and overthrow them by arming the anti-communist White Army. Unfortunately, we failed to crush and eliminate that evil scourge! After WWII, the "Communist Menace" began to spread in Europe. We couldn't fail again! We would have to gear-up and do what it takes. The Nazis had been eliminated and now it was time to eliminate the new "Axis of Evil," whose goal was to eliminate—us!

After the war, the Russian Bear was expanding and conquering Eastern European countries. It pounced on the weakened nations. Josef Stalin's communist regime was eliminating the Old Order and instituting state ownership of private enterprise wherever there were Russian troops. Communist Russia was also physically eliminating by execution all my acquaintances and like-minded friends!

Z: Say, what? What happened? How come the change from a friendly ally to a menacing predator? Less than 1,000 days earlier, England's Winston Churchill and Russia's Josef Stalin were allies who had secretly met "behind closed doors" to discuss post-WWII war issues.

Let's look behind the scenes at a friendlier time. It's time for a little levity:

The Winnie and Joe Parody
Carving up Europe: *Behind Closed Doors*

W: Look at all the honey!
 J: I want some
W: You got pots of honey: Estonia, Lithuania and Latvia
A treaty between Hitler and Stalin in 1939 illegally ceded these countries and eastern Poland to the Soviet Union, Russia. [See Internet: Nazi-Soviet Non-aggression Pact].
J: I want more. Let us share.

W: O. K. Here is a map. Let us talk. What do you want to take?
[In 1944, England's Winston Churchill secretly flew to meet with Josef Stalin (without telling their ally President Roosevelt) to discuss post-war Europe. Each wanted to protect their borders and/or financial interests.]
J: I want honey pot from Romania. Is that legal?
W: O. K. I want honey pot from Greece. Is that legal?
J: Let us share honey pots: Bulgaria, Hungary, Yugoslavia
W: Do we tell the people?
J: Do not tell. It is a secret!

The pencil written note shows how these two carved up Europe [View Internet: Churchill/Stalin, "Percentages agreement."] It is known as the "Naughty document" or "Percentage Agreement," that outlined divvying up post-war European countries.

In the movie, *The Mouse that Roared* starring Peter Sellers, English and Russian diplomats are playing Monopoly, trading real countries instead of real estate. It was supposed to be satire, but was actually reality!

W: It is a naughty, naughty secret
J. Do not tell the people.
...a few months later after WWII is over in Europe and the Agreement is not working out...
W: Oh, this is messy!
J: It's "hammer time!"
W: My hands are dripping...what? Honey?
J: No, no, no. Honey is not red. The people said, "No! Time for a smack down. I do it all the time.
W: I am mad. I will send in Redcoats! [see below]
J: I do it all the time! Ask the Ukrainians.
W: I want to take the honey pots back.
J: I do not want to be your friend!
W: Time to un-friend!

The Cold War Begins after WWII

Also, the communist ideology and influence were spreading throughout the world. Restless populations were joining communist and socialist political organizations. They were organizing and getting weapons! They wanted to throw off the yoke of colonialism. Communists/socialists were winning parliamentary and mayoral elections in France and Italy and threatening to win elections in Greece.

All our colonies that we had swiped "fair and square" from native peoples and sucked out their wealth, were soon in open rebellion: India, Algeria, Indo-china (Vietnam), Kenya, and other African colonies. They were demanding independence. Our way of life was being terminated by state-controlled totalitarianism in Communist Europe and later in Red China. We were being physically terminated by arrests and firing squads. All our accumulated assets and profits were being confiscated. We fled for our lives from communism. We, the survivors in the "Free World," had to draw "a line in the sand," a "line in the jungles," et al. and begin to staunch the unchecked, spreading threat of worldwide communism.

What to do? We had to crush all efforts to expel us from our lucrative colonies. We had to crush all challenges to our control and influence in other nations. We had to eliminate any ideology that promoted state control of natural resources, (especially oil) and infrastructure. There's no profit in that! We had to crush any rebellion by millions, actually billions, of people opposed to our control and way of doing business.

We had to create a New World order to save the Old World Order. The "clarion" call went out March 5, 1946, at Westminster College. In a speech, former British Prime Minister Winston Churchill proclaimed that "from Stettin in the Baltic to Trieste in the Adriatic, an iron curtain [Iron Curtain] has descended across the [European] continent." He "threw the gauntlet" down and challenged the United States to join England in joint counter measures against the spread of communism.

It was obvious we couldn't trust Russia and the communists to keep their word. Soon civil war broke out in Greece between non-royalists wanting changes and royalists wanting to re-establish the monarchy and the pre-WWII Old Order. We backed the Old Order!

Opposition by socialists and communists were labeled as an "uprising." We took sides. Our side was losing. Scheduled elections would have voted our allies and us out. Churchill set up "Operation Manna" to quell resistance. He sent British parachutists [Royal Expeditionary Forces] and the navy commanded by Lt. General Ronald Scobie. On October 18, 1944, the exiled Greek Prime Minister had been flown in by the British government and re-installed under the umbrella protection of British troops. Churchill's handpicked "man" was in power! And we approved! He could be trusted to do things the way they had always been done! Make money for my friends, British investors and bankers. And profit for us.

The Melos Solution: Crush Crush Crush

But, there was armed resistance. We acted decisively! No namby-pamby; it was Hammer Time! And so the Universal Churchill Dictum a.k.a. Melos Solution [see below] was proclaimed:

> *"Do not hesitate to act as if you were in a conquered*
> *city where a local rebellion is in progress."*
> —Winston Churchill to General Scobie, December 1944

The "Melos Solution" was to be applied to all resisters. If we decide to move in with superior forces, it's best for resisters to "throw in the towel!" History is replete with those who did not choose wisely!

In his History of the Peloponnesian War, Thucydides, wrote a fictionalized conversation of a meeting in 416B. C. between an Athenian delegation of negotiators who wanted the leaders of the island of Melos to quit remaining neutral and join their Delos League, an alliance against Sparta. However, the island leaders hoped to remain neutral and to be left alone. The Athenians demanded an acceptance of the alliance or suffer devastating consequences.

The vastly overwhelming military power of the Athenians could not be matched. And yet Melos declined to join the Delos League pleading the case for peaceful neutrality and insisting it had a right to such a claim. The Athenians "schooled" Melos with the following quote:

> "(r)ight is only in question between equals in power, while the strong do what they can and the weak suffer what they must."

Melos still resisted and after a loss in battle all captured males were executed and the women and children sold into slavery.

Q: What would be a good title for the above scenario?
A. Neutrality is so "iffy"
B. Can't we Get Along?
C. Crush! Crush! Crush! Kiss my derrière or die.

Z: The Churchill Dictum and the Melos Solutions produce the same results. They mean rulers have to do whatever it takes to put their boot on the neck of any resister. Remember King George's massive effort to crush Americans? The British sent 5,000 Redcoats [Royal Expeditionary Forces] to subdue the American rebels. But, they failed to use a widespread scorched earth policy against civilians and kill, kill, kill until they ceased rebelling. Fortunately, during the American Revolutionary War, English General Howe dilly-dallied with the ladies while George Washington built up his armed forces!

The King failed to factor in that Americans were armed with rifles (muskets) unlike peasants around the world who were unarmed and were slaughtered when they rebelled. Those muskets helped make it a "fight between equals in power." Unarmed protestors of tyranny of unequal strength are always defeated.

In 1947 a brutal civil war broke out in Greece. U.S. military aid and support defeated the communist opposition. The monarchy (backed by those in the Koloniki district) was restored. Greece remained non-communist after a brutal civil war.

The Churchill Dictum is the "marching orders" of all conquerors and rulers. They are the same ones given to generals thousands of years ago to hold the land and possessions for conquerors and rulers. Of course, when natives become "restless" and resist, it is necessary to smack them down— to crush them! Otherwise, we lose control. A "namby-pamby" response to armed resistance would fail!

It was obvious after WWII that Communist Russia's Josef Stalin was not going to mellow or change. The communists were going to continue to try to change our way of doing things any way and anywhere on earth. But, England did not have the resources to keep fighting and informed President Truman his government was pulling out of Greece. Oh, my! It looked like another country would soon fall to communism if no measures were taken to suppress it. Italy and France and Turkey would probably have been next! The Mediterranean Sea would have been opened to the Russian fleet!

Elsewhere, the natives in our colonies were growing restive. It was like the world was a giant plantation filled with rebelling "slaves" who wanted to be free—of us! This threatened everything. We had to act and act decisively with specific counter measures.

A Giant Leap into the Fray!

Our political allies went into action and set-up a united defense against the growing communist threat. How was this achieved? First there was an official declaration of "hostilities" against Russia: On March 12, 1947, before a joint session of Congress, President Harry Truman outlined the "Truman Doctrine" to aid Greece and Turkey. Military trainers and $400,000,000 in financial aid was the beginning. Next, the Marshall Plan was initiated years after war's end to help bolster economically impoverished countries. Third, a military Alliance called NATO was created—a "coalition of the willing" to prevent any direct attack in Europe by Russia.

Z: This alliance included former enemies who had just a few years earlier been blowing up each other's armies and citizens, especially Germany and Japan.

America has "never looked back" as she has gone from isolationist to interventionist. From minding our own business to a "long and winding" road of death and destruction for those who resist: Greece, Vietnam, Cuba, Chile, Guatemala, Iran, Afghanistan, Iraq, et. al. [See especially, Part Three: Kiss(inger) of Death]

PART TWO

CRUSHING GAMES

Who to Crush? Why?

Restore Stability. Restore the status quo.
Restore us. — Yachta Yachta Yachta

To Right the "World Turn'd Upside Down"

After devastating worldwide wars we are the ones who pick up the pieces to restore and set the world upright and functioning again. After wars, everyday citizens go back to everyday mundane affairs to earn a living. They can't conduct international relations with other countries of the world. They hope we, as leaders, know what we're doing. And we do! And we do things for our selfish reasons. We have already discussed that our ultimate goal is to make profit anyway we can. To that end we have supported any government and/or political faction including dictatorships. Why, some of our best friends are dictators—actually, most!

Today, our goals are the same as those espoused in many Mission Statements of today's privately funded Think Tanks. The following excerpt from the Lexington Institute's website succinctly states our worldly objectives:

By promoting America's ability to project power around the globe, we not only defend the homeland of democracy, but also sustain the international stability in which other free-market democracies can thrive. (Institute)

In summary, our foreign policy goals are:
1. Stable governments
2. Free-market economies
3. Defend the homeland

But we are not concerned with free elections or democracy. We have never wanted democracy to spread. We don't want citizens voting and opposing us. However, we do want international stability around the world for "our guys" to go forth and prosper with assistance from friendly foreign leaders! We never intervene to help the "little guy." We intervene to prop up and/or place a "Yes Man" in a government friendly to our ways.

Stability and *status quo* were being challenged around the world. It's too bad the millions of natives of the world didn't see it our way. They had helped fight against the Axis powers of Germany and Japan during WWII; and after the war, they wanted payback! They wanted independence from us. We wanted to keep our colonies. After all, we had spent lots of money and made major military efforts to swipe them.

We wanted to keep doing what we have always been doing throughout history: making money by sucking in the world's resources and wealth from everyone. Previously, we succeeded in "slicing-up" the territories of the world with treaties made by the world's major powers including the United States. Our predatory rights had been established for decades. They are outlined below to show the vast dominions that we seized and possessed. We were not going to give them up without a fight! After World War II, we would use citizens' taxes, resources and of course manpower to hold on!

In the past we had spent many decades carving up the world into our very profitable colonies. European leaders made many treaties and pacts. These are outlined below and illustrate how we "gobbled-up" territory and populations that had no means to resist us militarily.

UNIVERSAL RIGHT TO COLONIZE

"The higher races have a right over the lower races; they have a duty to civilize the inferior races." —French state funeral, 1884 Miles Ferry

They believed they were bringing civilization to 'savage people.' They introduced Christianity, trade, education, justice and a good deal of looting and forced labor.
—Richard Dowden, Director of Royal African Society in Britain

Steps to Colonization

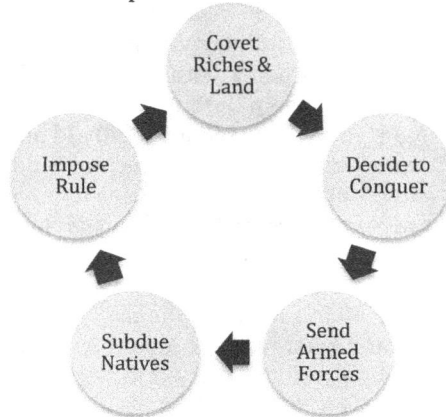

We always make-up some kind of a rationale for invading and occupying territories and taking what we want from the original inhabitants who had less firepower. [Review Chapter Six, *Swipers*] It looks better when our bloody endeavors are bleached clean in the history books. Citizens, especially in democracies, have to ignore the bloody downsides of conquest if they are going to "beat their chests" in prideful exultation over their country's (tribal) victories. The Fixxed Media does not emphasize what happens to those on the receiving end. Of course, we can't reveal the true nature of our conquests. The Gooderites would complain and protest! In reality we have intervened to promote what I humbly label, "Yachta's Way." We weren't there to help the natives. The Fixxed Media in every country has ignored challenges to this view. Citizens aren't told what's going on. They're powerless to change anything, anyway.

Hopefully, after seeing the events outlined in the following sections, citizens will relinquish their delusion that somehow their particular country acted innocently in dealings with their colonies or subjugation of native peoples. We have helped every government in history to subdue restive populations with every weapon possible. Do you think we really cared about people who had different skin color; who had different languages; who had different religions; and who lived in different lands?

Colonization began in earnest during the nineteenth century. Major countries agreed to avoid competitive armed conflict over the mineral riches of the world. How did these arrangements occur? Several European conferences and treaties affected tens of millions of inhabitants who had no say in how the European powers would intervene to govern them. As major players, we did not want to go to war to fight over new sources of trade and natural resources. So we agreed to "divvy-up" the potential goodies and avoid armed conflict! We spread a world map across the table, licked our lips, pointed a finger, and selected our new territories! The U.S. would also get into the act of overseas expansion to take its share of goodies!

(Prologue) Pacification in the Pacific

Z: In 1898, U.S. General Otis, military head of U.S. Expeditionary Forces, was charged to suppress the rebellion by the Filipinos after the Philippines were taken at the end of war with Spain. Emil Aquinaldo and the Filipino natives had fought against the brutal Spanish rule and then against U.S. Expeditionary Forces and their brutal repression. Many letters by soldiers sent back home and stories by reporters told of brutal torture, killings, and repressive methods to quell resistance to U.S. rule. [Soldiers were ordered to write letters to newspapers to recant and say they were lying, and to renounce their observations and earlier letters sent home as false!] Otis ordered all corralled and interred inhabitants in resisting areas beyond a "dead line" of 300 to 800 yards to be shot. He told reporters that the troops were ordered to shoot anyone old enough to carry a gun [but not actually having a gun] if found outside the restricted zone. When asked at what age, he replied, "ten years old." This information is from the book Little Brown Brother: How the United States Purchased and Pacified the Philippines, by Leon Wolff, (1960). Native deaths were estimated at several hundred thousand to 1,000,000. A letter by A. F. Miller, of the 32nd Volunteer Infantry Regiment, published in the Omaha World-Herald in May 1900, told of how Miller's unit subjected a prisoner to what he and others called the 'water cure.' "Now, this is the way we give them the water cure," he explained. "Lay them on their backs, a man standing on each hand and each foot, then put a round stick in the mouth and pour a pail of water in the mouth and nose, and if they don't give up [information] pour in another pail" (2008). [View picture and article: Paul Kramer, **The Water Cure,** The New Yorker.]

China: "Spheres of Influence," 19th century

France, England, Germany, Russia and Japan carved out territories for trade and influence in China. "Gunboat Diplomacy" through bombardment of Chinese ports enforced submission by the Chinese emperor. The Empress Dowager wrote they "descended like vultures upon the mainland for spheres of influence." "The various powers cast upon us looks of tiger-like voracity, hustling each other in their endeavors to seize upon our innermost territories" (Wolff, 1960).

The Berlin Conference of 1884-85

Germany, France, England, and 12 other countries carved up Africa into various colonies. Eventually, 50 countries would be arbitrarily created. Lines of demarcation were super-imposed on territory that disregarded over 1,000 indigenous cultures. Their efforts are related in the article by Charles Davis, **Colonialism and the 'scramble for Africa,'** (2010).

Sykes-Picot Asia Minor Agreement 1915-1916

England and France agreed to carve up the Ottoman Empire if they won WWI. Remember the slogan: "WWI was fought to make the world safe for democracy?!" It really was fought to make the world safe for us! The oil reserves of the Middle East "beckoned" and were divvied up. Syria and Iraq and other kingdoms would be artificially created within a few years. But there was armed resistance. Mark Pruszewicz, discusses the British efforts to colonize Iraq through massive bombing. **The 1920s British air bombing campaign in Iraq,** BBC News Magazine, (2014).

The mandates were a ruse so we could take the land and get control. We told the public through the Fixxed Media that the independence of these new colonies "would be postponed until the peoples of the region were considered ready to rule themselves." Of course, we would determine the time for that! [heh, heh, heh!] In May 1920, an uprising by Shia and Sunni tribes had to be crushed in Iraq. One hundred thousand British and Indian troops "were deployed...thousands of Arabs were killed." —along with hundreds of British Expeditionary Forces.

Winston Churchill, War Secretary, initiated "aerial policing"[massive bombing of opposition fighters and civilians]. He had outlined this policy in a speech in the House of Commons in March 1920. He told the government that aerial bombing *"would get the military expenditure down...until the present critical state of affairs* [viz. the Iraqi Rebellion] *passes away."* [NOTE: Adolf Hitler and Winston Churchill would blame each other for initiating massive air raids and indiscriminate bombing of civilian targets in their cities during WWII.]

Spanish American War 1898-1901

We encouraged a war with Spain after the Battleship Maine was sunk. The Yellow Press led by the Hearst newspapers and the Fixxed Media called for revenge. The United States defeated Spain and "swallowed" the following colonies: Cuba (Guantanamo Bay), Philippines (Manila Bay), Puerto Rico, Guam, Wake Island. Invading U.S. Marines had previously invaded and conquered Hawaii (Pearl Harbor).

EXPEDITIONARY FORCES CRUSH THE UNWILLING
The Tragedy of Vietnam and Other Tales

After WWII, the natives were restless!
Our colonies rebelled.
Everywhere!

After World War II we had to fight, not formal military armies, but whole populations of resisters. Where? Anywhere in the whole world! We had to control and dictate all challenges: suppress and expunge! Who would our enemies be? Anyone that challenged us! No one was beyond our reach. We went everywhere with efforts to suppress any challenge to our control and our ways of doing business!

Unfortunately, within a few decades we lost control of all our hard fought for colonies. We sent [fill-in country's name] Expeditionary Forces to try to subdue the "restive" natives. The following revelations illustrate our "tough-minded" efforts that some flaky government leaders condemned.

Z: The movies and news media stories always portrayed the British (et.al) colonial masters as benevolent and "giver of civilization" to the heathen and/or primitive, lesser humans of the world. Like Prometheus feeling sorry for the "mud" people of the world who were living in "darkness," they supposedly set forth to "enlighten" them. They developed schools and brought in missionaries [always supporters of the colonial masters] to provide the "right" religion. They educated a native civil servant class to carry out the wishes of each colonial power. Appointed colonial governors were supported by the military Expeditionary Forces dressed in their smart, impeccable uniforms. The Fixxed Media in newspapers, cinema and books portrayed each ruling government's actions as paternal and kind. A nation's citizens responded with pride of superiority and of conquest over the lesser "breeds." There's that "Herd" thing again!

Unfortunately for the natives, "Enlightened Benevolence" was spread and maintained through Fixxed bayonets. And torture. And massacres. And starvation. And imprisonment. And slavery. The British and American narrative on suppressing their conquered natives was never seriously revealed in history books or the Fixxed Media. All colonial actions were given a calculated "amnesia" whitewash. [See below, "Civil Wars, Uprisings, and Rebellions."]

Civil Wars, Uprisings, and Rebellions. Oh, my!
Stand Your Ground After Stealing It

Well, it's true there were excesses. But, the natives wanted to keep or take back all the colonies and assets we had taken and developed. And we had made better use of those than the original uneducated primitive tribes. Progress marches on! However, we must admit things were a little "messy" at times. Well, if they hadn't resisted us we wouldn't have had to use such drastic measures we later have had to apologize for! Several of our excesses are outlined below and relate "compelling force"[torture, see below].

*"the Herero nation must now leave the country. If it refuses, I shall compel it to do so with the 'long tube' [cannon]. Any Herero found inside the German frontier, with or without a gun or cattle, will be executed. **I shall spare neither women nor children."***
[emphasis added]

Recent court actions and public acknowledgment by former colonial "masters" have revealed the Standard Operating Procedures for "quelling" the restive populations. My response to recent apologies is this: Well, we had to try to keep our colonies! There were so many natives and so few of us! We (in our respective governments) gave the "Marching Orders" to our troop commanders and they used "Compelling Force." **Pages 98-99** list several repressive actions we engaged in, in order to try to stop the loss of our colonies. The following list of brutal actions were recently revealed by David M. Anderson in his article in *The New York Times* which lists a litany of actions we took. **Atoning for the Sins of Empire** (2013).

Malaya: (Malaysia) 1948 Batang Kali massacre
Cyprus: torturers' electrocutions and pulled nails
Aden: [now Yemen] massacre against Yemeni tribes   British governor fled firing pistol from steps of plane, 1965
Northern Ireland: "Bloody Sunday" killings Northern Ireland, 1972, an apology given by England
India: 1919 massacre "regret for loss of life" English Prime Minister
Algeria: no French apology for brutal Algerian war

Kenyan Cache of Documents

Kenya: 1,500 files of secret cache of smuggled documents, 1957 revealed systematic torture.
   Torture as a "Compelling force" was authorized at the cabinet level in Harold Macmillan's government. Survivors recount Kenyans being "savagely beaten, castrated, sexually assaulted" and witnessing murders. NBC reports, **Colonial sins return to haunt former world powers,** by NBC News' Ian Johnston, Nancy Ing, and Ploy Bunuesliip (2012).
Namibia: German extermination order in Namibia in 1904, German General Adrian von Trotha gave an order that:

> *"the Herero nation must now leave the country. If it refuses, I shall compel it to do so with the 'long tube' [cannon]. Any Herero found inside the German frontier, with or without a gun or cattle, will be executed. **I shall spare neither women nor children**" [emphasis added].*

Scroll down the above article to see a picture of a starved and emaciated family allowed to return. Germany issued an apology for the atrocity of the Herero tribe in 2006 and gave millions of Euros to "compensate for the German Army's genocide against the Herero tribe."

Algeria: 1954-1962 revolt, "a million lives were lost and people were murdered, raped, and tortured by both sides…" (France has publicly refused to apologize.)

Indonesia: Dutch apology for massacre of December 9, 1947 killing of 430 boys and young men by Dutch troops during 1946-1947 suppression. Claimants by families in court decision to receive ~$26,600. The Dutch ambassador had formerly apologized to the widows of Capt. Raymond Westerling's troops' counterinsurgency operation. **Dutch apologize for colonial killings in Indonesia** (Karmini, 2013).

Kenyan aftermath: English courts in 2011 awarded compensation to 5,228 Kenyans tortured during the Mau Mau uprising and fight for independence totaling £20 million, or £3,000 each only to living survivors. Mina Akrami reports in her article, **59 Years Later, Mau Mau Torture Victims Receive Compensation** (2013).

To keep control of their colonies in post WWII, our like-minded friends had planned ahead. The governments of France and England had signed a WWII pre-war secret agreement to restore each other's colonies after war's end. That is why the English government ordered British troops to restore the colonies of Indochina to France after they defeated Japanese troops.

Z: These two countries had just used their citizens' war efforts in WWII to vanquish the dictatorships of Germany and Japan. After the war, French Expeditionary Forces were sent in with the assistance of British troops to re-install unpopular colonial dictatorships! If the French hadn't returned to their colony in Vietnam to regain possession and impose their control, no one in the US would have ever heard of……………

THE TRAGEDY (τραγεδία) OF VIETNAM

"Never in the history of the United States…have we intervened against a native population, [in Vietnam] *and in support of a power* [France] *which has maintained colonial control."*
— Senator John F. Kennedy April 1954

'When I came back from Vietnam I no longer believed that it was necessary for us to get involved in Vietnam [after talking to US military personnel]. *I'd just had the greatest brainwashing that anybody can get."* —
Governor George Romney, Republican candidate running for president August 31, 1967. [Father of four sons]

The unwilling [draftees], *led by the unqualified, doing the unnecessary for the indifferent and the ungrateful.*
— Anonymous Graffiti Opposing the idea of commemorating that tragic war: ['Commemorating' the Vietnam War: One Marine's Perspective, Camillo MacBica *Truth-out]* (2014)
*Vietnam War Memorial November 10, 1982
[end of war March 29, 1973]

Z: On Tragedy: Put on a Happy Face

"Forest Gumpism:" touchy feel good feelings that masks the truth, and like morphine, camouflages and muffles the screaming pain of those who live and survive the physical and mental wounds of war. — Aegis

Commemorative War Memorials validate massive amnesia by those who live for those who died. War Memorials and ceremonies are the "Forest Gump" stamp of approval and justification to barbaric wars of death and destruction. — Aegis

Vietnam draftees did not "give" their lives willingly for their country. They were forcibly yanked (by threat of imprisonment) away from civilian life. They did not sacrifice. They were sacrificed! — Aegis

Citizens provide their children we need for our wars and Expeditionary Forces to conquer and suppress. Taxpayers pay for their guns, uniforms, burials, rehab, etc. Ernest taxpayers and citizens hope elected leaders tell the truth about the reasons for war. But, our allied interests and us don't reveal the truth. We decide where troops go and...who to kill.

Citizens trust us in times of war. The Fixxed Media provides the rationale. Their headlines and broadcasts provide the rallying slogans for a frightened or angry populace. They're designed to stir the jingoistic "herdal" instinct. They're laced throughout the history books:

> Remember the Alamo
> Remember the Maine
> Make the World Safe for Democracy, WWI
> Stop the Huns
> Better Dead than Red (communist)
> ISIS is coming!
> Make the World Safe for Democracy WWII
> (*redux, 2015*)

"Never in the history of the United States ....have we intervened against a native population, [in Vietnam] and in support of a power [France] which has maintained colonial control." Senator John F. Kennedy April 1954

We react decisively to any threat to our way of doing business. It was obvious that after WWII our way of doing business was challenged throughout the world! The U.S. and colonial powers had to quash all rebellious efforts by "restive" citizens who wanted to implement democratic reforms. They also wanted to throw us out and throw out our friendly, accommodating leaders that we approved of. [Review: Expeditionary Forces Crush the Unwilling.] We had to suppress all efforts that would lead to the end of our lucrative profiteering throughout the world.

Our associates and friends in the U.S. drew "a line in the jungles" of Asia after WWII. We committed to aid the French, and that failing, jumped in militarily into the fray. We would apply the Melos solution to all who resisted our efforts. [See: Part Three, *Kiss(inger) of Death*.]

My friends and I were very candid when outlining our desire and reasons to "move in" and maintain control of Vietnam and other Asian countries. We took action when the Vietnamese defeated France and she couldn't re-conquer her colonies. After the French were defeated at Dien Bien Phu, the Geneva Agreements (treaty) allowed for Vietnam to be divided temporarily into two sections, North and South. The struggle for political control over a divided Vietnam began in 1954 after the French left. We installed a "flyover" exile [see below] named Ngo Dinh Diem to be an alternative to the communist leader, Ho Chi Minh in the north. A plebiscite was to create one Vietnam and elect a president for all Vietnam. And then all foreign combatants were to leave.

The so-called valid reasons that we cared about had nothing to do with freedom for the Vietnamese in this French colony [France had colonized Indochina ~1887.] The U.S. had already given millions in aid to help France maintain control over her colony after WWII. When French control collapsed, we intervened to "save" Vietnam—for us!

The reasons are spelled out below in the section: *Freedom to Profit*

Z: A U.S. veteran of the Vietnam War proffers his assessment as to why we went to war in Vietnam where 58,000 military personnel were killed. "There were valid reasons for us to attempt to aid that incipient democracy [in Vietnam]. Everyone who stepped forward to serve can feel a sense of mission or sense of completion having done that." —(former) Senator James Webb AARP, Vo. 5 No. 4 (Wilson, 2014).

My friends and I have a different perspective on the above proffered rationale for our intervention! The following quotations explicitly detail what my friends and I were hoping to achieve. The true "valid reason" for <u>our</u> mission was the same that I have explained to you for all our actions, all the time. Wherever! We went after the profits!

For: Freedom to Profit

[The quotes used below (pp. 101-103) are excerpted from Felix Greene's <u>Vietnam! Vietnam!</u> (1966).]

"Diem [U.S. installed "flyover" president, See below]...has announced his reliance on private initiative for the future economic and social advancement of South Vietnam (and for this advancement there was only one source) "of capital and know-how...American private enterprise...we hope that this conference [set-up by American Friends of Vietnam] will directly stimulate increased private capital investment in Vietnam." John W. O'Daniel wrote in a November 29, 1957 Letter, *New York Times*,

> One of the world's richest areas is open to the winner in Indochina. That's behind the growing U.S. concern...tin, rubber, rice, key strategic raw materials are what the war is really about. The U.S. sees it as a place to hold—at any cost.

The magazine <u>US News & World Report</u> April 4, 1954, tells **Why the US Risks War for Indochina: It's the Key to the Control of all Asia.**

Geographically, Vietnam stands at the hub of a vast area of the world—Southeast Asia—an area with a population of 249 million persons...He who holds or has influence in Vietnam can affect the future of the Philippines and Formosa to the east, Thailand and Burma with their huge rice surpluses to the west, and Malaysia and Indonesia with their rubber, ore, and tin to the south...Vietnam does not exist in a vacuum—from it large storehouses of wealth and population can be influenced... —Henry Cabot Lodge, Boston Globe, *February 28, 1965.*

Incipient Democracy (not)

After WWII "Flyover Presidents" were installed by Communist and non-communist governments to govern their respective colonies and spheres of influence. Many of the leaders had fled their own country when invaded and did not stay and fight Nazi Germany or Japan. They were installed by Communist Russian armies in Eastern Europe and western armies in their colonies. They had no wide support from their countrymen because they hadn't stayed and fought their country's respective enemies. Naturally, citizens who stayed and fought a resistance movement against invading forces resented such imposed leaders who had gone into exile, away from harm's way. We had to work hard to bolster our handpicked collaborators.

Ngo Diem was such an exile. He was well educated in French schools. His brother was a bishop in Vietnam. He did not fight against the Japanese or French. He did not even fight against the communists. Part of the time he spent hanging out at a Big Ten campus and eating at Kewpie's cafeteria. He was a guest of the university's president. He was promoted by many influential Americans as an alternative to the popular communist, Ho Chi Minh, for the presidency of a united Vietnam (including Senator John F. Kennedy, Senator Mansfield, Joseph Kennedy, and Cardinal Spellman.) Robert Scheer provides more details in his booklet, **How the United States Got Involved in Vietnam** (1965).

Z: If the U.S. government had not flown Diem in on a U.S. military plane to Saigon, installed him in the presidential palace and guarded him with marines, there would not have been a war in Vietnam. Diem was not a popular viable alternative to the communist Ho Chi Minh, who had stayed and fought against the Japanese. He had led the armed fight and had helped drive out French colonial rule. After the French departed, there was supposed to be a vote by the Vietnamese to select a president and reunify Vietnam. Diem, whose family and supporters had sided with French colonial rule before the war, had no widespread popular following. The U.S. and Diem did not allow an election required by the Geneva Agreements.

Don't Have an Election If You're Going to Lose

President Diem refused to hold a plebiscite to elect one president and reunite North and South Vietnam. We realized Diem would lose, so we backed him when he refused a free election. After all, we [*viz.*, the U.S. taxpayer] were paying for his army and police force. Our side committed to "saving" Vietnam from communist rule. The Fixxed Media supported his refusal to abide by the Geneva Agreements. Published May 1, 1957 in <u>Life</u> magazine,

> *Diem saved his people from this agonizing* prospect [of losing the election] *simply by refusing to permit the plebiscite and thereby avoided national suicide.*

Even the US government knew the truth:

> [Everyone] *agreed that, had elections been held at the time of the fighting, possibly 80 per cent of the population would have voted the Communist Ho Chi Minh as their leader... the mass of the population supported the enemy.*
> — President Eisenhower, <u>Mandate for Change</u>, p. 372.

Z: After fighting and defeating the French, support had diminished for the communists. The communists' tactics in the north alienated some groups in the opposition. Controlling the north through brutal repression by the communists was spreading terror and eliminating all opposition. They were also crushing freedom of religion. Terrorized refugees were transported on U.S. ships to the south. They were offered the prospect of land and other rewards. Approximately 800,000 refugees fled to the south.

To this day there has never been a free election in Vietnam. There never has been an "incipient" democracy. Diem used the professors and administrative resources of his friends at a Big Ten university to set-up a civil administration to consolidate his oppressive dictatorial rule. Unfortunately, the professors' idealistic efforts to staunch the flow of communism were corrupted by Diem and his fellow dictatorial henchmen. [i.e. political opponents were thrown into open-air pits ("tiger" cages) and doused with lye].There was brutal repression by his secret police [trained by university professors] and suppression of all civil liberties.

We were total failures in trying to militarily secure the riches of Vietnam and Cambodia <u>exclusively</u> for our business interests. Our U.S. Expeditionary Forces and allies had to abandon a thoroughly botched military campaign known as the Vietnam War. U.S. taxpayers footed the bill for hundreds of billions of dollars to pay for the war.

Oh, yeah! A lot of people got killed. Their names are on the Vietnam War memorial. Of course, as usual, none of our own children suffered. [Review, "The Artful (War) Dodger"]. But, here's the really good news as reported by Margie Mason, (Vietnam Celebrates 40th Anniversary Of War's End With Enormous Parade, 2015).

> *The U.S. normalized relations with Vietnam in 1995. More than 16,000 Vietnamese students now study in America, and the U.S. has become one of Vietnam's biggest foreign investors. Bilateral trade exceeded $36 billion last year. The two countries have also hosted high-level visits...*

So in retrospect, I guess we can say that 60 years ago we should have allowed that election to unify Vietnam. The communists would have won and we would have been trading with them from the beginning. I guess you could say, "We were <u>for</u> the killing of Vietnamese communists before we were <u>against</u> it." Secretary of State and Vietnam War Vet hero, John Kerry, recently visited Vietnam *sans* guns. Hey, go with the [profit-cash] flow!

Kumbaya (f. Swahili = We get to keep it all)

Luckily, my business friends in South Africa dodged a bullet. Why? The African majority in South Africa was about to take over the reins of government in 1990. They all thought they would have to give up their assets and flee black majority rule when Nelson Mandela became president. Other recently freed colonies had seen "white flight" and disastrous efforts to nationalize natural resources such as the copper mines of Zambia. However, Mandela's negotiations with F. W. de Klerk and white business leaders helped to defuse the situation. We were able to keep all our "goodies" (assets) without any kind of reparations to those we had exploited for centuries!

Thank goodness Mr. Mandela moderated his more radical views of nationalization and government ownership. Noah Feldman reported,

> *after centuries of being robbed of possibly the greatest mineral wealth the world has ever known, not to mention decades of being repressed by apartheid, black South Africans got almost no compensation for what should rightfully have been theirs when the old regime was swept away for the new South Africa* (Was Mandela Right to Sell Out Black South Africans, 2013).

Feldman writes,

> *Indeed, the basic deal Mandela struck from prison with F.W. de Klerk... and* [that has] *essentially guaranteed the existing property rights of white South Africans in exchange for an end to apartheid.*

We were relieved when Nelson Mandela had previously told an audience of 300 white businessmen at a Johannesburg meeting, May 24, 1990:

> *"The view that the only words in the economic vocabulary that the* [African National Congress] *knows are nationalization and redistribution is mistaken"* **Mandela Conciliatory in Talk to Business Leaders** (Wren, 1990).

We knew with those words we were "home free." Our fears of losing all our assets in South Africa were abated. As usual, we would "land on our feet!"

Is South Africa a great country or not!
Kumbaya! = Business as usual!

PART THREE:
Kiss(inger) Kiss(inger) Kiss(inger)
Of Death

OPERATION MENU: [put] *"anything that flies on everything that moves!"*
—*Henry Kissinger, 1969 directive to illegally "carpet" bomb Cambodia*

"I think sooner or later we are going to have to crack the Cubans,"
—*Henry Kissinger recorded in President Ford's Oval Office, 1976*

Individuals in government make the decisions to take tax dollars and supply Expeditionary Forces to go forth and secure our goals and personal interests. The East India Company convinced King George to send a British fleet of Expeditionary Forces to "smack-down" George Washington, Thomas Jefferson, Thomas Paine, and the Sons of Liberty and all Freedom Fighters. Members of Parliament and the Crown were making a whole lot of money off the colonies. They made money for themselves and influential and well connected English aristocrats.

Like Freedom Fighters everywhere, citizens rebelled against colonial rule and/or arbitrary influence within their respective countries. As noted earlier, things began to change after WWII when Churchill and the British intervened in Greece. We tried to maintain our control so the money would keep flowing to us in our respective personal purses and countries' coffers. (Review, "Tragedy of Vietnam".)

We've succeeded in making sure the Fixxed Media supported our worldwide efforts. Stories were "planted" (and/or approved by editors) that railed against rebelling civilian populations that opposed us. We waged war against the Bad Guys: atheists, communists, liberals, unionists, democrats, patriots, etc. They were to be spied upon, hunted down and killed if necessary. Decisions to intervene were made by a few individuals ruling in each country "at the highest level" of power. Their aim: to suppress opposition using any tactic necessary so that we could maintain control. We "painted" <u>all</u> resistance as evil and atheistic and Marxist! In Kenya we even gave them a special name: Mau Maus.

Z: Generals and troops take orders; they don't make them. Government leaders do. Secret agencies [CIA, MIG] don't initiate subverting foreign governments on their own. They get their "marching orders" from government leaders and do their bidding. Leaders make secret decisions and do not inform their own citizens what they are doing. They hide behind "Plausible Deniability," especially in democracies. Congressional investigations are stymied, thwarted and defunded. The Fixxed Media is in on the "fix." And colludes by default. Citizens don't know what "goes on behind closed doors!" They don't know their taxes are funding massive military suppression tactics in countries around the world! They especially are not told of billions in funding that support and underpin brutal, cruel military dictators.

I could not understand why the U.S. was opposed to helping all the colonies throw off the yoke of European colonialism after WWII. After all, that's what the American Revolution was all about! I found it even harder to believe that U.S. government leaders engaged in decades-long efforts to block the growth of democracy. They crushed all those efforts by supporting dictatorships that suppressed all opposition.

How to Get Away with "Murdering" Democracy
Exhibit One: IRAN, "Poster Child"

After WWII and the beginning of the Cold War, we began an all-out effort to smash all pro socialist/liberal/communist opposition. We opposed any one making any effort to challenge our way of doing business. We especially hated democratic elections that elected governmental leaders we couldn't control. Any ideas hinting of government regulation/control over resources or government spending to alleviate harshness of life were labeled as Marxist or communistic.

"In the middle of the Cold War, the United States played a role in the overthrow of a democratically elected Iranian government."
— President Barack Obama, Cairo, Egypt 2009

We especially squashed any popular effort by citizens in the Middle East to "swipe" back our oil assets. We had previously seized these through "friendlier" governments arbitrarily set-up by Europeans enforcing the Sykes-Picot Agreements after WWI.

Unfortunately, the natives in Iran had become restless and worked to gain complete independence from England. New leaders wanted to regain control of their government and their oil reserves! We had to stymie that! In 1953, the democratically elected government of Prime Minister Mohammed Mossadegh tried to nationalize our oil interests. With the help of leaders in the U.S. and England we were able to stir up opposition and organize army units and religious leaders to move against him.

Z: Released documents show that U.S. governmental leaders at the highest level sponsored, approved, financed, and set in motion a CIA initiated coup to destabilize Iran's democratically elected government, the first democracy in that region. Millions of dollars were spent bribing people to demonstrate and riot. On August 19, 1953, a U.S. backed army coup overthrew, arrested and imprisoned President Mossadegh. The Shah [a flyover exile living in Paris] was set-up by England and the United States and imposed as the newly installed compliant leader. These events are outlined in the following articles: **The Moment the U.S. Ended Iran's Brief Experiment in Democracy**, by Robert Scheer, *Truth Dig* (2013) and **In declassified**

document, CIA acknowledges role in '53 Iran Coup, by Dan Merica and Jason Hanna, <u>CNN</u> (2013).

The CNN article states:

> *The military coup that overthrew Mossadeq and his National Front cabinet was carried out under CIA direction as an act of U.S. foreign policy, conceived and approved at the highest levels of government...*

The Shah's brutal dictatorship [i.e. SAVAK secret police torturers banged metal head gear worn by victims] eventually spawned another popular revolution. If the U.S. had not intervened in 1953, a future revolution led by the religious fundamentalist and strong anti-American Ayatollah Khomeini would not have risen to power. The U.S. embassy would never have been occupied in Tehran. Democracy might have flourished. Iran might have been a "shining guiding star" for democracy in the Middle East, a first.

We were able to maintain the rule of the dictatorial Shah Pahlavi against discontented opposition. The CIA sent in experts to set-up his secret intelligence agency SAVAK. Researching online for "SAVAK and torture" does show some gruesome stuff! Its secret police arrested and used "enhanced interrogation" techniques to repress and/or eliminate all opposition. As in Vietnam, our hand picked presidents/dictators couldn't stand-alone against their respective populations! That's why we crush all efforts for genuine democratic elections <u>wherever</u> we can! Our forcibly installed dictators would lose out in any free election!

Henry Kissinger influenced several American presidents. He pushed actions to help us maintain control of our assets throughout an unstable world. He supported every dictator trying to suppress any kind of expansion of democratic principles.

CAMBODIA: The Kissinger Killing Fields 1969-73

Operation Menu: [put] *"anything that flies on everything that moves!"*
— Henry Kissinger, 1969 directive to illegally and indiscriminately inflict massive bombing on Cambodia

We tried to stop enemy infiltration of war materiel into Vietnam to win that war. As a super power, the United States couldn't afford to lose. We'd lose face and look impotent. So we "dropped the hammer" on Cambodia by doing the following:

- 20,000,000 gallons of Agent Orange [field tested in Okinawa] were dropped on an area the size of Florida [**See: www.agent orange record.com**]
- Kissinger/Nixon ordered B-52 bombers to "carpet bomb" Cambodia and dropped the equivalent of five "Hiroshimas" (1969-1973) more than all tonnage dropped in WWII --2,756,941 tons with 230,516 sorties. **From Pol Pot... Everything that moves,** by John Pilger, *Truth-out* (2014).

- The bombing was the "first stage in a decade of genocide." Finnish Government Commission of Enquiry estimating 600,000 Cambodians died in ensuing civil war. [Further research is fairly gruesome including: Cambodia Killing Fields; Torture; Bone Collection. Pictures of torture techniques are particularly grisly!] Hundreds of villages were leveled. Survivors "froze up and they would wander around muttering for three or four days." Pol Pot and the Khmer Rouge seized power from a government that was destabilized by the United States' massive, unrelenting bombing. They systematically imprisoned and tortured to death 1,000,000-1,500,000 people. They depopulated the cities and murdered at will to snuff out Western influence and create a utopian agrarian society. Today museums with thousands of stacked skulls are on exhibit. Shades of Hitler! [View victims on the Internet: Pol Pot.]

Henry Kissinger's "Jane Fonda" Moment

Z: Henry Kissinger's "Jane Fonda" moment occurred while Americans were still being killed in Vietnam with weapons and war materiel supplied by Communist China. He was Nixon's National Security Advisor. He made a secret back-channel trip to Red China in July 1971. He met with communist leader Zhou En Lai while the war was going on. Over 100,000 Chinese personnel were helping North Vietnam sustain its war effort at this time against U.S. troops. Billions in supplies and armaments and weapons were "Made in China" including the anti-aircraft guns that shot down several hundred American pilots. Illegally expanding the war into Cambodia, (April 1970) extending the war until it ended January 1973. Failing to end the war meant more deaths. Forty percent of war casualties occurred after Nixon and Kissinger were in the Presidency. It also meant longer years in captivity for prisoners-of-war. Almost 1,500 days passed from Nixon's inauguration (January 1969) to January 1973. The war ended with the Paris Peace Accords, January 27, 1973. Kissinger and Nixon made a trip to Red China while the war was still going on. They exchanged toasts with Red China's Communist leader Mao-tse Tung while the war was still going on and Americans were still being killed. [You Tube, **"Nixon Bows to Mao tse-Tung,"** one minute.]

CUBA
Oink! Oink! Oink!

Fidel Castro had to go!

He took our assets, our land and businesses.

We never willingly give back. Victims have to be taken back by using force.

Castro took all our lucrative casinos! Many were mafia owned. He nationalized all foreign-owned business enterprises. He promised to reimburse my friends and me based on our own yearly tax filings. I'm sure they were rather low-balled! [heh, heh, heh!] He eliminated private ownership and even expropriated all Church lands. That action got him excommunicated! He is probably the only dictator in South America to suffer such a fate. Cuba's model of state-owned socialism and state ownership of everything had to be stopped! He was eliminating private property and taking back all the assets we had accrued since we swiped Cuba and Guantanamo Bay from the Spanish. Such radical philosophy had to be stopped dead in its tracks! DEAD was the operative word!

U.S. Invades Cuba: "Bay of Pigs"

Z: Cuba had not invaded Florida or killed any Americans. It was no direct threat to the U.S. However, Cuba's communist philosophy was anathema to the "free world" ideal of private property and freedom. U.S. government leaders [including Eisenhower, Dulles, Kennedy] ordered the CIA to train and arm an invasion force made up of Cuban exiles. They had fled Cuba after Fidel Castro betrayed the ideals of creating a democratic Cuba. He had set-up a personal dictatorship with no free elections and imprisoned and killed political opponents. However, Cuba is an independent sovereign nation and was no imminent threat to the United States. The U.S. led invasion in 1961 was a clear violation of international law. It was designed to overthrow and assassinate President Castro.

After the failed CIA invasion at the Bay of Pigs, President Kennedy ordered a military study on what it would take for U.S. troops to invade and overthrow Castro [reportedly 250,000 troops]. Castro asked Communist Russia for military help and protection. Prime Minister Khrushchev sent nuclear missiles creating the "Cuban Missile Crisis." [Off shore in the Atlantic Ocean, American subs were facing and ready to sink Russian ships delivering missiles; troops in Europe were on alert and poised for WWIII. Students on college campuses cancelled class and threw "Annihilation Parties!"] This nuclear war threat never would have occurred if the U.S. would have done what we have subsequently done with the thug nations of Communist Russia and Communist China—send in trade delegations! Today we trade with those thug regimes that slaughtered and starved tens of millions of their citizens to death to get and keep power! Those countries have never had free elections. All efforts at democratic reform are crushed.

Update: President Obama continued to suppress a report by the CIA that gives a rendering of its [and U.S.] role in the invasion of Cuba. He sent assistant U.S. Attorney Mitchell P. Zeff to an appellate court to argue that the time is not right to release the documents. Zeff argued that the "passage of time has not made it releasable." Almost 50 years after the illegal invasion, President Obama continues to block transparency and the truth! **Lawsuit seeks to unlock CIA'S secret history of Bay of Pigs invasion,** by Michael Doyle (2013).

CUBA, Redux,
Boink! Boink! Boink!

Kissinger was furious that Castro had scorned his earlier efforts at détente and normalization in the Ford presidency. According to official inner White House **recorded** transcripts, amongst governmental leaders, a furious Kissinger wanted to "smash"[boink!] Castro.

> *"If we decide to use military force, it must succeed. There should be no halfway measures—we would get no award for using military power in moderation. If we decide on a blockade, it must be ruthless and rapid and efficient."*
> —Kissinger, 1976, White House contingency plans.

The *New York Times reported,* **Kissinger Drew up Plans to Attack Cuba, Records Show**, (Robles, 2014).

Those invasion plans were abandoned when Jimmy Carter defeated President Ford. He wouldn't go along with the plan. What a whuzz! We could have smashed Cuba, put our chosen leader in power, and reclaimed all our lost possessions, especially the casinos! *¡Qué lástima!*

Q: What do you think is the best way to resolve the problem of Castro's Cuba?
A. Nuke Cuba when the wind is blowing south
B. Drop enough bombs to sink it
C. Designate it as a destination point for Spring Break students and reopen the casinos for U.S. seniors

---

KISSINGER ON STEROIDS, KO'S DEMOCRACY

Unfortunately, the majority of people in most countries don't like our philosophy of "What's Best for Me!" Since the end of WWII, we've tried to suppress them in every way. It's been a mammoth effort, especially in Central and South America. We've had to crush citizens who have tried to implement democratic ideals. We've used threats and military coups and brutal slaughtering of civilians to maintain control.

We've managed to crush most democratic efforts by indigenous citizens who wanted to install democratic governments. Why do we oppose them? They want to take from me—and my friends! They want to dictate conditions of nationalization of industries and taxation. We did some rather nasty stuff in the past decades and kept things well-hidden thanks to the Fixxed Media. The American people did not know what was going on.

It was either Us or Them [the "bad" guys]! U.S. tax dollars paid for all our sneaky and nefarious efforts. Those who resisted paid with their lives!
¡Muchísimas Gracias! Mega Thanks for Mega Dólare$!
We had the lethal "blessings" of Presidents and Kissinger.

KaPOW! Chile September 11, 1973

Setting up machinery for exterminating people

I don't see why we need to stand by and watch a country
[Chile] go communist due to the irresponsibility of its people.
— Henry Kissinger [assists overthrow of freely elected President Allende]

Z:

Estadio Chile*

Six of us were lost
As if into starry space
One dead, another beaten as I could never have believed a human being could
be beaten
The other four wanted to end their terror
One jumping into nothingness
Another beating his head against a wall
But all with the fixed stare of death
What horror the face of fascism creates!

*Poem "Estadio Chile," 1973 by Victor Jara, excerpts. He was one of
thousands rounded up into Chile Stadium, beaten, tortured and murdered.
The poem survived, but not the poet. Rounded up teachers, professors,
unionists, and reporters were imprisoned, tortured and killed. The article
and complete poem is a graphic depiction of the brutal military suppression
of those opposed to the military coup (MahMag.org, 2008) **Victor Jara and
the Story of His Last poem**. Alert! Brutal written graphics!

Kissinger:
*"We cannot let
Chile go down
the drain."*

Helms:
"I am with you."
—1973

We always knew Henry was our friend! But now
everyone can read and **hear** about it in recently
declassified documents and tapes from the National
Security Archive as reported in John Pilger's article
from *Truth-Out* (Kissinger and Chile: In an Age of
Vigilantes, There Is Cause for Optimism, 2003). Like
us, Henry shows his concern that the democratically
elected President Salvatore Allende and his reforms
would have a "model effect." He was afraid Allende's
example "can be insidious" in its influence in other
South American countries. On tape he plots with the
CIA director Richard Helms to overthrow Chile's new democratically elected
government.

Z: The Chilean military led by General Augusto Pinochet attacked the
presidential palace and assassinated President Allende. Afterward, on tape,
Kissinger is heard praising Augusto Pinochet. "You did a great service to the
West." Pinochet dismantled government regulations and social services
such as social security. Milton Friedman, professor from the University of
Chicago, promotes the beliefs in The Road to Serfdom by Friedrich Von
Hayek, and flew several times to Chile to provide advice on deregulation for
the dictatorship. Kissinger, Friedman, and dictator Pinochet worked hand in

hand to dismantle remnants of government regulation and social services. [View on the Internet: Friedman and Pinochet; Kissinger and Pinochet; to see their pictures with the brutal dictator in Chile.] They were trying to create a "Randian" retro paradise *al la* Ayn Rand.

Naturally, there was resistance to the dictatorship. Vicious suppression occurred. A military **Caravan of Death** was sent by Pinochet's military to show no mercy to "extremists." U. S. made and funded Puma helicopters flew into towns rounding-up and killing resisters to the coup. Such happenings were reported by the BBC, **Chile Caravan of Death: Eight guilty of Murder,** (2013).

Sally Sara reports that more than 3,000 Chileans were rounded up, tortured and killed. Recent trial testimony revealed a super-secret extermination center called Simon Bolivar. Estela Ortiz, whose university professor husband was murdered, asks of the torturers,

> *How can they do it? How can they live with the eyes, the screams, with the horror? How can a human being be part of this machinery of exterminating people?* **Facing the Past,** *ABC News* (Sara, 2014).

KaPOW! ARGENTINA:
Baby Snatchers & *Los Desaparecidos*
People simply disappeared, always at night—Orwell, <u>1984</u>

"Look, our basic attitude is that we would like you [Argentina coup generals] *to succeed...The quicker you succeed the better...We want a stable situation. We won't cause you unnecessary difficulties."*
—Secretary of State Henry Kissinger October 7, 1976

Once again Henry would have our back. He and U.S. governmental leaders provided critical political and military support for our illegal military junta in Argentina. Our friends succeeded in crushing the "civilian support mechanism" with much needed military aid from the U.S. The following information was released from the National Security Archive as revealed in **Kissinger approved Argentinian 'dirty war,'** by Duncan Campbell, *The Guardian* (2003).

Verbatim transcripts of a meeting between Kissinger and Argentina's foreign minister on October 7, 1976, reassured the foreign minister that he had the U.S. backing in whatever he did.

> *"Look our basic attitude is that we would like you to succeed ...I have an old-fashion view that friends ought to be supported. What is not understood in the United States is that you have a civil war. We read about human rights problems but not the context."*

A senior state department official, Charles Robinson, pointed out that Americans did not approve of dictators' needs to be "tough." However he noted,

> the problem is that the United States is an idealistic and moral country and its citizens have great difficulty in comprehending the kinds of problems faced by Argentina today.

Z: Why are we so decent and opposed to brutal dictatorships? We just don't want to get with your killing program! Of course there was a civil war in Argentina fought against the unlawful junta that overthrew the legitimate government! Over 30,000 "students, labor leaders, intellectuals, and leftists disappeared" who believed in democracy and civil liberties. They were rounded up, tortured and killed. Innocent people were picked-up and never heard from again.

> *Los Desaparecidos*
> *...people who had incurred the displeasure of the Party, simply*
> *disappeared and were never heard from again.*
> *One never had the smallest clue as to what happened to them*
> —*Orwell, 1984*

The following information is from civilian trials in Argentina:
Two former dictators [and doctors] were found guilty of "systematically stealing babies from political prisoners [who were murdered] and of giving them new identities."
Argentina tries doctors for 'baby theft' during military rule (2014).
"Former dictators found guilty in Argentine baby-stealing trial." CNN Wire Staff... (2012)

> With this trial we'll be able to learn what they did with our mothers the day after we were born...know that there will be punishment and justice because we are living proof of the crime...36 year old Francisco Madariaga...

The mother, Silvia Quintela, a leftist militant, has never been found.

A la Coup *et al*

> *"If you don't spout off you won't get harpooned!"*
> Advice from Mother Whale to Baby Whale

> *U.S. helicopter gunships are the rescuing "angels"*
> *for thug dictators.* — Aegis

Why do individuals with that accursed Gooderite philosophy have to go and try to change the natural order of human kind? We worked so hard to establish our way of life—the Good Life, La Dolce Vita! For five hundred years (half a millennium) we've ruled the Americas unchallenged. We've had to "drop the hammer" and eliminate, as in expunge, the ungrateful and discontented. We've had to repeatedly quash "restive" peasants [farmers] and democratic followers. Fortunately, the unaware American taxpayer has footed the bill to fund our efforts! U.S. leaders spent billions in citizens' taxes to squash rebellious citizens everywhere. Their government and the Fixxed Media chose not to inform them of our ruthless and bloody interventions. The world is a dangerous place and there's no need to tell the taxpayer! [See: Fixed Media statement by Washington Post editor.] We never sit idly by when our material interests are challenged and at stake. The following are some of our other very successful efforts.

Guatemala, 1954 *Coup d'état*

In 1951 President Truman authorized a *coup d'état* against the popular agrarian reformer, President Jacobo Árbenaz Guzmán. His foolish "Decree 900" expropriated large tracts of land from us to be given to small farmers. Almost half the arable land was owned by our friends at the United Fruit Company. Fortunately, our buddy John Foster Dulles, had large stock holdings in the lands threatened to be distributed. He ordered the CIA to initiate "Operation PBSUCCESS" to overthrow the Guatemalan president. The Fixxed Media portrayed ["painted"] him as a dangerous Marxist and therefore Russian controlled. This trumped-up charge was used as a legitimate excuse to intervene. Our efforts worked. On May 24, 1954, the U.S. Navy launched "Hardrock Baker," a blockade on all ports using submarines and surface ships to intercept all ships. The CIA trained an invasion force in Florida called, *El Ejército de Liberación*. CIA pilots bombed the country. U.S. citizens never even knew that their tax dollars had been used to coordinate the overthrow of a democratically elected government. We hand picked the new president who agreed to rescind all laws that took the United Fruit Company's land. We even made sure to get rid of the law that required paying farm workers 50 cents a day! The Fixxed News went along with our efforts and supported the trumped-up charges that communists had taken over Guatemala!

¡Se fue Árbenaz!

El Salvador, 1980

Every now and then some members of the Catholic Church hierarchy have decided to "break ranks" and advocate for our enemy on the other side. Some of our supporters took extreme measures against such nonsense! It had to be stopped! "Unfriendlies" had to be eliminated!

"Harpooning" the Archbishop

Z: Archbishop Oscar Arnulfo Romero was gunned down March 24, 1980, while saying mass in the Church of the Divine Providence.

He committed two "sins:"

1. He had preached against the military dictatorship
2. He had promoted social justice for the poor and landless farmers.

The motive for his assassination was clear. His was the most outspoken voice,

> *against the death squad slaughter gathering steam in the U.S.*
> *backyard. The ranks of El Salvador's leftwing rebels were being*

swelled by priests who preached that the poor should seek justice in this world, not wait for the next. Romero was the 'voice of those without voice,' telling the soldiers not to kill.

Tome Gibb reported in *The Guardian* (2000), **The killing of archbishop Oscar Romero was one of the most notorious crimes of the cold war. Was the CIA to blame?**

¡Se fue Romero!

Others opposing the military dictatorship and trying to promote social justice were intimidated and murdered. On December 2, 1980, four U.S. nuns were kidnapped, raped and murdered. Those later convicted of the crime said they got orders from their military superiors. The "killings came as the United States was beginning a decades-long $7 billion aid effort to prevent left-wing guerillas from coming to power..."

4 Salvadorans Say They Killed U.S. Nuns on Orders of Military, Larry Rohter, *The New York Times* (1998)

Those pesky civilians in Central America just kept on challenging us! Thank goodness for the U.S. government leaders' support. We wiped out the rebels' "civilian support mechanism" using U.S. Huey helicopters, trucks, jeeps, etc. Some called our efforts "bloodbaths" or "massacres" as we suppressed popular citizen uprisings. We call it, "doing what is necessary to protect ourselves and our way of life!" We "painted" all rebel resistance as "Marxist" or communist controlled. These violent armed revolts frightened U.S. citizens. Our scare tactics and planted articles in the Fixxed Media helped to hoodwink unsuspecting U.S. taxpayers into passively paying the billions for our antidemocratic suppression of the populace.

¡Muchiima Gracia$!

The death toll from our interventions: El Salvador, 70,000; Nicaragua, 20,000; Honduras, 200 political disappearances; Guatemala, 100,000. CIA documents reveal "the social population appeared to fully support the guerillas... and the soldiers were forced to fire at anything that moved."

How Reagan Promoted Genocide, by Robert Parry. *Consortium News.* (2013). [In the TV show "Bones" reference is made to Temperance's efforts to identify body remains of massacred civilians.] As always we had to support our allies who were crushing and suppressing all civilian opposition to our way of ruling. Dictatorships made it easy!

Boinking Grenada and Venezuela
"A piece of the truth to justify a lie." —David B., 2015

We'll use any excuse to justify military intervention into a country. We have to fabricate something if we want to get rid of the leaders of a country that we don't like. Overthrowing the government of itsy bitsy Grenada is an excellent example. President Reagan, without consulting Congress, secretly sent in several thousand U.S. Expeditionary Forces (contrary to the war provision of the Constitution) to invade Grenada in the military operation, "Urgent Fury." The population of Grenada was less than 90,000. It is only

132 sq. mi. in area, one-fifth the size of Butte, MT! The socialist government was using Cuban engineers to help expand the airport's runway. This was true. As always we were committed to crushing any left-leaning government that did not comport to our way of doing things. We "trumped up" the phony excuse that the expansion of the runway could be a threat to the U.S. national security! It is a piece of the truth to justify a lie. What was the lie? It was that the airport could be used as a threat to the U.S.! Such a canard is a favorite ploy that we use all the time. We come up with <u>any</u> excuse to overthrow a government we don't like. Imagine itty-bitty, Grenada a threat! Americans don't even know where Grenada is! They don't even know how many Americans, Cubans, or Grenadians were killed in the invasion! Those deaths are minor details.

President Obama's National Emergency Order issued March 9, 2015, enacted sanctions against Venezuela because of: "the unusual and extraordinary threat to the national security and foreign policy of the United States posed by the situation in Venezuela **Obama Declares Venezuela A Threat to U.S. National Security**. (Mason & Rampton, 2015). Venezuela is 2,000 miles from Washington D. C.! Do you really believe Venezuela is a threat? What we're really after is the Western Hemisphere's largest oil reserves located in Venezuela! We're mad because President Hugo Chávez nationalized the oil reserves that we had previously staked out for <u>us</u>! For years we've been trying to destabilize the government with negative stories in the Fixxed Media. Obama cited real human rights abuses by the government. That is a piece of the truth used to justify the lie that Venezuela is a threat to the United States!

We breathlessly await a coup against the government! Boink! Boink!

We certainly haven't worried about constitutional rights or even life itself for citizens around the world. Obviously, we have never been adverse to dumping the rights of U.S. citizens, including the original natives! We have used all means to wrest control of the continent from the original landowners. We uprooted millions of people from Africa and enslaved them. With such a track record, it is obvious we will have no qualms in doing anything to suppress all opposition to us. The next chapter relates how we suppress all who oppose us even internally in the United States.

As we shall see, we respect no constitutional rights!

CHAPTER NINE

ROUNDUP ROUNDUP ROUNDUP
Weeding out the Dissidents
Crushing Constitutional Rights

CRUSHING CONSTITUTIONAL RIGHTS

Who is Janat Gul?

Before Gulags were filled, lists were made. —Aegis

*The Eyes of Saruman: "Concealed within his fortress,
the Lord of Morda sees all."* —<u>The Lord of the Rings</u>

We Can Hear You Now, 24/7
We know who you are.
We know where you live.
We know where you go.
We know who[m] you meet.
When we want you… gotcha!
—Yachta's e-mail/text to <u>everyone</u>

*"When I am president, we won't work in secret to avoid honoring
our laws and Constitution…that means no more illegal wiretapping of
American citizens. No more national security letters to spy on citizens
who are not suspected of a crime."* —candidate Barack Obama, 2007
Obama's Path from Critic to Overseer of Spying,
The New York Times, (Baker, 2014).

"[Bush] was in fact an integral part of the *[CIA enhanced
interrogation]* program, he had to approve it before
we went forward with it."
— Dick Cheney, December 2014 *Fox News*

<u>DON'T GET ON OUR NAUGHTY LIST</u>

Santa has his Lists. We have ours.

Our criteria for inclusion are quite different!

Do not get on our Naughty List.

In a democracy, constitutional civil liberties can be revoked when we choose. Nothing's guaranteed except <u>our</u> <u>right</u> to revoke and ignore them. We can draw up and utilize lists of names at any time. We can designate anyone on them as an "Enemy Combatant," terrorist, subversive, or traitor.

We can "Rendition" you, anytime.

We can "No Fly" List you.

We can "Enhance interrogate" you.

We can "Blacklist" you.

We can "Drone" you, too! [Ayn Rand's "Thompson Harmonizer" is obsolete.] We can "cull" you from the herd!

It's easier to do these things in a dictatorship (no questioning allowed). But, in a democracy we have to manipulate public opinion to support us. [Review, *Fixxed Media.*] We've been quite successful. We never let the ideas of abstract constitutional rights deter us.

Defending the Homeland (*viz.* Us)
Stop us if you can!

When our way of conducting business is threatened or challenged, we must set-up counter measures. We have to take steps and figure out how to persuade citizens to rally behind us and to fear our opponents. Our pliant and supportive political leaders in government take actions to help suppress and/or eliminate citizen opposition.

Jingoism is good to use to stir the patriotic juices against an overseas enemy [Review, *Gird the Herd*]. Without its effects we would not be able to rally the people to pay for and "man" the military for battle against...

> The Huns!
> The Bolsheviks!
> The Mau Maus!
> The Occupy Wall Streeters! [heh, heh, heh! Just kidding!]

Well, regarding the latter, we couldn't take any chances! Our friends at the FBI coordinated with large banks and law enforcement officials to spy on largely peaceful protesters who were considered potential terrorists! (Wolf, 2012) **Revealed: how the FBI coordinated the crackdown on Occupy**.

Xenophobia [f. Gk: ξενος = foreign; φοβois = fear] is a great tool for frightening the populace to rally against all things foreign. Irrational behavior, inflamed by headlines and misinformation by the Fixxed Media and calculating politicians, instigate hatred and provoke violence against a current foe, domestic or foreign. The Fixxed Media helps to "channel our innermost thoughts" into action against our designated enemy. "Herdal" instincts kick in and irrational, unquestioning support ensues. For millennia, we've used these scare tactics to misinform the public. It helps to rally citizen support against our designated enemies.

Rounding-up (Suppressing) Restive Workers
Hitler dissolved all trade unions May 2, 1933

At the beginning of the twentieth century, many workers began to organize and form labor unions. There were strikes and violence and even thrown bombs. Many strikes were not peaceful and deaths even occurred. Many immigrants were avowed socialists who led the workers and tried to organize them into unions. Some preached the violent overthrow of the government as had recently happened in Russia (1917).

Those pesky immigrants were "huddled masses yearning to breathe free" and forced us to pay more wages to them. They also wanted to force us to pay to improve their working conditions! They were forming labor unions to challenge our absolute right to dictate pay and working conditions for those ungrateful laborers. They wanted to dictate to us in our own businesses! Our businesses!!! Many of the workers' leaders were of German ancestry. Once the U.S. declared war against Germany, (WWI) they were viewed as traitors and vilified. Speeches were made even calling for the death of alleged traitors. We figured out a "patriotic" way to go after our opponents <u>and</u> crush the growing union movement.

Our political friends in Congress passed the *Espionage Act* (1917) and the *Sedition Act* (1918). These laws gave Attorney General Mitchell Palmer and his assistant John Edgar Hoover the "legal" weapons and excuse to round-up radicals and professed anarchists and <u>anyone</u> trying to organize unions. On November 7, 1919, 10,000 left-leaning suspected "communists and anarchists" were arrested and rounded-up without warrants. Most were held for many months and never tried or even charged with a crime and eventfully were released. On January 2, 1920, another 6,000 were arrested and held without trial according to John Simkin's article, **The Palmer Raids** (Simkin, n.d.). Many union leaders of the Industrial Workers of the World (IWW) were arrested. All those arrests were part of what is called the "Palmer Raids." Citizens welcomed them to thwart the feared imminent violent revolution by supposed revolutionaries. Russian citizens recently had overthrown the Czar of Russia in a violent Revolution in 1917 led by the Bolsheviks (communists). The Fixxed Media headlined impending revolution in the United States and frightened the voting public! Constitutional rights were suspended with impunity.

Long ago we learned that the voting public really didn't give a damn about constitutional rights when we frightened them enough. American citizens supported the "Palmer Raids" enthusiastically!

A Scrap of Paper

Z: In 1787, many Americans resisted the Founding Fathers' efforts to ditch the Articles of Confederation. That first "constitution" created a weak central government with few powers. In school and with the "Fixxed Media" we have been taught the distortion that the Founding Fathers wanted a weak central government. In the 18th century, Americans had been afraid to strengthen the authority of the central government. They remembered the British monarchy's power to wage expensive wars, heavily tax everyone and arbitrarily suppress opposition and torture them in dungeons! Therefore, the Bill of Rights was voted on and attached to the new Constitution. It was supposed to be a protective bulwark against abuse of power and make centralization of power more palatable. The Bill of Rights was supposed to curtail potential governmental abuse. Thus, the myth was started that our civil liberties were constitutionally guaranteed and protected. Actually, they are "abstract principles" dependent on the whims of politicians and the manipulated voters. [See Roosevelt's quote below about Indian rights.]

In reality, the Constitution is "merely a scrap of paper." Governmental leaders can choose not to recognize and enforce the alleged constitutional guarantees.

Life, Liberty, Pursuit of Happiness (NOT)

Well, of course if anyone looked at our historical track record, he/she would see that we do not abide by any "paper" restrictions such as the

"What do I care about the law? H'aint I got the power!"
—Vanderbilt

"noble" ideals and **abstract principles** of the Bill of Rights of the U.S. Constitution. At any time, whenever we choose, we can suspend any supposed legal protection against arbitrary governmental actions. Our actual view of the pretentious concept of limited governmental power is encapsulated in Robber Baron Commodore Vanderbilt's succinct boast, "What do I care about the law? H'aint I got the power!"

We don't recognize constitutional rights that delimit our power, our absolute right to rule. Our righteous attitude is that of Teddy Roosevelt's toward the millions of inhabitants, "citizens," of the 500 independent nations forcibly expelled from 9,631,420 square miles in North America. [Review, Swipers, Swipers, Swipers]. He observed,

> *"This continent had to be won. We need not waste our time dealing with any sentimentalist who believes that, on account of any **abstract principle** [emphasis added] it would have been right to leave this continent to the domain, the hunting ground of squalid savages [Indians]. It had to be taken by the white race."*
> — Theodore Roosevelt ~1892 Lowell Institute Lecture

If we had been "sentimentalists" respecting the "Rights of Man," (and women and children), then we never would have been able to amass great wealth and profits. Remember that, that great "sucking sound" is the mooted swooshing of profits into our tills! [Review, *Profits, Profits, Profits*] Consider the following examples of wholesale violation of human rights against totally innocent victims. We were not deterred by sentimentalism!

Case One: "Out of Africa"

It's true that tribal nations of Africa were forcefully depopulated through the lucrative slave trade. Millions of lives were lost. But, we made good money. We were totally lacking in empathy for the victims of our lucrative trans-Atlantic transactions. President Clinton went to Africa to apologize for the slavery institution that had ended 150 years earlier! Must be that "touchy-feel" legacy thing [heh, heh, heh!] But, we really regretted that slavery was ended. We "felt a lot of pain" at its demise—and loss of profit!

Z: Millions of Africans died and/or were captured, enslaved, and forcibly removed from their homeland. Estimates range up to 15,000,000! There was good profit in the Slave Trade. All European monarchies, including England's, invested in it. Cooperating African kings/chiefs were enriched and were mortified when slave trading was eventually banned by England. (Once England's slave-owning southern colonies were lost with American independence, the monarchy took the high moral position against slavery.

Better late than never!)

My history books [Fixxed Media] depicted the Africans as "fortunate" to get food and shelter and to be taken care of by their masters in the United States. They supposedly had been "rescued" from their primitive life! Also, as they were heathens, they got to "see the light" with Christian conversion. Slaves were depicted ("painted") as docile and non-rebellious. The Fixxed Media did not relate slave resistance and numerous rebellions. Later, I read of captured Africans on slave ships resisting by going on hunger strikes. They were forced-fed using hot irons rammed down their throats and inserted funnels to pour food in them to keep them alive.

Resistance was futile.

Slaves were denied any constitutional protection against their owners. Laws stated they were property. They could not even be legally married. They could not prevent their own children from being sold off. Slaves had to acquiesce and let their masters/overseers rape their children and any woman at will. Our Founding Fathers, including Patrick Henry who had proclaimed, "Give me Liberty or give me death," voted to consider each slave as three-fifth a person to give the southern slave states more voter representation in Congress. Thus, slaves weren't even designated as a whole human being! There are many books depicting the real brutality of slavery. The Peculiar Institution by Kenneth Stampp is an eye-opener.

Case Two: Into Reservations

Infidel Indian savages had to bend to our will! The movie, "Dancing with Wolves," was a sentimental rewrite of history to make people feel guilty. But, we made good money taking and selling their land. We feel no guilt or remorse. The Great White Fathers in Washington, like President Teddy Roosevelt, were always on our side. [Review, Swipers]. Who do you think negotiated dozens of treaties whereby every Indian nation signed and surrendered all the good land and then were forcibly moved to designated reservations? Natch, it was our friends in high places and our allies, the land speculators. And the politically connected. And the railroad companies!

Z: The rights and homelands of the natives were systematically crushed and eliminated in over 500 American Indian nations. Resistance meant physical annihilation! It is estimated that there was a decline of approximately 2,000,000 inhabitants before the end of American fulfillment of "Manifest Destiny" which was preached by ministers and land speculators. Sentimental views of their right of "life, liberty and the pursuit of happiness" were never contemplated for them.

The Fixxed Media has "painted" the Indians as lazy and heathen and "scalp hungry!" Such portrayals helped Americans overlook the travesty of Indian de-population of their nations. It was the British in the colonies who initiated the practice of purchasing scalps of their Indian enemies to help subdue them. The public was given justifications to gloss over the brutal suppression of the American natives: they couldn't compete, that's progress, they were incorrigible savages who ravished innocent women, and the white man's trek westward was inexorable and couldn't be stopped!

Case Three: Inward into Camps,
Order #9060

So, OK, you can argue "illegal Indians" [heh, heh, heh!] and "relocated" Africans never had legal status of citizenship bestowed upon them. Therefore, their rights were not violated because they didn't have any! So, you ask, "What's all the "hullabaloo?" And besides, you argue, that was a long time ago when everybody was doing the same thing we were doing. And the thousands of arrests by J. Edgar & Co.'s raids were not a serious breach of the Constitution. Why not? Most of those illegally arrested and detained were soon released from jail without trial. No serious harm done.

So let's get down to "brass tacks." The "truthiness" is we can suspend all rights at any time. We simply scare the public with the help of the Fixxed Media and politicians "waving the patriotic" flag (for political gain). After the attack on Pearl Harbor by Japan in 1941, President Roosevelt signed Order #9060 which expunged all constitutional rights of 127,000 citizens of the U.S., including 70% who were natural born citizens. In essence he declared citizens of Japanese ancestry to be "enemy combatants." As has been shown before, the Constitution is viewed as "a scrap of paper" when necessary! The order was to be carried out through the military, as it was to protect the "Homeland." Headlines proclaimed the immediate invasion by Japan. Politicians such as Attorney General Earl Warren of California portrayed Japanese-Americans as potential saboteurs and traitors. (Warren later was Chief Justice of the Supreme Court.)

Fait accompli

Z: Even the Supreme Court acquiesced in its responsibilities to be a bulwark against an attack on the Bill of Rights! The Supreme Court would not declare the wholesale roundup of U.S. citizens to be illegal! It was pedaled as a military measure. War hysteria, "egged on" by inflammatory newspaper headlines, in the Fixxed Media "fanned" the hysteria and doomed anyone of Japanese ancestry to years of illegal, unconstitutional, communal internment.

It was easy to round-up unarmed innocent civilians even though none had committed a crime. That "Constitutional thingy" did not get in our way! There were no arrest warrants. There were no trials. Citizens were ordered to report to designated areas under threat of imprisonment and fine. There was no "due-process," only the mass processing of non-guilty citizens. All family members were under armed military escort. They were put into several concentration camps. Military guards and barbed wire facing inward surrounded them.

Real Americans were relieved! Patriotic "herds," egged on by scary headlines howled, "Good riddance!" [Researching the Internet for "Japanese internment" provides pictures and stories.]

The Diaper Ruse

Z: The "Onionette News" had an explanation as to why all Japanese family members had to be Rounded Up including babies, pregnant women, toddlers, and seniors. An "authoritative" anonymous source had reported that the cloth diapers (Pampers hadn't been invented yet) of babies were going to be used in an elaborate ruse to trick defending American soldiers. Deceptively innocent-looking, slow-paced sneaky seniors were going to cane-walk hidden white cloth diapers to the invading forces. Then the Japanese soldiers were going to wave them in a fake pretense of surrender! With no visible rifles, they were going to approach the U.S. military and attack the unsuspecting American soldiers with samurai swords! The shouted signal for the surprise attack would be:

Banzai! Banzai! Banzai! [f. Arabic= Benghazi! Benghazi! Benghazi!]

I remember reading in a textbook that the Japanese were moved from their homes for their own protection against very angry, "100% true-blue" Americans who might attack them! But someone has pointed out that the barbed wire surrounding the camps where they were imprisoned was turned inward, not outward. So much for propaganda! The Civil Liberties Act, 1988, a half-century later, paid survivors $20,000 totaling $1.2 billion. On Pearl Harbor Day 1991, President Bush apologized again.

It's easier to round up and control and move millions of people based on some different "herdal" physical characteristics!

(perceived) Red = Indians
(perceived) Black = Africans
(perceived) Yellow = Japanese.

It's much easier to run roughshod over citizens' rights in a dictatorship. No one dares challenge a tyrant! However, in some countries like the U.S., we must judiciously tread carefully to maintain an "appearance" of a constitutional democracy with checks and balances.

MISSION: TO CONTROL—WE HAVE A PROBLEM

We never willingly give up power. History is replete with examples of a weakened dictatorship failing to maintain control and stability. We have seen what happens in countries around the world when a strong central government slackens the reins of control. Lina Khatib has suggested that instability in Arab countries has made things worse since the Arab Spring (Was the Middle East better off with its dictators?, 2015). Stability collapses if rulers don't "drop the hammer" on protestors and dissidents. Chaos may follow.

- Marshal Tito died and communist Yugoslavia splintered into Croatia, Bosnia, and Serbia with civil wars
- Saddam Hussein was removed and chaos has ensued
- President Mubarak's moderate dictatorship was removed by the Egyptian army. Chaos!
- The Arab spring "blossomed" into armed fighting in Syria and Libya.

We try to avoid chaos and civil war! No ruling dictator in the world will <u>ever</u> give any real democratic power to rebelling subjects!

It is seen that throughout history, rulers in control <u>never</u> willingly give up power and possessions. They must be forced by an overpowering military force or threat to their physical existence to abdicate any control. Rulers, either win or lose. We either stay in power or not, *N'est-ce pas?*

Entrenched Powers Lose When Overpowered

The English King John reluctantly was forced to surrender some power when surrounded and challenged and outmanned by armed nobles (lords). Fearing for his life, he signed the *Magna Carta* at Runnymede, 1215. It abolished the concept of absolute rule of the monarchy. It delimited his power. Had the king's men had a few AK-47 firearms, the nobles would still be kissing a king's ring! But, he was outnumbered.

Unhappy American colonists, like the armed nobles, signed a petition to redress grievances and sent it to their king. He wouldn't even accept it. On October 25, 1775, His Majesty King George III responded before Parliament with the "Proclamation of Rebellion." He promised to crush the growing rebellion. Thomas Paine published <u>Common Sense</u> in January, 1776, outlining reasons for independence. In February 1776, Parliament had passed the "Prohibitory Acts." These Acts blockaded American ports and declared American ships to be enemy vessels. The British refused to compromise. The king rejected all compromise. Lord North stated in 1775 that, "Blows must decide whether they [the colonies] are to be subject to this country or independent." The British sent 5,000 troops [Expeditionary Forces] to help lay siege to Boston and to smack-down the rebellion. But, the rag-tag troops of the Continental Army eventually won. Why? They didn't dress-up in easily targeted scarlet red uniforms! But, more importantly, they had a lot of firepower with highly trained sharpshooters. Many had honed their skills doing a lot of squirrel hunting! With a "little help from [a] friend" the French, (actually a lot of help!) a rare event occurred in the history of the human race: citizens in open rebellion, won against a vastly superior military expedition that existed at that time!

Entrenched Powers Win When Overpowering

We usually win when militarily challenged. During the widespread rebellion of the 1381 Peasants Revolt, a frightened and surrounded King Richard was threatened at Mile End. Fearing for his life, he acceded to the demands of rebelling peasants. One demand included ending serfdom. He made promises of amnesty and friendship. He was allowed to return to his castle. Later he mobilized 4,000 soldiers, moved against the peasants and their leaders, and quashed the rebellion. As a warning, the body parts and heads of defeated rebels adorned castle walls. The revolt ended. If the rebels had had a few AK-47s they would have been victorious. All the acceded demands were rescinded. "It ain't over til it's over!"

A hundred thousand peasants were killed fighting against their rulers during the German Peasants Rebellion, 1524-1525. The rebels fought with scythes, axes, and flails. The threatened nobles formed the Swabian League to defeat the rebels. Nine thousand armed men and 2,000 horsemen overpowered and quashed the revolt. It was "soon over, over there!"

The slave Spartacus rallied 70,000 poorly armed slaves ~70 B. C. into rebellion against the Roman government and slave-owners. The end result: total defeat and 6,000 captured slaves crucified and displayed along Appian Way. They truly were "hung out to dry!" [die]. The movie, "Spartacus" starring Kirk Douglas, portrays the event.

In the United States in 1878, disgruntled heavily indebted farmers led Shays' Rebellion against the state government. There were military attacks. There was no federal standing army to counter the armed dissidents. The uprising was put down after some battles by a private, *ad hoc* army. George Washington, a private citizen at the time, led the armed forces. In a letter to Henry Knox, Washington wrote,

> *...if three years ago any person had told me that at this day, I should see such a **formidable rebellion** [emphasis added] against the laws & constitutions of our own making as now appears I should have thought him a bedlamite— a fit subject for a mad house.* (Gilder Lehrman Institute, n.d.)

He wrote that if the government "shrinks, or is unable to enforce its laws ...anarchy & confusion must prevail."

That fear of armed rebellion by discontented citizens is why the following clause was put into the new Constitution written in Philadelphia:

> *The Congress shall have Power To ...**raise and support Armies,*** [emphasis added] *but no Appropriation of Money to that Use shall be for a longer Term than two Years....*

As was illustrated in the examples above, entrenched powers win when overpowering rebelling citizens. We've known this for thousands of years. Whether it be dictatorships or democracies, rulers need to have the necessary military might to repel rebelling citizens. Contrary to popular belief [falsely created by the Fixxed Media], the Founding Fathers wanted a <u>strong</u> central government, not a weak one like that under the Articles of Confederation. They wanted to be able to enforce laws against "anarchy and confusion." They needed a military option to: Crush! Crush! Crush!

The problem with armed rebellion is that an outcome is so uncertain. We like things to move quietly along our way. Uprisings and civil wars can be messy and so destructive. In a democracy it's best to maintain control without overt conflict. The populace votes and peacefully, if not grudgingly, accepts the results. "Armies" of voters peacefully "battle" it out in the voting booth and then "retreat" to lament and mourn the outcomes!

Thus, we must remain vigilant and must control the information that citizens receive so they can make wise choices. [Review Fixxed Media] We don't want citizens to vote against <u>our</u> interests. Throughout history, those heading powerful institutions, whether secular or religious, have suppressed alternative belief systems or ideology. We try to control correct thinking. In times of crisis we use the same processes that various European inquisitions have used to try to "snuff out" threatening beliefs which challenge the *status quo* of entrenched religious Bailiwicks.

Inquiring Minds led to the Spanish Inquisition.

[ROUNDUP: PART TWO]

SHUTTING DOWN INQUIRING MINDS
HERESY   HERESY   HERESY

"No one expects the Spanish Inquisition" —f. Monty Python

Who is Janat Gul? Snap! Crackle! Pop! [Sounds of torture].

"[U.S. Rep] *Pike will pay for this...we'll destroy him for this.*"
—CIA special counsel, 1976. [See below]

'Internal enemies' can be as great a danger to the people as external ones...Perhaps even greater. —f. Ayn Rand, Atlas Shrugged

We strive to maintain our belief system and practices that will advance our desire to prosper and profit. We try to snuff out any contrary challenges. When necessary, we engage in *extra-constitutional* means. Our nefarious methods parallel those of leaders of religious Inquisitions that beseeched *"extra-terrestial"* heavenly forces, *viz*, God. Like them, we suppress and eliminate those who are opposed to us. In a democracy we have to "use the velvet glove" approach to subdue opposition. Operators of the Inquisition "took the gloves off" to eradicate blasphemers. Their goals were the same as ours: suppress evil, heretical ideas using any means necessary. We warn challengers: We rule! You rue!

We'll cull you from the herd!

We think of a "heretic" [f. Gk. αιρετικός = one who chooses] as someone who has a strong disagreement with established religious church doctrine. All leaders of countries and major institutions engage in an inculcation process for their established respective belief systems. They don't want dissenters. They demand absolute loyalty. They attack and suppress those who challenge the views of the religious and/or political institutions. They suppress because their personal positions might be threatened—not because they oppose the actual writings and beliefs of others.

Scoured & Scourged

Rulers and leaders of nations also use the same various processes to dominate and control. Those who disagree are labeled as "heretics" or "traitors." Their very existence threatens the *status quo,* and they are

127

condemned as heretics or traitors or mal-contents. Two of the greatest threats to established institutions have used the same tactics to suppress and eradicate their opposition in order to survive. Different religious institutions such as the Inquisition went after heretics; the U.S. went after Communists. [f. Gk κομίνιστας = we want what you have]

In both cases, victims committed no crimes. They broke no laws. They physically threatened no one. They stole nothing. They harmed no one. They only thought differently. But established authorities feared the mantra, "Thinking Makes It So!" (Enquiring minds want to know.) Fearing a revolt against their established privileges, leaders sought the eradication of heretical thinking and practices. The Inquisition's interrogators literally crushed the bones of perceived heretics by placing a wooden board across the ribs and adding one rock at a time until...Crack! Crack! Crack! [Research further on the Internet: Inquisition torture; the "Pear;" WARNING: disturbing graphic images of torture.]

In early Christianity, correct, rigid doctrines such as the Nicene Creed were formalized through special Councils. Tribunals were set-up to judge dissenters. The most famous was in Rome after Martin Luther "posted" his Ninety-five Theses at the Wittenberg Cathedral in 1517. Luther's defiant action is considered the beginning of the Protestant Reformation against papal authority. Charges were made. Judgments made. Luther was summoned to Rome by church officials to be interrogated in a forum and questioned for his actions. It did not go well for him!

The church decreed: *Exsurge Domine*

Bull of Pope Leo issued June 15, 1520

Arise, O Lord, and judge your own cause...for foxes have arisen seeking to destroy the vineyard [Church]*...The wild boar* [Martin Luther] *from the forests seeks to destroy it and everyday wild beast feeds upon it. Their tongues are fire, a restless evil, full of deadly poison...He is like the heretics* [who] *start spewing out a serpent's venom with their tongue...* [*We can*] *no longer tolerate or overlook the pernicious poison of the above errors...*

In other words they thought his actions and ideas stunk! His "best sellers" got him and his followers officially condemned by the officiating tribunal. They were decreed illegal and heretical.

The Church officials acted as all threatened rulers and leaders of institutions do: they went into "a full court press" against heretics and/or dissenters. Armed with official "legal" condemnation, "Official Enforcers of the Inquisition" scoured the countryside gathering "testimony" from informers and spies. The Inquisition was previously authorized in different countries by Pope Sixtus IV, November 1, 1478, by papal bull, *Exiget Sinceras Devotionis Affecxtus.* Gruesome tortures were used to garner confessions and expiate the sins of the accused "heretics." [View on Internet: *Man of la Mancha* (1972) Movie Clip: "The Edict of the Inquisition" which shows the arrest of Miguel Cervantes and other harmless, unarmed members of a theatrical troupe. They're being arrested for the "crime" of mocking the Church. They are taken to a sinister building (which resembles NSA Headquarters) to be questioned. Also view the "Spanish Inquisition the Brutal Truth by the BBC"]. Suspected heretics were eliminated through confessions, burning at the stake, imprisonment and excommunication. Their books and writings were burned. Their crime: thinking differently! Church officials wanted them to think (politically and religiously) correct! They sure knew how to inflict earthly "divine" intervention! We believe in expunging political heretical thinking.

Cold War: Counter "Reformation"
Better Dead than Red

We have done the same processes, *sans* torture, to extirpate our "enemies in our midst" who challenge us. Naturally, we prefer to use methods that we can convince voters are legitimate. Torture is so "rear view mirror."

After WWII, we went after those who thought differently and threatened us. We had to suppress the threat of the spread of Russian communism. Once again we shelved the Constitution. We prepared to deal with the political "heretics" who disagreed with the way we were running things. They had very harmful views promoted by Marxists, socialists, communists, unionists etc. The Communist Manifesto, written by Karl Marx and Friedrich Engels a century earlier (1848), terrified us with the proposed dumping of my associates and I into oblivion—and dispossession of our possessions [heh, heh, heh!] Their proclamation, "Workers of the world unite! You have nothing to lose but your chains!" sent shudders through our ranks. They wanted to end private property and have government control over the resources of a nation. Such a philosophy would shut us down and shut us out—of our profits!

As brutal communist regimes were established post-WWII in East European countries occupied by Russian troops, we feared the same thing would be happening in the U.S. The communists had eliminated free enterprise and nationalized the means of production. Our way of doing business would be destroyed along with us! Through the Fixxed Media we promoted fear of a communist takeover so we could rally the citizens against any threat. These threats included a highly unlikely invasion by Russia [U.S.S.R.] and/or possible communist–supported rebellious uprisings from within. The term Cold War is a descriptive term encapsulating our all-out efforts to suppress the spread of communism. If you don't know what this term means, ask someone over 50 years old. We had to "roll up our sleeves" and take proactive measures to eliminate all perceived threats. We took measures that would totally crush the essence of civil liberties. The Constitution would be "scrapped" again. Frightened American citizens acquiesced and gave us a "pass" to crush constitutional rights written in the Bill of Rights. *¡Asì es la vida! ¡Viva la Inquisición!*

RENDER UNTO CAESAR AND INTO U.S. CAMPS

*There is no excuse for any American citizen becoming affiliated
with a group on the Attorney General's list today.*
—1947 Elks Magazine, November 1956 cite f. (Goldstein) "The Making of a
Blacklist," Prologue Magazine, Fall 2006, Vol. 38, No. 3.

How Will Our Laws Against Traitors Work? —Beverly Smith,
Saturday Evening Post, January 3, 1951.

Who got on the "Naughty List" in December 1947?

Who is Janat Gul?

How was the list made up? What were the criteria for listing groups? What right did anyone, including the Attorney General, have to compile and publish any list of citizens' activities? Well, we did have the right!

President Truman's "Executive Order 9835" of March 21, 1947, was to be used to find disloyal federal civil service employees. Essentially, any citizen would be disloyal if they had had "membership in, affiliation with or sympathetic association [that the attorney general found to be] totalitarian, Fascist, Communist or subversive." The FBI and the secret police compiled dossiers of suspected traitors and/or commies.

All accumulated names were used to help President Truman, J Edgar Hoover, and the attorney general make up a list of Americans to be rounded up. Truman's Executive Order 9835 authorized Hoover to make a list of potential disloyal Americans. In August 1948, attorney General J. Howard McGrath and J. Edgar Hoover drew up a plan, "Security Portfolio," to authorize the arbitrary arrest of 20,000 citizens who were considered disloyal Americans. Hoover wanted to arrest and detain without court approval in the event of a Russian invasion or communist "terrorism." Truman wanted to get legal court approval to round up Americans into camps authorized by the acts of Congress. [See below, McCarran Act]

Hoover had his "J'accuse List" [apologies to Émile Zola], which he compiled from hand-written white index cards. According to Kathleen Sharp, he alone, judged the level of loyalty of citizens. He categorized and classified each on his "Security Index." He indexed Dorothy Comingore, movie star of *Citizen Kane.* She was put in "category C" which meant she could be rounded up at his discretion. Her mail was opened, her phones tapped; she was followed and "blacklisted." Hoover considered her dangerous. Add her to the list! **Living the Orwellian Life,** *Truth-out* (Sharp, 2013).

Z: Thus, the secret police spied and infiltrated any legal organization they wanted to. Faceless bureaucrats decided who were "true blue" Americans. Dossiers were made. Lists were made. Mistakes can easily be made by government spy agencies. Faceless, unaccountable bureaucrats can wreak havoc on innocent citizens. The no-fly list is a good example of secret lists made by unseen, judgmental bureaucrats.

No-Fly List: More Than 750,000

The following event occurred according to the article in *USA Today*. "**15,000 want off the US terror watch list,**" by Mimi Hall (2007)

Actual event

Ticket agent "flags" (with stern voice): "Who is John A_ _ _ _ ?

Mother: [points to stroller.]

Family must personally check in to fly so officials can see that the person on the "No Fly" list is just 6 years old and not a terrorist!

Mother: "No one can give any answers to why my son is on the list."

AGLOSO AGLOSO AGLOSO

(Attorney General's List of Subversive Organizations)

*"Dear subscriber, **you are registered** [emphasis added] as a participant in a mass disturbance"* —Ukrainian government E-mail warning sent directly to thousands of anti-government protestors' phones

Our Secret Police spied and made files on citizens who committed no overt illegal activity against the state. Unknown faceless government agents made dossiers in secret. They helped ready the lists. We were getting ready to intern citizens whose way of thinking we did not like. Citizens were perceived as a threat even if they had broken no laws. We were getting ready to act. We've done it before: Remember Roosevelt's Order #9060?

Camp McCarran

The McCarran Act (Internal Security Act of 1950), *Subversive Activities Control Act* gave the president authority [power] to apprehend and detain

*each person as to whom there is a reasonable ground to believe that such person **probably** will engage in, or **probably** [emphasis added] will conspire with others to engage in, acts of espionage or sabotage.*

The Part II *Emergency Detention Act* set-up detention facilities.

Q: Which of the following U.S. Congressmen voted for the Internal Security Act of 1950 (McCarran Act) for setting up internment camps and rounding up innocent U.S. citizens without trials on the FBI's pre-established list of subversives? McCarran Act passed by over 89% of Congress; 268-48 in the House; 57-10 in the Senate

    A. John F. Kennedy, future senator and President

    B. Hubert Humphrey, senator and future VP

    C. Lyndon Johnson, future Senator, VP and president

    D. Richard Nixon, future VP and President

    E. All of the above

In December 1952, Attorney T. Howard McGrath set up 6 sites, including the Tule Lake site that had encamped Japanese Americans during WWII. Would the roundup of citizens have been initiated if the Ruskies (Soviet Union) had made an amphibious invasion landing near Wasilla, Alaska? [by kayak, canoe or ice floe?! "Yer dern shootin'!" heh, heh, heh!]

ERADICATION OF "RADICAL" THOUGHT
Who Decides Who Is Subversive?
Who is Janat Gul?
The Ferris "Persuader," torture device, f. Atlas Shrugged
They're coming to take me away....

During the Cold War we had to "cleanse" those with their radical ideas who wanted to subvert our way of doing things. We "painted" them with names: subversives, sympathizers, traitors, or communists. We told a frightened public that the commies were everywhere covertly planning to take over the country just as they had done in many European countries! Through the Fixxed Media and political and religious leaders' exhortations, we fanned the fear that, *"The Russians are coming! The Russians are coming!"* [This was the name of the 1966 Cold War comedy.] A panicked public, like Foxy Loxy and Henny Penny, *et al,* falsely feared an imminent violent confrontation with internal and/or external communists' forces. *¡Viva la Revolución!*

There's no doubt that Russia was assisting U.S. commies with funds and setting up spy networks. However, we made sure that several thousand undercover FBI agents swelled the Communist Party ranks to spy on their every move! We made sure to keep an eye on them! [Review above, "Camp McCarran" and See, below: "Whacked by HUAC."] The truth is, domestic communists never were a threat! They were never even strong enough to storm and capture even a single police station! They didn't even have the wherewithal to storm a local PTA meeting in Wasilla and seize the dais!
¡La Revolución está muerta!

Little guys plowing in the fields or throwing darts in a pub don't promulgate decrees against an enemy. Who Does? We do! The rulers and leaders of institutions do. First, we perceive a menace that threatens or challenges our positions such as the dangerous ideas of Martin Luther or Karl Marx. Then, we establish legal justification through laws, decrees, and papal bulls. [Review, Heresy! Heresy Heresy!] This provides legal authorization to "drop the hammer" on anyone considered a threat.

Next, we have to accumulate evidence with an elaborate spy network of paid secret agents and willing informers. They funnel collected evidence to officials who "roll up their sleeves" and begin the process of hunting down the designated "Enemy of the State:" heretic, heathen, traitor, etc.

Then, we convene Official Interrogation Tribunals. In the 16th century it was the Inquisition. In the United States it was HUAC, House Un-American Activity Committee. Politicians in Congress set-up an investigative committee to ferret out the bad guys. The committee members could subpoena anyone. It was a Win-Win well-publicized victory for them. They were charged with rooting out the "traitors in our midst" and tracking down purveyors of "heresy." Their "marching orders" were to "Stamp Out Traitors!" Through televised hearings they exposed the threat. They won the admiration <u>and</u> votes of a grateful citizenry. As a result, we succeeded in crushing any thought, ideology, or challenge to our way of doing things.

Life was going to continue to be good—for us!

Life was not going to be so good for those we targeted!

They got on our Naughty List!

YOOISM: If you're subpoenaed, you're guilty!

WHACKED BY HUAC (HEW-ACK)!

We have always kept tabs of dangerous thinkers and activists who might challenge our right to rule. In a democracy citizens believe they have a right to free speech and free association. Karl Marx visited the United States in the 19th Century. He believed that through the democratic process the Communist Party might win a majority in elections, and the United States might become a communist country. [In your radical dreams! heh, heh, heh!] We make sure such a horrendous nightmarish possibility would never, never, never, never happen! Some Americans didn't get the message! During the Cold War we, went on an aggressive hunt for commies and their sympathizers. We set our investigative tools to work. We set up the House Un-American Activities congressional committee called HUAC. Our secret police (FBI) provided the dossiers and data to haul anyone we wanted before the committee.

Evidence was surreptitiously gathered by thousands of secret career FBI spies. Willing neighbors reported suspicious behavior. Phones were tapped. Mail opened. Suspects tailed. It's easier in a dictatorship to eliminate pesky troublemakers. The absolutist monarchs of France could simply sign *"lettres de cachet"* to arrest any citizen for <u>any</u> reason. They would be imprisoned in the Bastille fortress without trial. In the era of the Divine Right of monarchs, [*L'Etat c'est moi*] there was no pretense of any rights of the accused if a king was offended or angry with one of his subjects.

Z: Imagine the whole world watching while you are seated in front of a panel of solemn-faced House congressional politicians. Through their power to subpoena, they have commanded your appearance before them. Those politicians are going to determine if you are a loyal American. They have the power to declare you worthy and to give their "stamp of approval." They have the power to condemn you as unworthy and "cull" you from the herd. The odds were against you. Las Vegas didn't take bets!

Out of 151,325,798 citizens (1950) how did the politicians know who on the list of individuals should be subpoenaed? What were their political transgressions?

A list of actors known as the "Hollywood 10" and three hundred other actors and artists were called before the committee. As a result, many were blacklisted and unable to find work. They were fired and/or shunned by Hollywood producers. They were "excommunicated." They were culled from the 100% true-blue American "herd!"

One of those actors was Burgess Meredith. He was blacklisted and therefore unemployable. He was unable to ply his trade and earn money for several years. Review his bio on the Internet. The reader can see his numerous awards and his illustrious career of six decades in movies. He portrayed the Penguin in the Batman TV series and "Rocky" Balboa's trainer in the "Rocky" movies.

The highly acclaimed Meredith had the proverbial "last laugh!"

Yuk! Yuk! Yuk!

The Penguin's Wings Get Clipped

We're sorry the Penguin got roasted
And all the others got toasted
We got you blacklisted
Crushed with our fisted (*sic*)
And with high poll numbers we boasted!
— Preening Politicians on HUAC Committee

Guilt by Association

*... the subjecting of men to punishment for things which,
when they were done, were breaches of no law* [is among]
the favorite and most formidable instrument of tyranny."
—The Federalist, no. 78 discussion of *ex post facto* laws

Past behavior by citizens was suspect even though their past activities were not illegal behavior. Being a member of an organization *ipso facto* made a person "guilty."[YOOISM: If you're subpoenaed, you're an *ipso facto* traitor.] Basically, freedom to associate and engage in free speech were considered un-American if tainted with radical ideas. Some Americans had joined political organizations in the past, which were later designated communist fronts but still were not considered illegal. Their "crime" was thinking differently. Past activities were considered treasonous and subversive. These actions were mainly attending meetings and having personal associations.

No one was hurt.
No violent crime was planned.
No caches of arms were found.

> **Q:** Write a story, "The Naughty List," include dialogue in which you are unjustly dragged before an accusing governmental tribunal. You have been falsely accused. Get ideas from the book Darkness at Noon by Arthur Koestler and Arthur Miller's play, "The Crucible."

The beat (down) goes on! "Witch" hunt in China

[The current Chinese dictatorship has]"taken down professors, journalists and others deemed disloyal to the Communist Party orthodoxy." [The Old Guard conservatives]"have declared open season on Chinese academics, artists and party cadres seen as insufficiently red" (communist). Chris Buckley and Andrew Jacob reported the Chinese government's cracking down on dissidents, **Maoists in China, Given New Life, Attack Dissent,** *New York Times*, (2015).

Marian the (Spyarian) Librarian
(f. "The Music Man")
Thought Control Police

"Enquiring minds want to know. Shut them down!" —Yachta

Orthodoxy (f. Gk. Ὀρθόδοξία = "straight," correct thinking)

Z: J. Edgar Hoover, an unelected bureaucrat, determined what a citizen should read. The FBI contacted some librarians to spy on those checking out "subversive books" that he didn't approve of. There is great *irony* in the FBI asking librarians to spy and compile lists of citizens who checked-out certain books that they wanted to read! Today, the title The Great Crash by John Galbraith might have been misinterpreted as code for a terrorist plot to attack and crash planes!

CENSORSHIP: Oppressive governments always try to expunge dangerous reading material. The Spanish Bishop of Yucatan burned hundreds of Mayan manuscripts and plays written on deerskin. He decreed them works of the devil. The movie, "Indiana Jones: Raiders of the Lost Ark" depicts a public book burning in Hilter's Nazi Germany. In the Ray Bradbury futuristic novel and movie, Fahrenheit 451 (1953), there were "search and destroy" book burners as firemen and fire engines went to homes to set seditious books on fire. The hero "fireman" started taking and reading the forbidden books out of curiosity. That action was viewed as treasonous!

During the Cold War, we citizens were told that the dirty rotten good for nothing Russian commies, read mail, "bugged" phone calls, spied on their citizens, and tracked what they could read. I didn't realize the U.S. government through the secret police (FBI) did the same! In high school I was curious about the communist Karl Marx's book, Das Kapital. I checked it out of the library and tried reading that cumbersome tome. I was puzzled as to what was written. All students in Russia (Soviet Union) were required to read it. I distinctly remember feeling sorry for those Russian students because I couldn't make heads nor tails what it was all about! I think I didn't get past page twenty! Was I put on a list? A teenage subversive!

In 1965 an individual told me he always bought magazines from a news stand because he didn't want the government knowing what he read if he subscribed to it. How quaint! I thought he was paranoid! Today, with the NSA spying on us, we all are paranoid—or should be!

Whoops! J. Edgar Hoover perceived Martin Luther King (and also Nelson Mandela) as sympathetic to communism and attempted to destroy his leadership of the Civil Rights movement. One secret FBI agent wrote:

> In the light of King's powerful demagogic speech ["I Have a Dream," March on Washington]... We must mark him now, if we have not done so before, as **the most dangerous Negro** [emphasis added] of the future in this Nation from the standpoint of communism, the Negro, and national security.

The Dark Side of 'I Have a Dream' The FBI's War on Martin Luther King, Mother Jones, FBI Memo (Korn, 2013). The NSA spied on Martin Luther King and Senators Frank Church and Howard Baker, Muhammed Ali, and anti-Vietnam war protestors and tapped phones on their "watch lists." They also bugged, *The New York Times'* columnist Tom Wicker and even jocular *Washington Post* columnist Art Buchwald! [Surely you jest!] **Power of One, BBC, NSA spied on Martin Luther King, documents reveal** (BBC, 2013).

[ROUNDUP PART THREE]

I SPY, THEREFORE I AM

THE NSA: INTERNAL SPY AND CONTROL NETWORK

The goddess Athena was birthed from the head of Zeus;
The omnipresent NSA mystically was birthed from.......????

YOOISM: In a free society, secret spying must remain secret otherwise, it's no longer secret and we're no longer free.

"HOUSTON, WE HAVE A PROBLEM!"

The whole country is getting restless.

We must maintain a watchful eye.

We have developed a universal means of keeping an eye on everyone! It's the "Internal Spy and Control Network." We call it the NSA for short. It's enthusiastically supported by members of Congress, political leadership and the Fixxed Media. We don't need to use the archaic means employed during the Cold War to keep track of dissenters. We just listen in! We claim that we're fighting terrorists. But, actually with new technology, we're going to be able to suppress any strong organized domestic effort to challenge us. Why install secret spying machinery? "The natives are restless!"

Checks and Balance, R.I.P.

Edward Snowden rained [heh, heh, heh!] on our (data collecting) parade when he fled the country with government NSA data in 1.7 million intelligence files. He alerted the citizens of the world that, "We can hear you now wherever you are!" His exposé was very disconcerting to say the least. We had to rally lots of Congressional and governmental leaders to defend the spying by NSA. In unison they shouted: "National Security! National Security!" in front of the TV cameras to try to rally the citizens against Snowden and to defend massive, invasive spying! We were evasive about civil liberties' infractions, as usual. We tried to paint Snowden as a traitor. Anyone challenging us is!

Suppressing the truth about our efforts to spy on citizens is not new. Being openly exposed and challenged is. How did we get away with spying in the past? We didn't tell anyone. We decide if we need to know things about any citizen. How do we find out? It's none of your business. We have a "free hand" in gathering info and intel. Even a duly elected member of Congress can't force the President and the Executive to kowtow to the Checks & Balances system setup by the Constitution. Congressional mavericks are no match in our efforts to thwart their inquiries into our nefarious "spy apparatus!" We helped a defiant Executive and its spy agencies to refuse to answer questions and honor a Congressional subpoena. Mark Ames reveals how we went after and "brought down" a troublesome Congressman in his article, **The first congressman to battle the NSA is dead. No-one noticed, no-one cares**, (Ames, 2014).

Legally, government action and laws must have a "written" proof of their validity no matter how farfetched the linkage. Thus, President Eisenhower approved funds for the interstate highway system and justified it as a matter of national defense. Hundreds of billions of taxes have been spent. There is no mention of a highway system in the constitution! But, funds were legally approved by Congressional authorization as a national defense necessity. There is a legal basis for it.

House Committee Chairman Rep. Otis Pike wanted to find out more about the Cold War intelligence expenditures. He wanted to know the purpose of the CIA and the NSA, and what were the expenditures, procedures, and efficacy of the programs. He couldn't find out the legal basis as to how the NSA was authorized and how it had come into existence. Why? We had successfully concealed the means of its creation as if it were a national secret. It was! We didn't want anyone to know about it!

WARNED: "I'm serious, there will be retaliation. Any political ambitions that [Rep.] Pike had in New York are through. We will destroy him for this." - Michael Rogain, Special Counsel to CIA Director George Bush.

CIA director William Colby admitted for the first time "that the NSA was routinely tapping phones." The head of the NSA, Lew Allen Jr., publicly admitted that NSA was <u>legally</u> entitled to wiretap Americans' phone calls overseas. Pike wanted to see the document authorizing the creation of the NSA and its goals. Pike issued a National Security Council Intelligence Directive No. 6 order for NSA to produce the charter. Albert Hall, the Pentagon's intelligence head, appeared before Pike's committee without the document. He agreed it could be viewed at another building so that the secret document would not be entered into the official Senate record. Pike refused saying,

> "You're talking about the document that set up the entire N.S.A., it's one which all members [of Congress] are entitled to see without shuttling back and forth downtown to look at."

Defense Secretary Hall refused to bring the document because it "has secret material in it." Pike exploded:

> "It seems incredible to me, very frankly, that we are asked to appropriate large amounts of money for that agency...

without being provided a copy of the piece of paper by which
the agency is authorized."

Pike summoned Secretary of State Henry Kissinger to testify, but with presidential support, he refused to appear. The subpoena was ignored and Kissinger was held in contempt. For Pike's rebellious actions, we "sicced" the Fixxed Media on Representative Pike and ruthlessly attacked him. He threatened to issue a scathing report. We retaliated!

We rallied House members and the House voted to quash the Pike "Committee Report." [The Wrath of Con(gress), heh, heh! Heh!]
The rest is history and so was Rep Pike! After we organized the Fixxed Media and political opponents against him, Pike chose not to run for re-election. He realized our motto was true! "We rule! You rue!"
¡Se fué! ¡Así es la vida! Pike = *¡Desaparecidio!*

Q: **Write an essay on this topic:** Should a U.S. Congressional committee chairman be allowed to ask for and receive documents from the Executive Branch as part of the Checks and Balance system?

Fein[ken]stein & Rogers: Roger that!

After those public attacks we "dodged a bullet" and continued spying unabatedly and in secret upon the "free" citizens of America until...................... Edward Snowden! In the latest spying revelations [2013], our allies in Congress led the way in attacking Snowden's character and motives. Rep Mike Rogers on "Meet the Press" implied Snowden, by fleeing to Russia, is a traitor working for Russian spy services. "I don't think it was a gee-whiz luck event that he ended up in Moscow under the handling of the F.S.B. [formerly the K.G.B]." Eric Schmitt and David E. Sanger reported adverse congressional reaction to Snowden, **Congressional Leaders Suggest Earlier Snowden Link to Russia** (Schmidt & Sanger, 2014). Rep Rogers also accused Snowden's friend Glenn Greenwald of looking for personal gain, "He's now selling his access to [leaked] information...A thief selling stolen material is a thief!" **Intelligence chairman accuses Glenn Greenwald of illegally selling stolen material** (Gerstein, 2014).

Senator Feinstein "ran interference" for us as she "pooh-poohed" the hullabaloo about citizens being spied on. She did not call it a spy program. She said, "It's not a surveillance program, it's a data-collection program." [Define euphemism! heh, heh, heh!] *The Hill's* Kate Tummarello wrote, **Feinstein blasts critics of NSA phone program** (2014). The Senator cited the efforts of 10,000 FBI people doing intelligence work. "It's called protecting America." **Dianne Feinstein on NSA: 'It's called protecting America.'** (Mak & Meredith, 2013). We always get a "pass" from the Senate Intelligence Committee. Its motto should be, "See no Evil!"

We're lucky there no longer is any real "Checks and Balances" by Congress. Actually, there never was. Thank goodness members of Congress simply are "toothless" or whole-heartedly support us when it comes to overseeing our nefarious activities. They either agree with us or don't have the [fill-in the blank] to fight us! Niccolò (the Prince) Machiavelli in his <u>Discourses</u> observed,

> *He who desires or attempts to reform the government of a state, and wishes to have it accepted and be capable of maintaining itself to the satisfaction of everybody, must at least retain the semblance of the old forms; so that it may seem to the people that there has been no change in the institutions, even though in fact they are entirely different from the old ones.*

All our past secret spying was "hunky-dory" without checks until Edward Snowden rained on our (data collecting) parade!

But, but…It was a wrong number "butt" dial!
We can "hear you now" even if you whisper!

> **Q: View the You Tube trailer and then write a short paragraph describing your emotions while viewing it.**
>
> Who Knew? —Snowden Did!
>
> "Know that every border you cross
> every purchase you make
> every call you dial
> every cell phone tower you pass
> every friend you keep
> every site you visit
> and every subject you type
> is in the hands of a system whose reach is unlimited but
> whose safeguards are not."
>
> View You Tube: "Citizen Four Trailer" by Edward Snowden (over 1,000,000 visits)

Keep your eyes on our spies

The government has easy access to our tax information, stock trades, phone bills, medical records and credit card spending and it is just getting started.— WSJ

We like keeping tabs on you. Knowing what you're up to keeps us safer. The NSA gathers nearly 5 billion records a day from hundreds of millions of devices according to Barton Gellman and Ashkan Soltani, **NSA tracking cellphone locations worldwide, Snowden documents show**. (2013) Andy Kessler writes, **In the Privacy War, It's iSpy v gSpy** that, "The government has easy access to our tax information, stock trades, phone bills, medical records and credit-card spending, and it is just getting started." (Kessler, 2013). Citing <u>Wired</u> magazine, he reports that in Bluffdale, Utah, the National Security Agency is building a $2 billion, one-million-square-foot facility. "Some estimate the facility will be capable of storing five zettabytes of data…so that's like five billion terabyte drives, which would be enough to store every email, cellphone call." We think that should be sufficient to track everyone!

> **Q: Do you agree or disagree with Snowden? Discuss the pros and cons in Edward Snowden's YouTube "Moment of Truth" Virtual Interview.** [See: YouTube] (Summary: If citizens discuss in an open, public debate and pass laws and give their consent, then that's OK. But, citizens should decide on the spying network. And know that the government is spying on everyone and everything and have been lying about it.)

I suggest a law requiring all citizens to wear a digital wristband so all movements and transactions would automatically be monitored. Citizens might have a "bit of a fit" being forced to purchase and wear a hand bracelet (band) monitoring system. License fee charges and fees to download printouts would be mandatory. Of course my friends and I would get a piece of the action [heh, heh, heh!] Ratings based on a matrix of factors could be used to categorize behavior. Thus, citizens could be classified as to their security threat level. Possible use of universal monitoring bracelets: the government's secret monitoring agents could emit an electronic pain to deter sit-in protestors and bad behavior. An "Internal Special Forces" unit could be trained and manned to hunt down malcontents. Imagine a drone flying overhead that can detect aberrant behavior of any kind. And then, Zaaaaaaaaaap! The program could be called Max Pacification and the weapon used could be called the Pacifier. [f. Pacifier = Shut up!] Of course mistakes might be made. [View YouTube: "Collateral Murder."]

[Scott Walker: Muzzletov! *Faire ses adieu à liberté*]

Z: I suggest the NSA have a monitoring system on <u>all</u> individuals in Washington D.C. involved with crafting and making laws, such as politicians and lobbyists. All conversations involving official business would have to be transmitted "real time" or have to be recorded. Citizens could have access to them to monitor the influence of any interest group or individual. No FOIA would be needed.

What's "good for the goose is good for the gander!"

We need to keep track of all malcontents. There are more and more and more. Tough economic conditions with more foreclosures and poor economic opportunities and low, subpar wages have created an angry public. The demonstrations in the "Occupy Wall Street" movement provided overt manifestation of that anger. We have to keep "tabs" on this seething, bubbling threat. Our friends at the FBI and the NSA are assisting us with secret surveillance. The danger to us is spelled out in Chuck Collins book, <u>99 to 1</u> (Collins, 2012). The title to chapter eight, "The Sleeping 99 Per cent Giant Wakes Up" succinctly summarizes our dilemma—we're outnumbered! Thankfully, our elaborate spy apparatus will help keep a watchful eye on a "restive" citizenry.

Edward Snowden correctly warned of our concern when he stated

"Once you've lost a certain degree of power you can no longer oppose that power. There can be no revolutionary political movement when the government knows what everybody is doing, what everybody is saying, what everybody is thinking." (Curbing of US spy powers is 'historic': Edward Snowden, 2015).

We have to stay vigilant against those who oppose our rule and way of doing things.

Citizens are outraged because not one of us who perpetrated fraud and cost the nation hundreds of billions of dollars went to jail. We almost crashed the whole economic system with our massive, fraudulent "Grand Theft" schemes. And none of us went to jail! Is this a great country or not!

How did we get away with it? The next chapter explains how we got away with a mere "slap on the wrist" with a wet noodle (*al dente*).

CHAPTER TEN

MEET THE
FIXXERS FIXXERS FIXXERS

If you do the crime, just pay a fine.

As ye sow, so shall ye reap. — Galatians 6:7
We do the "sowing." You do the "weeping!" — Yachta Yachta Yachta
Thy Liberty in law, "America the Beautiful" —Katherine Lee Bates
Justice ~~Delayed~~ Never — Att. General Eric Holder's view

CONNECTIONS, CONNECTIONS, CONNECTIONS
(f. Latin: = Arugula! Arugula! Arugula!

Say the magic words and rub the magic lamp and the genie will send up an
invisible smoke screen to shield us from stealing trillions and trillions!
— Consortium of Bankers, Yachta's Friends

In a democracy we struggle to gain access to positions of power. What is the objective? It is winning (procuring) political power. Gaining power is a means, not an end in itself. Power holders like us utilize options (means) to achieve our hidden true political-economic objectives.

Remember we "seize" governments to help us channel (suck) citizens' wealth into our coffers. Fortunately for us, citizens don't want to believe they have been a "mark" in a sophisticated political "con" game. Well-palmed hands through political contributions purchase politicians' votes and governmental access. Naturally, this process is well hidden. The game is the same as it's always been: redirecting wealth from citizens to us. We don't need bombs or guns. We just need access to friends in high places in the "Establishment" to smooth the way and run interference for us.

We have succeeded in being in a position to pass any law that we want that is favorable to us. Our people in government do our bidding because they are our friends. With "a little help from our friends," we completely avoided any prosecution of all our criminal activity that led to a complete meltdown of the economy in 2008. We expiated our fraudulent banking "sins" simply by paying fines, a form of "indulgence." Even Martin Luther [the original one] would gasp at the purchase price [billions in fines] for forgiveness! Attorney General Eric Holder's rationale is the "Mother of all Yooisms" in his rationalization for not pursuing any <u>criminal</u> prosecution of our banking friends. His statement below is emblematic of how we can rationalize <u>any</u> thievery and get away with it. [See quotations and question below.]

Axis of Access: Vortex of Complicity

Gatekeepers guard the doors.
Gatekeepers possess the keys.
Gatekeepers unlock or block the entryway.

Whoever "seizes" control of the presidency appoints his own personnel to staff his administration's gatekeepers. They do the bidding of a president. An attorney general is such a pivotal linchpin. He's supposed to uphold the concept of "liberty and justice for all." But, in reality, "It's justice for us, the well-connected!" Students recite the Pledge of Allegiance one thousand times. The ending should be "and justice for all...who are well-connected and can afford it!" [heh, heh, heh!] We are well connected!

Z: "Restless" citizens rebelled in the 2008 presidential election. They tossed the dice for a virtually unknown politician from Chicago. Politically non-aligned independents (neophytes) actually physically worked *ad hoc* phone banks to help elect him! [Talk about fish out of water!] His dazzling smile bedazzled voters. His words of promise gave them HOPE he would begin to set the listing "Ship of State" upright. When president, the voters waited…and waited…and waited…and waited…for him to draw his mighty sword and "slay the beast" of "Too Big to Fail" bankers and political corruption and secrecy and suppression of civil liberties. Unfortunately for them, their knight in shining armor had emerged from the shadowy *milieu* of Chicago politics. He was already a buddy with Jamie Dimon, Banker *extraordinaire*. [See below: "Whassup?"] Soon many voters realized they had rolled "snake eyes!" The Executive Branch of government failed to prosecute the culprits who had "tanked" the economy. The chief legal authority of the United States, the attorney general, said they were too big to fail! Angry voters rebelled against the party in power and "fifed" in the rebellious Tea Partyers in 2010! In 2014, voters again "socked it to 'em" and the established leadership by rejecting their party.

The president had appointed Eric Holder as a key gatekeeper with the keys for unlocking or blocking the pathways to justice. His favorable attitude toward us is spelled out in the following limerick:

Don't <u>Hold 'em</u> (accountable). <u>Fold 'em</u>!
(If you do the crime, just pay a fine.)
Eric says, "Too big to fail,"
Eric says, "We cannot jail."
Although I'm a crook
And billions I took
Eric asks, "A thief? Au contraire!" (Sic)
—The President's Fixxer-in-Chief

Read the following quotations and then answer the question. The first is by Attorney General Eric Holder in testimony before the Senate Judiciary Committee (Holder Admits That Department of Justice Believes Big Bankers Are Above the Law, 2013).

Theory of "collateral consequences"
"I am concerned that the size of some of these institutions
[large banks] *becomes so large that it does become difficult*
for us to prosecute them when we are hit with indications
that if we do prosecute—if we do bring a criminal charge—it
will have a negative impact on the national economy, perhaps
even the world economy. I think that is the function of the fact
that some of these institutions have become too large."

The second is by David M. Uhlmann, University of Michigan Law School.

Theory of "deterrent value"
…the use of deferred prosecution and non-prosecution
agreements [settling with fines] *erodes corporate criminal*
liability and undermines the rule of law. [These agreements]
limit the punitive and deterrent value of the government's law
enforcement efforts and extinguish the societal condemnation

that should accompany criminal prosecution. —Maryland Law Review, Vol. 72. No. 4 (Uhlmann, 2013).

> **Q**: Do you agree that the U.S. government should not prosecute bankers' criminal wrongdoing for fear of economic repercussions? Do you think that public shaming and fear of getting a bad "rap" and condemnation from citizens would really deter criminal behavior?

The Audacity of Chutzpah (f. Hebrew = Yes, we con)

Z: Holder had developed this concept of "too big to fail" years earlier while working in private business at Covington & Burling. Reaction to his testimony was one of disbelief:

> *Collateral Consequences was out of the bag. After years and years of mysterious non-prosecutions and expertly negotiated cost-of-doing-business fines, we finally had the policy it all led to.*
> —Matt Taibbi, *The Divide* (2014, p. 68).

Also flabbergasted by this concept of law and order was Randall Forsyth writing in *Barron's*, "The nation's chief law enforcement official admitted the decision to prosecute depends not on the law, but on the impact on the financial markets" [as quoted by Taibbi, See: article, "Too Big to Jail" *Barron's* March, 2013].

I personally believe that all the banks and their executives who got off "scot-free" are laughing at us. After making settlements with no jail time, I picture them backslapping and clinking glasses of toasts with guffaws and salutatory congratulations! And this especially after Holder's testimony! We, the people, waited and waited and waited. We wanted "justice [to] roll down like waters in a mighty stream" [Amos 5:24] and to dispense justice through the courts. While we waited for justice, they, the flouters of the law, received bonuses and "forgiveness!" They paid for the absolution of their "sins" with billion dollar fines to purchase secular "indulgences." They didn't even have to publicly "confess" to remit their sins! Even a bank robber has to elocute crimes when pleading guilty in a plea bargain!

We are thoroughly happy with the attorney general's convoluted thinking that let's us off "scot-free." Now, we don't have to worry no matter how outrageous our behavior is! We should have been hammered in court trials for our disgraceful (and illegal) banking shenanigans. Instead, we were "graced" with TARP money and bailouts and some very doable fines. Our profits, like our bonuses, and income since 2008 have had an inexorable upward trajectory! Too bad about the rest of you. We landed on "top of the mountain" while you and the economy got buried with "underwater" mortgages! Our bonuses are greater than ever! Only in America.

We've used the critical governmental gatekeepers to "pull the strings" and help us rake in billions and billions. The following examples provide some details of how we have managed to get things done.

MOTHER OF ALL GORDIAN KNOTS

Connection In High Places = No jail time

It's "a riddle, wrapped in a mystery, inside an enigma" and fueled with greed. How come none of us went to jail after we made hundreds of billions and successfully blocked any prosecution for the roles of the Big Players in the 2008 meltdown of the economy? Answer: Connections! The following three parts lay out loose banking behaviors that eventually helped lead to the 2008 economic meltdown. Then, we succeeded in gently "crushing" any legal challenge to our trillion dollar illegalities.

Part One: Tear Down This (regulatory) Wall!

First we needed Congress to change the restrictive regulatory laws for Wall Street investors. The Glass-Stegall Act was passed in 1933 to prevent the financial banking interests' abuses of the 1920's. For decades bankers have chafed at government restrictions. Robert Rubin, President Clinton's treasury secretary, had pushed for passage of legislation lifting those restrictions and helped the president and Congress to pass legislation to eliminate them.

Poof! The Gramm-Leach-Biley bill removed restrictions on comingling of investment banking, insurance companies and commercial banking, which collected and used citizens' deposits. Veto proof majorities in Congress by the politicians overwhelmingly passed the legislation and the President signed it. The new law ended the Depression Era Glass-Stegall Act to prevent use of depositors' money for unsound and reckless behavior. These practices had helped lead to the Great Depression and the banking collapse in 1929. Of course with restrictions removed, we proceeded to make oodles and oodles of money! Unfortunately, for the U.S. taxpayers and pensioners this led to the financial debacle of 2008! But, we made billions! Taxpayers were left with an empty bag while we filled ours! Our "cup runneth(ed) over!"

Senator Byron Dorgan had warned in 1999: "I think we will look back in ten years' time and say we should not have done this but we did because we forgot the lessons of the past." *Viz.* causes for the Great Depression! Rubin left government and "slid" over to Citigroup as chairman. He got an annual compensation package of $40 million! He has been labeled the "quintessential revolving-door man" moving from one governmental position into private business. He's made a lot of money (and so have we) through his efforts as related in these two sources: All the Presidents' Bankers: The Hidden Alliances that Drive American Power by Nomi Prins (2014); **Rethinking Robert Rubin** by William D. Cohan, *Bloomberg Business Week* (2012).

Part Two: Cash for Secrecy

Do whistleblowers really think they can make a difference? Not if we continue to have friends in high places! Our friends, the gatekeepers of political power, protect us and gently "crush" any challenge to us. According to Matt Taibbi in his article, **The $9 Billion Witness: Meet JP Morgan Chase's Worst Nightmare,** Rolling Stone, (Taibbi, 2014). Alayne Fleischmann was ready and willing to testify under oath against our shenanigans relating to the subprime mortgage fiascos. She had first-hand knowledge as a transaction manager at JP Morgan to see that at one time around 40% of mortgage loans "were based on overstated incomes." [One manicurist applicant allegedly had an income of $117,000.] She saw the systematic fraud involved. She warned her superiors about "toxic" mortgages and the fraud in selling them off to investors [such as pension funds]. Of course she was ignored then and later. Her revealing testimony was never utilized in court trials. Why? Our Fixxers were at work.

*This past year she watched as [Eric] Holder's Justice Department struck a series of historic settlement deals with Chase, Citigroup and Bank of America. The **root bargain in these deals was cash for secrecy** [emphasis added]. The banks paid big fines, without trials or even judges—only secret negotiations that typically ended with the public shown nothing but vague, quasi-official papers called "statements of facts," which were conveniently devoid of anything like actual facts...* (Taibbi, 2014).

I could lose my license to practice law. I could lose everything. But if we don't start speaking up, then this really is all we're going to get: the biggest financial cover-up in history.

Poor "innocent child." She doesn't get it! She has gone public knowing that we could grind her down. She's defiantly told her story and told in detail how fraud was perpetrated. She vowed to expose the truth! She defiantly proclaimed, "*I could lose my license to practice law. I could lose everything. But if we don't start speaking up, then this really is all we're going to get: the biggest financial cover-up in history!*" To her exposé we say, "Ho, hum!"

Part Three: 65,000,000,000 Winks
Backstreet Boys Load the Dice

A recent *New York Times* article, **A Standoff of Lawyers Veils Madoff's Ties to JP Morgan Chase,** observed that Bernard Madoff's Ponzi pyramid "...remains one of Wall Street's most puzzling mysteries..." It asks: **What exactly did JP Morgan Chase bankers know about Bernard L. Madoff's Ponzi scheme?** (Protess & Silver-Greenberg, 2014). Anyone reading my book should be able to answer that question: Have friends in the right places!

Bernard Madoff's principal bank, JP Morgan Chase, has for years obstructed federal bank examiners trying to ascertain what it knew about his [Madoff's] gigantic Ponzi scheme... The Justice Department [Holder's bailiwick] refused to pursue criminal wrong-doing. (Protess & Silver-Greenberg, 2014). [The Justice Department] *refused to back up*

*Treasury inspector general staff who wanted a court order
to enforce a subpoena, in effect shielding JP Morgan from
law enforcement...* (2014).

Denying granting a subpoena by Holder's Justice Department effectively shut down any meaningful investigation. This meant all my associates involved would not undergo any criminal legal actions. Investigators had wanted to gain access to "interviews with 90 JP Morgan employees." (New Revelation that AG Eric Holder Is Protecting JPMorgan Chase NYC From Criminal Investigation, 2014), *Buzzflash* at Truth-out citing David Cay Johnston's <u>Newsweek</u> article, (Johnston D. C., 2013).

JP Morgan agreed to pay $2,600,000,000 (billion) to settle. Jamie Dimon said, "It was in the best interests of our company and shareholders for us to accept responsibility, resolve these issues and move forward." I wonder if he said that with a straight face and a wink-wink [heh, heh, heh!]. Thanks Jamie! Of course no one will go to jail! Good job, Jamie! Get your bonuses!

Z: "[Madoff] was a knowing predator. He would show up at weddings, funerals. At funerals, he would put his arm round the grieving widow and say, 'I'll take care of you' and of course he did, he'd wipe her out...he was a predator." He wiped out many pensioners too! Harry Markopolos tried for many years to get different officials including those in the SEC to listen to him about the Madoff fraud he had uncovered. In an interview by Andrew Clark, he says, "I knew I had to be right. And the risk-return ratios had never been seen in human recorded history. They were off the charts." **The Man Who Blew the Whistle on Bernard Madoff**, (Clark, 2010). And of course, no one will go to jail! For further details see Markopolos' book, <u>No One Would Listen</u>; also, JP Madoff.com and **The Unholy Alliance between America's Biggest Bank and America's Biggest Crook** (Chaitman & Gotthoffer, n.d.). Drug cartels must marvel at that "laundering" set-up!

How do you keep a $65,000,000,000 Ponzi scheme quiet? Funnel the money through banks whose officers have friends in [very] high places.

Whassup?

Obama's Favorite Banker* (Prins, 2014). New King of Wall Street*
Linked-In: Friends in High Places

*Coined in <u>All the Presidents' Bankers</u> by Nomi Prins, (pp. 412-413) referring to Dimon who's made over fifty-nine trips to the White House.
<u>Golf links</u>: golfed with Jamie [View Image: Dimon, Obama golfing]
<u>Cuff links</u>: **White House Resident Jamie Dimon's Presidential Cufflinks A Gift From A White House Resident** (Bradford, 2012).
<u>LinkedIn </u>Obama: (Jamie Dimon) is "one of the smartest bankers we got." <u>The View</u> May 2013. Praise: "I know both these guys [Dimon and Blankfein], they are very savvy businessmen." Obama: JP Morgan "is one of the best-managed banks there is" (May 2012). Despite billions in fines!
<u>Fixxed media link</u>: Dick Daley's comments—former board member of JP Morgan and Obama's chief of Staff who joined Fixxed media's CBS in October 2013. His interview ran "interference" for JP Morgan's legal

problems with the Justice Department: "They make a great target because they make a lot of money and they've done real well. Jamie's as good a CEO as there is in any industry."[As a hired CBS analyst opposing the government's close scrutiny of behavior of JP Morgan.]"I think there is a bit of an aggressiveness here…" on *CNBC* "Squawk Box" October 10, 2013. Note: after meetings with Holder, several billions in fines were agreed to, to settle charges with banks. And no one went to jail!

===

Z

Yachta Yachta Yachta and his friends' tales have been told. His observations and revelations have been well documented. In the next chapter I tell of continuing business as usual. The control of government by vested interests is complete. They will continue on their avaricious course despite public opinion. The views and opinions of citizens are irrelevant to them. Private billionaire donors are spending billions to purchase our representatives' votes. They want to maintain the system that redirects the wealth of the nation into their coffers. They continue to suppress legitimate concerns of the citizens. Their donor-owned elected politicians do their bidding. They crush our dreams for progress. They suppress all efforts for legitimate discussion of issues relevant to the American people.

The final chapter offers specific courses of action to help rid us of the Dark Money "infestation."

Billions of campaign dollars are like a biblical plague that infiltrates and clogs and stifles our democratic process. It controls our political institutions because it controls politicians' votes through wealthy donor contributions.

CHAPTER ELEVEN

KRYPTOCRACY VS DEMOCRACY
Democracy on the Ropes

*Whoever seizes the reins of government, seizes the wealth
of the nation* —*Yachta Yachta Yachta*

*Everything the State says is a lie,
and everything it has, it has stolen* — *Friedrich Nietzsche*

[Aristocrats] *are "those who fear and distrust the people,
and wish to draw all powers from them into
the hands of the higher classes."* —*Thomas Jefferson*

Democracy's toast! Let's toast! — *Yachta & Co.*

CITIZENS LAMENT THE FIXXERS
Atlas ~~Shrugged~~ Shriveled

Everything "looks" legitimate. But, the "sting" is going on right before our eyes. Citizens want to elect good leaders. But, elected politicians and their supporters want the "goods!" Our goods! They pursue the Golden Rule: "Gold Rules." Leaders can't say that out loud. They can't reveal what's really going on. They can't "let the cat out of the bag!" They use highfalutin' ideas disseminated through books, media, academia and TV personalities. Their main fear is that an angry electorate will curtail their free wheelin' stealin' ways. Thus, they try to bamboozle people with words like "liberty" and "freedom." They use fear and slogans to limit <u>any</u> efforts by government agencies from interfering with them. President Ronald Reagan's quote summarizes their view, "The most terrifying words in the English language are: 'I'm from the government and I'm here to help.'"

Frederick Hayek feared oppression from elite bureaucrats controlling society in a strong, regulated central government. He outlined his concerns in his book, <u>The Road to Serfdom</u>. He failed to acknowledge or see the corrupt influence of moneyed interests, politicians and lobbyists. Milton Freidman believed the capitalist system would prevent abuse of government. Therefore, little or no governmental regulation was needed and even was to be feared. These two authors believed in the concept of limited government to prevent oppression by an ever-interfering state with little or no regulation by the state or a central government. Theoretically, this would prevent oppression by a political class. Their followers talk of "freedom" and "liberty." They feared the highly regulated totalitarian states of Communist Russia and Nazi Germany. They feared the growth of the "nanny state" and an ever-growing dependency on welfare benefits. Ironically, their writings are used by Yachta and his friends as philosophical "fig leafs" to cover up their own actions. The writings help justify the simple truth of their heartless avaricious consequences. Oh, also Ayn Rand's writings present saccharine sweet fictional representations of big businessmen as the "good guys" fighting dictatorial governmental Looters, *viz.* regulators. Unlike today's extravagant billionaires [my yacht's bigger than your yacht], in Ayn Rand's <u>Atlas Shrugged</u>, they lived extremely modest utopian lives with self-generated electricity—off the grid! They grew their own food and, like life in a medieval manor, were completely self-sufficient with no government at all. No McMansions or car elevators! Or bundling of their millions to "purchase" a politician! Utopia reigned only in an author's imagination! [Someone should alert Congressman Paul Ryan.]

Yachta's friends talk of "freedom" and "liberty" but they never have believed in democracy. Why not? It allows citizens to vote to improve their lot and provide social services. Robert Michels in his book <u>Political Parties,</u> p. 46 (1962) outlines how the ruling elite in Europe over a hundred years ago <u>had</u> to participate in the democratic electoral process even though they didn't believe in it. The name of the game by the privileged was conning the voters to vote for them so they could preserve their own wealth and privileges. They never have believed in broadening the electorate for the majority of citizens. Viewers of Downton Abbey have seen the abhorrence by the aristocracy to the rise of the Labour Party's "seizing" power in England. The moneyed interests have sought self-preservation through the pretense of accepting democratic principles and electoral participation. As Michels observed one hundred years ago in 1915,

> *Thus, the aristocrat is constrained to secure his election in virtue of a principle which he himself does not accept, and which in his soul he abhors.* [He tries], *"the maintenance of a restricted suffrage"* [by citizens who challenge] *"traditional privileges". And* [to win elections]*"he dissembles [hides] his true thoughts, and howls with the democratic wolves in order to secure the coveted majority* [election victories].

They make false promises with enticements to voters. They spend billions on campaigns to hide the true nature of their intent to suppress democratic tendencies and "raid" the public treasury. Through ads and the media they beckon the trusting innocent (voters) to cast their lot (ballot) with them. Innocent voters are deceived like the poem about innocent, trusting oysters illustrates in Alice's old song. The hungry walrus and Carpenter entice them to shore for a feast [Through the Looking Glass by Lewis Carol].

"O Oysters, [citizens] *come and walk with us!"*...
[soon their fate is revealed that they are the feast]
"But not on us!" the Oysters cried [*too late*]...
It seems a shame," the Walrus said,
  "To play them such a trick.
After we've brought them out so far........" [but]
                    Gulp! Gulp! Gulp!
   They were "going down," down our gullets! —Yachta

TALES FROM THE KRYPTOCRACY

Yachta is still gulping. More is never enough! Remember his earlier warning: "I am a predator and you are my prey." Recent political developments show we are continuing to be "thrown to the wolves" by our compliant and/or purchased elected officials.

President Obama has sent his handpicked negotiators for secret negotiations for a new trade treaty. The Trans-Pacific Partnership Agreement [TPP] currently being negotiated would curtail U.S. jurisdiction and regulation of foreign companies doing business in America. He wants Congress to be allowed only to vote yes or no without any altering amendments or debate. Think NAFTA! Robert Reich writes that,

> *the TPP is a Trojan horse in a global race to the bottom, giving corporations and Wall Street banks a way to eliminate any and all laws and regulations that get in the*

way of their profits. **Why the Trans-Pacific Partnership Agreement is a Pending Disaster,** (2015).

Many of the negotiators for the secret treaty had recently received multimillion-dollar bonuses from banks as revealed in the article, **Obama Admin's TPP Trade Officials Received Hefty Bonuses from Big Banks** (Fang, 2014).

The "vortex of complicity" between campaign donors and politicians also continues. The Congress passed [December 2014] and the president signed into law the repeal of the 2010 Dodd-Frank financial reform law. The provision in the new law allows "banks to use savings accounts of ordinary Americans to gamble in the stock market on behalf of hedge funds, corporations, and the rich." **President Obama and Congress Just Gave Your Savings Account to JP Morgan** *Truthdig*, (Editor, 2014). Citigroup drafted the legislation that benefits five of the largest banks in the country. **Citigroup Wrote the Wall Street Giveaway The House Just Approved** (Eichelberger, 2014). Jamie Dimon personally called up legislators to lobby by phone for the legislation! **Jamie Dimon himself called to urge support for the derivatives rule in the spending bill,** (Mufson & Hamburger, 2014). The bill allows for the government (the taxpayers) to guarantee the risky derivatives market trading. Think 2008 collapse and bailout! Rep. Nancy Pelosi was outraged and opposed the bill:

> *What I am saying is: the taxpayer should not assume the risk...*[it would] *privatize the gain, nationalize the risk. You succeed, it's in your pocket. You fail, the taxpayer pays the bill. It's just not right.*

There were no hearings or debate on the provision. The politicians willingly passed the bill and their donors were pleased! It was a "slamdunk!"

The "revolving door" that allows the flow between politicians, lobbyists and economic interests continues. There's no pretense of serving the public interests or doing what's good for the country. It's getting much worse! Many newly hired congressional aides "are former lobbyists and executives [who] are working crucial [congressional] staff positions in the new (2014) congress." Lee Fang observes that,

> *On almost any big issue coming up for debate during the final two years of the Obama administration—surveillance, trade, healthcare, entitlements, tax reform, climate change—corporate lobbyists will now be attempting to influence **their own former colleagues** [emphasis added], whose salaries are now covered by US taxpayers.*

(With These Hires, Congress Becomes Even More Like a Corporation, 2015).

Janine Wedel writes of "new players and networks of power and influence" that

> [as] influencers perform overlapping roles and networks of policy deciders [who] snake through official and private organizations, creating a loop that is closed to democratic processes... (Wedel, 2009).

Her book Shadow Elite: How the World's New Power Brokers Undermine Democracy, Government, and the Free Market documents in great detail the sweeping changes that have transformed our notion of democracy in the United States and its interactions in the world.

DARK MONEY: THE PLAGUE OF DEMOCRACY

Even more outrageous are the endosymbiotic relationships being deliberately embedded within the body politic [visualize growing parasitic alien life forms in the movie, "Alien!"]. Several banks are trying to "keep hidden their practice of paying executives multimillion-dollar awards for entering government service." Antonio Weiss "acknowledged in financial disclosures that he would be paid $21 million in unvested income and deferred compensation upon exiting the company for a job in government." David Dayen reveals the embedding of these employees in his article, **Wall Street pays Bankers to work in Government and it doesn't want anyone to know** (Dayen, 2015).

Prins decries the "symbiotic and costly relationship" between bankers and government that gives them "a seat at the table of power."

> You are either invited to the table, or on it!

Pam Martens noted that seven of Obama's [2008] campaigns' top donors were connected to those accused "with looting the public..." She asks, "Why is the "yes, we can" candidate in bed with this [money] cartel? How can "we," the people, make change if Obama's money backers block our ability to be heard?" Hopeless: Obama and the Politics of Illusion p. 14-22: **"Obama's Money Cartel."** (Martens, 2012) **See also, "The Wall Street White House,"** Hopeless, (Cockburn, 2012) p. 61-62 by Andrew Cockburn.

As Prins points out in All the Presidents' Bankers, p. 423:

> It no longer matters who sits in the White House. Presidents no longer even try to garner banker support for population friendly policies, and bankers operate oblivious to the needs of the national economies. There is no counter balance to their power. (2014)

Private individuals and corporations also divvy up contributions to gain access to the public "trough." Other secret large donations to public officials circumscribe citizen influence. The Koch brothers unabashedly announced they are going to spend almost one billion dollars on the 2016 campaign for presidential and congressional races according to Nicholas Confessore, **Kochs Plan to Spend $900 million on 2016 Campaign,** (2015) Such spending would be a formidable force for purchasing access to the political reins of government! The Supreme Court's "Citizens United" decision has allowed campaign donations and spending by moneyed interests to influence and thus skewer election results. The title to an article by Senator Bernie Sanders and Robert Weissman hits the nail on the head! (2015) **Five Years after Citizens United, Billionaires are Buying Democracy.**

Even the courts in the judicial system are up for "auction." Alabama's Chief Justice Sue Bell Cobb gave the necessity of raising campaign contributions as her reason for resigning. **I Was Alabama's Top Judge. I'm Ashamed by What I Had to Do to Get There.** (Cobb, 2015). She writes of her reaction to a reporter's inquiries.

> [Judge Cobb], *"how does it feel to be the victor of the most expensive judicial race in the United States this year? And how can you assure the people of Alabama that the contributions you sought are not going to impact how you rule? And how can you convince the people of Alabama not to believe that their courts are for sale?"*
>
> *…The simple fact is: I had to. Judicial elections have become just as overwhelmed by money as all the other contests in American politics, even if we tend to forget that in Alabama and 38 other states, judges have to stand for election. And if you're running for office, it means you have to raise money. Lots of money.*

She and her opponent had spent $5,000,000 on the 2006 state Supreme Court election! It's "justice for all"…who can afford to contribute!

But the flow of donations (with strings attached) is pervasive for electing all public officials including judges and attorneys-general. Zephyr Teachout in an op-ed editorial in *The New York Times*, "Legalized Bribery" warns of the dangers to democracy. He writes, "The corruption that hides in plain sight is the real threat to our democracy" (2015).

He offers four reforms that are necessary for restoring our democracy: First, ban all outside income for elected officials. Next, expand public financing. Third, ban corporate spending. Finally, limit total campaign spending. He concludes that, "[C]orruption is about greed and private interests put ahead of public good."

Constitutional checks and balances at state and national levels are willingly cast aside by men and women in the following branches of government: executive, legislative, and judicial. Elected leaders and their appointees usher through self-serving legislation. Hired lobbyists and appointed regulators do their bidding behind closed doors.

Can anything be done to alter and change the status of our very challenged democracy? The final chapter offers some specific, practical, and doable solutions.

CHAPTER TWELVE

Battle to
TAKE BACK OUR DEMOCRACY

Freedom is participation in power —Cicero

*"the framers intended for our government, as Madison put it,
to be dependent on the people alone."* — Laurence Lessing

LET THE SUN SHINE IN: BLEACH OUT DARK MONEY

Traditionally, we've elected leaders thinking they would act in our best interests. Today, we know this is not so. We have what can be called "casino" democracy. Voters show up voluntarily to "play" the game. But no matter what their selected choice, they end up with a "losing hand!" Despite the choices offered, they seldom win. Today, we face the same dilemma when voting. Do we just sit back and accept our choices for leaders? Do we just resign ourselves to mediocrity?

That's not the American Way. We're fighters, not quitters!

As one of 320,000,000 Americans, your one vote doesn't count for much.

As one of 127,000,000 votes actually cast in the 2012 election for president, your one vote didn't count for much.

At the national level you're stuck with choices you may or may not like. The point is, that you don't have much choice. That's true at the state level, too. So why vote? Only about 50% of registered voters voted. The rest did not show up. Many say, "They're all the same! What's the use? My vote doesn't count for much. Money decides!"

Everyone [over 80%] agrees unlimited spending in political campaigns is out of control. Citizens want to curtail the money that flows from private interests, the so-called "Dark Money" that stains the fabric of our democracy.

We need to "bleach-out" that Dark Money. But, how? Elected politicians like the system. It works for them. It got them elected. They won't change it. Their minds are made up. Opinion polls don't persuade them.

I contend that within two to three election cycles, meaningful campaign finance reform can be enacted at the state level. But, we must make change at the state level. We must deploy the proper strategy to force (convince) state politicians to change their position. They must "wake-up" and realize they are going to lose out unless they change. How can we send them a "wake-up call?" Can "we, the people" regain our power?

It is an indisputable fact that every candidate has to win a primary of a political party. Then, the party's nominee must run for office and win an election. There are many electoral districts within a state. Politicians compete for state house and senate seats. Their main goal is to get elected or re-elected. It's easy if they're in a "safe" district unthreatened by competition from an opposition party. Many districts are "solid blue" or "solid red" with little competition from an opposing party. If they're not "threatened" by an electoral outcome, they do not have to listen to voters' concerns. We're not part of the solution. We're excluded. Only the "moneyed" interests and donors have influence. How can we change this cozy relationship with "Dark Money?" Can it be changed?

Yes We Can—LEVERAGE!

We can leverage our vote and make it more valuable. How is this possible? Let me give an example to explain. Let's look at a recent (2014) primary voter turnout for electing a state legislator. Turnout was abysmally low. In the district there was a contested primary to determine a party's nominee for state representative. Only 360 votes separated the winner from the loser. A switch of 181 votes in the primary would have changed the outcome. In that election a few votes was extremely important. A person's vote has more leverage in a primary, especially if it is a contested primary election. Your one vote has even more leverage if we "bundle" your vote and coordinate with like-minded citizens who want campaign finance reform. Is it impossible to bring about real, meaningful campaign finance reform? Shall we just throw up our hands and give in? It's a daunting task. But, it will be a lot easier than it was achieving victory in the American Revolution. And no one has to get hurt!

Let's look at that history of the American colonies to see how a long-term strategy by well-coordinated angry citizens can succeed against seemingly impossible odds.

Citizens in the colonies were angry at how they were being mistreated [informal opinion polls]. They beseeched [petitioned] King George to address their grievances [public forums]. They formed Committees of Correspondence to coordinate their actions [oppositional groups]. Those evolved into a "shadow" government that kept track of those supporting uncompromising British colonial rule [oppositional research]. They couldn't "throw the rascals out" by voting. So, they formed militias and declared independence in 1776 [commitment to the cause]. Seven years later, with the Treaty of Paris signed in 1783 [approximately three election cycles], they won! I do not trivialize the long, bloody suffering and hardships endured by the troops in the Continental Army and their arduous struggle for victory in the war.

They could not have defeated King George's troops without taking specific overt military actions and engaging the enemy "mano a mano." A militarily untrained retinue of farmers, teachers, shopkeepers, clerics, laborers, lawyers, townsmen, mothers and their teenage children coalesced to fight for a common cause. First, they made a public commitment to the cause through a written statement: *The Declaration of Independence.* Then, they devised military strategies. They engaged the enemy through armed conflicts. These battles eventually won the war for independence.

Like the American colonialists, we also must decide to make a commitment and take specific actions that engage the "enemy." Our weapons of choice will be the cell phone, the Internet, and all digital media. No one will get harmed. All Americans can participate in the effort to reform the system. Here are some ideas.

THINK OUTSIDE THE [BALLOT] BOX.

The cell phone is mightier than the pen and all other
archaic means of communication   — Aegis

A Unifying Goal

First, the one issue that must be agreed to is the commitment by a concerned citizen to vote only for a candidate that commits to campaign finance reform. This issue embraces many Americans' concerns and crosses the political spectrum. There's no "red" or "blue" divide. Other issues may be important to voters, but the primary concern must be campaign finance reform. It will be easier to join with other concerned Americans if no one gets "bogged down" arguing issues. This will make "bundling" your efforts with other concerned citizens much easier.

Next, you must get a few like-minded citizens to form a group [two or more] committed to reform. You should limit your efforts within a specific voting district or geographical area within a state. This will let you make as much personal contact as possible and leverage your efforts.

Then, select a name for your group. Mine is CARPERS UNITED!

Citizens
Arise!
Responsible
People
Enact
Responsible
Solutions

C-A-R-P-E-R-S United

We began by just kowtowing
Then, we did some open growling
Now we've learned the truth
And say to you, "Forsooth!"
Now we are mad and are howling!
(And we're "mad as Hell and aren't going to take it anymore!")

Launch Campaign to Conquer

Santa has his Lists.
We have ours.
Our criteria for inclusion are quite different!
Do not get on our Naughty List. — American Voters

Strategy: Fono "Bombing"

We must contact <u>any</u> elected official who needs to win an election. We need to get each individual to commit to reform. Yea or Nay! Are you for us or against us? Make public officials an offer they better not refuse: agree with us or we vote you out! It's "bada-bing, bada-boom!" If you won't support us, we won't support you. It's curtains for you [at the polls]!

We must make a concerted, long-term commitment to effect change. Our efforts could include the following steps:

1. Let's "bombard" with phone calls, e-mails, snail mail and also use personal contacts announcing our goals.
2. Record responses of public officials, visually if possible. Try to get "live" interviews including those at public meeting forums.
3. "Publish" or post responses of elected officials to <u>all</u> media.

These are first tier contacts: state reps, city council, and county officials. I obtained a printed list from the League of Women Voters. It has 75 local public officials' names with their phone numbers and/or contact e-mails. A second tier of contacts could include public leaders: chamber of commerce, religious leaders, charity associations, business associations, educational boards, student & college associations and any organized group.

Possible Ideas for Scripts

Announce that you are part of a coalition of voters in your district and we have organized to get political and campaign finance reform laws passed. Using Teachout's guidelines, ask:

Which of the following, if any, do you support?

1. ban all outside income for elected officials
2. increase public funding for viable candidates
3. eliminate all corporate and interest group donations
4. limit total spending amount by parties per campaign

A simpler script is a question proposed in a recent ballot poll in a Chicago election. (See below) Calling non-political citizens spreads the word that individuals are organizing. They can be encouraged to do the same.

Call centers: Anywhere USA

No one needs to "join up" to organize call-groups. Everything is informal. No meetings. No dues. Anyone with a phone device can make calls— individually or with friends. Potential supporters include: any retiree, veterans, the home-bound, pilots, mechanics, stewardesses, nurses, teachers, nursing home occupants, therapists, fast food workers, chain store workers, clerks, actors and movie personnel, TV personalities. Anyone!

Below are two recent successes involving citizens organizing and making their voices heard in recent elections at the polls. In Chicago, voters passed a resolution for campaign finance reform, *79% to 21%*. The voters endorsed a resolution that asked elected officials whether the city of Chicago and state of Illinois should,

> *reduce the influence of special interest money in elections by financing campaigns using small contributions from individuals , and a limited amount of public money.*
> **Chicago Voters Overwhelmingly Endorse Campaign Finance Reform,** (Levine, 2015).

In Tallahassee, Florida, the first city in the country passed an Anti-Corruption Act overwhelmingly by 2-1 margin. It is now the law! It can be read at: http://anticorruptionact.org.

> *A small but dedicated group of progressives, conservatives, and independents* **put aside their differences** [emphasis added] *to wage an historic battle against corruption in their community, and they won.* **One City. One Big Win. Now It's Your Turn** (RepresentUs, n.d.).

We can take heart from such voters' successes.

Can You Hear Us Now?

Hopefully, working together, we can move forward...
> *... to fulfill the American Dream*
> *... to restore belief in a country of, by, and for the people*
> *... to cast aside despair and doubt*
> *... to deny the naysayers their doom*
> *... to boldly promote the hope of a people*
> *... who fearlessly proclaim:*

We are here! Hear us now!

Flyover USA
Middle of the Mitten, 2015
E.J.S.

BIBLIOGRAPHY

Akrami, N. (2013, June 29). *59 Years Later, Mau Mau Torture Victims Receive Compensation* . Retrieved from News Record: http://www.newsrecord.co/59-years-later-mau-mau-torture-victims-receive-compensation/

Ames, M. (2014, February 4). *The first congressman to battle the NSA is dead. No-one noticed, no-one cares.* . Retrieved from Pando Daily: http://pando.com/2014/02/04/the-first-congressman-to-battle-the-nsa-is-dead-no-one-noticed-no-one-cares/

Anderson, D. (2013, June 12). *Atoning for the Sins of Empire.* Retrieved from The New York Times , Opinion Pages: http://www.nytimes.com/2013/06/13/opinion/atoning-for-the-sins-of-empire.html

Anderson, S. (2013, November 20). *Filthy Rich CEOs Are Lobbying to Cut Medicare, Social Security and Push the Retirement Age Back.* Retrieved from Alternet: http://www.alternet.org/economy/ceos-against-grandmas

AP. (1975, July 22). *New York Times Magazine.* Retrieved from Family in LSD Case Gets Ford Apology: http://www.nytimes.com/1975/07/22/magazine/750722OLSON.html

Argentina tries doctors for 'baby theft' during military rule. (2014, September 18). Retrieved from BBC News: http://www.bbc.com/news/world-latin-america-29248974

Baker, P. (2014, January 15). *Obama's Path From Critic to Overseer of Spying.* Retrieved from The New York Times: http://www.nytimes.com/2014/01/16/us/obamas-path-from-critic-to-defender-of-spying.html?_r=0

Bassett, L. (2013, December 12). *Michigan 'Rape Insurance' Bill Passes Into Law.* Retrieved from Huffpost Politics: http://www.huffingtonpost.com/2013/12/11/michigan-rape-insurance_n_4428432.html

BBC. (2013, September 26). *"NSA spied on Martin Luther King, documents reveal".* Retrieved from BBC: http://www.bbc.com/news/world-us-canada-24279394

BBC. (2013, December 13). *Chile Caravan of Death: Eight guilty of murder* . Retrieved from BBC News, latin America: http://www.bbc.com/news/world-latin-america-25499373

Bennett-Smith, M. (2014, January 23). *'Tsunami Bomb' In Development During World War II, Documents Note.* Retrieved from The World Post: http://www.huffingtonpost.com/2013/01/02/tsunami-bomb-in-development-world-war-ii-top-secret-documents_n_2397856.html

Berkowitz, B. (2013, October 11). *States Guarantee High Prison Populations for Private Prison Industry's Profits.* Retrieved from BuzzFlash.com: http://www.truth-out.org/buzzflash/commentary/item/18248-prison-populations-private-profits

Bernstein, C. (1977, October 20). *The CIA and the Media.* Retrieved from Rolling Stone: http://danwismar.com/uploads/Bernstein%20-%20CIA%20and%20Media.htm

Blum, S. J. (n.d.). *The National Experience.* New York: Harcourt Brace Hovanovich, 1985.

Bradford, H. (2012, June 15). *Jamie Dimon's Presidential Cufflinks A Gift From A White House Resident.* Retrieved from HuffPost Business: http://www.huffingtonpost.com/2012/06/15/jamie-dimon-cufflinks-presidential-seal-senate-hearing_n_1600335.html

Braxton, C. (2011, October 22). *Commentary: What Would King Do?* Retrieved from BET: http://www.bet.com/news/national/2011/10/22/commentary-what-would-king-do.html

Bronstein, S., Griffin, D., & Turk, M. (2014, april 14). *A fatal wait: Veterans languish and die on a VA hospital's secret list.* Retrieved from CNN Investigations: http://www.cnn.com/2014/04/23/health/veterans-dying-health-care-delays/index.html

Buckley, C., & Jacobs, A. (2015, January 4). *Maoists in China, Given New Life, Attack Dissent.* Retrieved from The New York Times: http://www.nytimes.com/2015/01/05/world/chinas-maoists-are-revived-as-thought-police.html?_r=0

Campbell, D. (2003, December 5). *Kissinger approved Argentinian 'dirty war'.* Retrieved February 15, 2015, from TheGuardian World News: http://www.abc.net.au/foreign/content/2014/s3971320.htm

Center for Responsive Politics. (n.d.). *Corrections Corp of America.* Retrieved March 4, 2015, from Open Secrets.org: http://www.opensecrets.org/orgs/summary.php?id=D000021940

Chaitman, H. D., & Gotthoffer, L. (n.d.). *The Unholy Alliance between America's Biggest Bank and America's Biggest Crook.* Retrieved February 17, 2015, from JP Madoff: http://jpmadoff.com/foreword/

Clark, A. (2010, March 24). *The man who blew the whistle on Bernard Madoff.* Retrieved from The Guardian: http://www.theguardian.com/business/2010/mar/24/bernard-madoff-whistleblower-harry-markopolos

Cobb, S. B. (2015, March/April). *I Was Alabama's Top Judge. I'm Ashamed by What I Had to Do to Get There.* . Retrieved from Politico Magazine: http://www.politico.com/magazine/story/2015/03/judicial-elections-fundraising-115503.html#.VP214CjFCOI

Cockburn, A. (2012). The Wall Street Whitehouse. In J. St. Clair, & J. Frank, *Hopeless; Barack Obama and the Politics of Illusion* (pp. 61-62). Oakland: AK Press.

Cohan, W. D. (2012, September 30). *Rethinking Robert Rubin.* Retrieved from Bloomberg Businessweek: http://www.businessweek.com/articles/2012-09-19/rethinking-robert-rubin

Collins, C. (2012). *99 to 1.* San Francisco: Berrett-Koehler Publishers, Inc.

Confessore, N. (2015, January 26). *Koch Brothers' Budget of $889 Million for 2016 Is on Par With Both Parties' Spending.* Retrieved from The New York Times: http://www.nytimes.com/2015/01/27/us/politics/kochs-plan-to-spend-900-million-on-2016-campaign.html

Congress, L. o. (n.d.). *George Washington to William Crawford, September 1, 1767.* Retrieved March 15, 2015, from Library of Congress: http://www.loc.gov/teachers/classroommaterials/presentationsandactivities/presentations/timeline/amrev/britref/crawford.html

Curbing of US spy powers is 'historic': Edward Snowden. (2015, June 2). Retrieved from Yahoo News: http://news.yahoo.com/curbing-us-spy-powers-historic-edward-snowden-211807673.html

Curt Devine, M. T. (2014, July 30). *More VA employees said they were told to falsify data.* Retrieved 2014, from CNN: http://www.cnn.com/2014/07/29/politics/va-audit/index.html

Davies, C. (2010, August 12). *Colonialism and the 'scramble for Africa'.* Retrieved from CNN: http://www.cnn.com/2010/WORLD/africa/08/02/independence.africa.colonialism/index.html

Dayen, D. (2015, February 4). *Wall Street Pays Bankers to Work in Government and It Doesn't Want Anyone to Know.* Retrieved from New Republic: http://www.newrepublic.com/article/120967/wall-street-pays-bankers-work-government-and-wants-it-secret

Doyle, M. (2013, December 12). *Lawsuit seeks to unlock CIA's secret history of Bay of Pigs invasion.* Retrieved from McClatchey DC: http://www.mcclatchydc.com/2013/12/12/211491/lawsuit-seeks-to-unlock-cias-secret.html

Editor. (2014, December 14). *President Obama and Congress Just Gave Your Savings Account to JPMorgan.* Retrieved from Truthdig: http://www.truthdig.com/eartotheground/item/the_federal_budget_just_gave_jp_morgans_ceo_your_savings_account_20141214

Edwards, D. (2012, August 21). *Akin rape theory rooted in Nazi death camp experiments.* Retrieved from Raw Story: http://www.rawstory.com/rs/2012/08/akin-rape-theory-rooted-in-nazi-death-camp-experiments/

Egan, P. (2014, July 14). *Maggots found in food at second Michigan prison.* Retrieved from Detroit Free Press: http://archive.freep.com/article/20140702/NEWS06/307020165/prison-food-maggots-aramark

Eichelberger, E. (2014, December 12). *Citigroup Wrote the Wall Street Giveaway The House Just Approved.* Retrieved from Mother Jones:

http://www.motherjones.com/politics/2014/12/spending-bill-992-derivatives-citigroup-lobbyists

Fang, L. (2014, February 17). *Obama Trade Officials Received Hefty Bonuses From Big Banks*. Retrieved from HuffPost politics: http://www.huffingtonpost.com/2014/02/17/obama-trade-banks_n_4805544.html

Fang, L. (2015, February 11). *With These Hires, Congress Becomes Even More Like a Corporation*. Retrieved from The Nation: http://www.thenation.com/article/197561/these-hires-congress-becomes-even-more-corporation

Feldman, N. (2013, December 13). *Was Mandela Right to Sell Out Black South Africans*. Retrieved from BloombergView: http://www.bloombergview.com/articles/2013-12-09/was-mandela-right-to-sell-out-black-south-africans-

Former dictators found guilty in Argentine baby-stealing trial. (2012, July 10). Retrieved from CNN Wire Staff: http://www.cnn.com/2012/07/05/world/americas/argentina-baby-theft-trial/index.html

Forsyth, R. (2013, March 9). *Too Big to Jail*. Retrieved from Barron's: http://online.barrons.com/articles/SB50001424052748704836204578340381145471280

Gaines, D. E. (2013, July 18). *Lawsuit by family of drugged Detrick employee dismissed*. Retrieved from Frederick News Post: http://www.fredericknewspost.com/news/crime_and_justice/article_8705f623-edfd-59b0-9e04-548b15a2c423.html?TNNoMobile

Gellman, B., & Soltani, S. (2013, December 4). *NSA tracking cellphone locations worldwide, Snowden documents show*. Retrieved from The Washington Post: http://www.washingtonpost.com/world/national-security/nsa-tracking-cellphone-locations-worldwide-snowden-documents-show/2013/12/04/5492873a-5cf2-11e3-bc56-c6ca94801fac_story.html

Gerstein, J. (2014, February 4). *Intelligence chairman accuses Glenn Greenwald of illegally selling stolen material*. Retrieved from Politico.com: http://www.politico.com/story/2014/02/intelligence-chairman-argues-selling-snowden-docs-a-crime-103100.html

Gibb, T. (2000, March 22). *The killing of Archbishop Oscar Romero was one of the most notorious crimes of the cold war. Was the CIA to blame?* Retrieved from The Guardian: http://www.theguardian.com/theguardian/2000/mar/23/features11.g21

Gilder Lehrman Institute. (n.d.). *George Washington discusses Shays' Rebellion and the upcoming Constitutional Convention, 1787*. Retrieved February 16, 2015, from The Gilder Lehrman Institute of History: http://www.gilderlehrman.org/history-by-era/creating-new-government/resources/george-washington-discusses-shays'-rebellion-and-up

Gill, V. (2013, January 28). *Victims of Nazi anatomists named*. Retrieved from BBC: http://www.bbc.com/news/health-21086388

Goldstein, R. J. (n.d.). *Prelude to McCarthyism: The Making of a Blacklist*. Retrieved April 22, 2015, from Prologue Magazine: http://www.archives.gov/publications/prologue/2006/fall/agloso.html

Goodstein, L. (2012, May 30). *In Milwaukee Post, Cardinal Authorized Paying Abusers*. Retrieved from nytimes.com: http://www.nytimes.com/2012/05/31/us/cardinal-authorized-payments-to-abusers.html

Goodstein, L. (2013, July 1). *Dolan Sought to Protect Church Assets, Files Show*. Retrieved from New York Times: http://www.nytimes.com/2013/07/02/us/dolan-sought-vatican-permission-to-shield-assets.html?_r=0

Greene, F. (1966). *Vietnam! Vietnam!* Fullton Publishing Company.

Gutting, G. (2013, September 29). *Why Conservatives Should Reread Milton Friedman*. Retrieved from New York Times Opininator: http://greenthinkboxsocialnetworking.blogspot.com/2013/09/why-conservatives-should-reread-milton.html

Hall, M. (2007, Novmber 7). *15,000 want off the U.S. terror watch list*. Retrieved from USA Today: http://usatoday30.usatoday.com/news/washington/2007-11-06-watchlist_N.htm

Hart, P. (2013, July 1). *Media Millionaires Journalism by and for the 0.01 Percent*. Retrieved from FAIR: http://fair.org/extra-online-articles/cover-story-media-millionaires/

Hasson, J. (2012, June 27). *Atomic Vet Benefit Long Time Coming.* Retrieved from AARP
  BULLETIN: http://www.aarp.org/health/conditions-treatments/info-06-2012/veteran-
  radiation-exposure-compensation.html
Hedges, C. (2013, March 24). *The Day That TV News Died.* Retrieved from Truthdig:
  http://www.truthdig.com/report/item/the_day_that_tv_news_died_20130324
History Place. (n.d.). *Genocide in the 20th Century.* Retrieved February 11, 2015, from The
  History Place: http://www.historyplace.com/worldhistory/genocide/stalin.htm
Institute, L. (n.d.). *LexNext.* Retrieved April 28, 2015, from Lexington Institute:
  http://lexingtoninstitute.org/
Jackovich, K. G., & Sinnet, M. (1980, November 10). *The Children of John Wayne, Susan Hayward
  and Dick Powell Fear That Fallout Killed Their Parents.* Retrieved from People magaine:
  http://www.people.com/people/archive/article/0,,20077825,00.html
Jacoby, J. (2014, March 12). *Eminent disaster Homeowners in Connecticut town were
  dispossessed for nothing.* Retrieved from The Boston Globe:
  http://www.jeffjacoby.com/14530/eminent-disaster
Johnston, D. C. (2013, December 23). *JPMorgan Doesn't Want to Talk About Bernie Madoff.*
  Retrieved from Newsweek: http://www.newsweek.com/jpmorgan-doesnt-want-talk-
  about-bernie-madoff-225067
Johnston, I., Ing, N., & Bunlueslip, P. (2012, Octobere 1). *Colonial sins return to haunt former
  world powers.* Retrieved February 13, 2015, from NBC World News:
  http://worldnews.nbcnews.com/_news/2012/10/01/13722339-colonial-sins-return-to-
  haunt-former-world-powers?lite
Karlin, M. (2013, March 13). *Holder Admits That Department of Justice Believes Big Bankers Are
  Above the Law.* Retrieved from Buzzflash: http://www.truth-
  out.org/buzzflash/commentary/item/17846-holder-admits-that-department-of-justice-
  believes-big-bankers-are-above-the-law
Karlin, M. (2014, December 26). *New Revelation that AG Eric Holder Is Protecting JPMorgan
  Chase NYC From Criminal Investigation.* Retrieved from BuzzFlash.com:
  http://www.truth-out.org/buzzflash/commentary/item/18387-new-revelation-that-
  attorney-general-eric-holder-is-protecting-jpmorgan-chase-nyc-from-criminal-
  investigation
Karmini, N. (2013, September 12). *Dutch apologize for colonial killings in Indonesia.* Retrieved
  from AP The Big Story: http://bigstory.ap.org/article/dutch-apologize-colonial-killings-
  indonesia
Kelo v. City of New London: Dissenting Opinion by Justice O'Connor. (2005). Retrieved February
  12, 2015, from Intellectual Takeout:
  http://www.intellectualtakeout.org/library/primary-sources/kelo-v-city-new-london-
  dissenting-opinion-justice-oconnor-2005
Kessler, A. (2013, January 3). *In the Privacy Wars, It's iSpy vs. gSpy Big Brother is watching us.
  But we are watching back.* Retrieved from The Wall Street Journal:
  http://www.wsj.com/articles/SB10001424127887323984704578206063994711952
Khatib, L. (2015, March 27). *Was the Middle East better off with its dictators?* Retrieved from
  CNN News: http://www.cnn.com/2015/03/27/opinions/yemen-mideast-
  dictators/index.html
Kingkade, T. (2014, October 23). *How Colleges Let Sexual Predators Slip Away To Other Schools* .
  Retrieved from HuffingtonPost.com:
  http://www.huffingtonpost.com/2014/10/23/college-rape-transfer_n_6030770.html
Kluger, B. (2005, November 24). *Phil Donahue got bounced off the air...* Retrieved from Timeout:
  http://www.timeout.com/newyork/film/out-in-left-field
Korn, D. (2013, August 28). *The Dark Side of "I Have a Dream": The FBI's War on Martin Luther
  King.* Retrieved from MotherJones: http://www.motherjones.com/politics/2013/08/j-
  edgar-hoover-war-martin-luther-king
Kovanis, G. (2014, January 26). *Cleavage rules! Enduring allure of women's figures gives them
  some measure of control over their lives.* Retrieved from Detroit Free Press:
  http://archive.freep.com/article/20140126/COL23/301260034/cleavage-season-
  kovanis-detroit

KPHO TV. (2010, September 2). *Jan Brewer, Arizona Governor, Has Ties To Private Prisons That House Those Locked Up By New Immigration Law.* Retrieved February 20, 2015, from HuffPostPolitics: http://www.huffingtonpost.com/2010/09/02/jan-brewer-arizona-govern_2_n_703251.html

Kramer, P. (2008, February 25). *The Water Cure .* Retrieved from The New Yorker: http://www.newyorker.com/magazine/2008/02/25/the-water-cure

Lachman, S. (2014, February 28). *Republican Lawmaker Apologizes For Saying Men Should Be Able To Rape Women If Abortion Is Legal.* Retrieved from HuffPost Politics: http://www.huffingtonpost.com/2014/02/28/lawrence-lockman-rape-_n_4874586.html

LaForge, J. (2013, April 12-14). *Inhuman Radiation Experiments: Contaminated Nation.* Retrieved from CounterPunch [Weekend edition]: http://www.counterpunch.org/2013/04/12/inhuman-radiation-experiments/

Larsson, S. (n.d.). *The Girl with the Dragon Tattoo.*

Levesque, W. R. (2009, May 29). *Camp Lejeune vets suffer from drinking water contamination .* Retrieved from Tampa Bay Times: http://www.tampabay.com/news/military/veterans/camp-lejeune-vets-suffer-from-drinking-water-contamination/1005564

Levine, G. (2015, February 24). *Chicago voters overwhelmingly endorse campaign finance reform .* Retrieved from The Scrutineer: http://america.aljazeera.com/blogs/scrutineer/2015/2/25/chicago-voters-overwhelmingly-endorse-campaign-finance-reform.html

Long, J. (2015, February 2). *My Journey With Securus: Prison Phone Monopoly Punishes Loved Ones.* Retrieved from Buzzflash @ Truth-Out.org: http://truth-out.org/opinion/item/28872-my-journey-with-securus-prison-phone-monopoly-punishes-loved-ones

Lutz, A. (2012, June 14). *These 6 Corporations Control 90% Of The Media in America.* Retrieved from Business Insider: http://www.businessinsider.com/these-6-corporations-control-90-of-the-media-in-america-2012-6

MacBica, C. (2014, March 21). *"Commemorating" the Vietnam War: One Marine's Perspective Friday, 21 March 2014.* Retrieved from Truthout: http://truth-out.org/opinion/item/22579-commemorating-the-vietnam-war-one-marines-perspective

MacPherson, K. (1999, November 21). *'The Plutonium Files' by Eileen Welsome .* Retrieved from Post-Gazette.com: http://old.post-gazette.com/books/reviews/19991121review372.asp

MahMag.org. (2008, October 6). Retrieved from Victor Jara and the Story of His Last poem: http://www.mahmag.org/english/worldpoetry.php?itemid=380

Mak, T., & Meredith, E. (2013, June 6). *Dianne Feinstein on NSA: 'It's called protecting America'.* Retrieved from politico.com: http://www.politico.com/story/2013/06/dianne-feinstein-on-nsa-its-called-protecting-america-92340.html

Marshall, A. G. (2013, April 12). *The Propaganda System That Has Helped Create a Permanent Overclass Is Over a Century in the Making.* Retrieved from AlterNet: http://www.alternet.org/media/propaganda-system-has-helped-create-permanent-overclass-over-century-making

Martens, P. (2012). "Obama's Money Cartel". In J. Frank, & J. St. Clair, *Hopeless and the Politics of Illusion* (pp. 14-22). Oakland: AK Press.

Mason, J., & Rampton, R. (2015, March 9). *Obama Declares Venezuela A Threat To U.S. National Security.* Retrieved from HuffPostPolitics: http://www.huffingtonpost.com/2015/03/09/obama-venezuela_n_6831890.html

Mason, M. (2015, April 30). *Vietnam Celebrates 40th Anniversary Of War's End With Enormous Parade.* Retrieved from World Post: http://www.huffingtonpost.com/2015/04/30/vietnam-war-40-anniversary-parade_n_7180270.html?utm_hp_ref=world

McAuliff, M. (2015, April 13). *Lawmakers Who Seem To Have Forgotten Iraq Insist They're Right About Iran.* Retrieved from HuffPost Politics: http://www.huffingtonpost.com/2015/04/13/iran-nuclear-talks_n_7044180.html

McCormick, J. (2014, January 23). *Yacht Owners Seek to Salvage Deduction for Second Home.* Retrieved from Bloomberg.com: http://www.bloomberg.com/news/articles/2014-01-23/yacht-owners-seek-to-salvage-deduction-for-second-homes

McDowell, A. (2013, September 29). *Saudi cleric says women who drive risk damaging their ovaries.* Retrieved from Reuters Yahoo: http://news.yahoo.com/top-saudi-cleric-says-women-drive-risk-damaging-092329183.html

Melville, H. (1851). *Moby Dick.*

Merica, D., & Hanna, J. (2013, August 4). *In declassified document, CIA acknowledges role in '53 Iran coup.* Retrieved from CNN Politics: http://www.cnn.com/2013/08/19/politics/cia-iran-1953-coup/index.html

Michels, R. (1962). *Political Parties.* New York: Collier Books.

Mirkinson, J. (2014, April 14). *The Media Is Still Dancing Around The Word 'Torture'.* Retrieved from HuffingtonPost: http://www.huffingtonpost.com/2014/04/14/media-torture-senate-report-cia_n_5138450.html

Mitchell, G. (2014, March 17). *A History of the "Friedman" Unit.* Retrieved from Pressing Issues: http://gregmitchellwriter.blogspot.com/2013/03/a-history-of-friedman-unit.html

Mitchell, J. (2012, May 18). *Agent Orange 'tested in Okinawa' Documents indicate jungle use in 1962 .* Retrieved from Veterans Today: http://www.veteranstoday.com/2012/05/18/agent-orange-tested-in-okinawa/

Mitchell, J. (2012, Dec 17). *Were U.S marines used as guinea pigs on Okinawa.* Retrieved April 1, 2015, from The Asia-Pacific Journal Vol 10, Issue, No. 2: http://www.japanfocus.org/-Jon-Mitchell/3868

Mufson, S., & Hamburger, T. (2014, December 11). *Jamie Dimon himself called to urge support for the derivatives rule in the spending bill.* Retrieved from Washington Post Wonkblog: http://www.washingtonpost.com/blogs/wonkblog/wp/2014/12/11/the-item-that-is-blowing-up-the-budget-deal/

Murphy, M. (2014, February 8). *BREKKIE WRAP: Miss Venezuela 2013 beauty queen contestant Wi May Nava sews mesh to tongue .* Retrieved from Gold Coast Bulletin: http://www.goldcoastbulletin.com.au/brekkie-wrap-miss-venezuela-2013-beauty-queen-contestant-wi-may-nava-sews-mesh-to-tongue/story-fnj90t7b-1226821177140

Nasiripour, S. (2015, April 26). *HuffPost Politics.* Retrieved from Troubled For-Profit Corinthian Colleges Shutting Down As Education Department Faces Bill: http://www.huffingtonpost.com/2015/04/26/corinthian-colleges-closing_n_7147380.html

NSC 5412, National Security Council Directive on Covert Operations. (n.d.). Retrieved from The Ratvil Times: http://www.ratical.org/ratville/JFK/USO/appC.html

OpenJurist.org. (2015, March 17). *Open Jurist.* Retrieved from Gavlick v Continental Can Company: http://openjurist.org/812/f2d/834/gavalik-j-a-t-w-w-e-c-a-h-j-a-b

Parry, R. (2013, February 21). *How Reagan Promoted Genocide.* Retrieved from Consortium News.com: http://consortiumnews.com/2013/02/21/how-reagan-promoted-genocide/

Patton, S. (2014, February 13). *A Little Valentine's Day Straight Talk.* Retrieved from The Wall Street Journal: http://www.wsj.com/articles/SB10001424052702303496804579369420198599600

PBS. (n.d.). *People & Ideas: Henry Ward Beecher.* Retrieved February 22, 2015, from PBS: http://www.pbs.org/godinamerica/people/henry-ward-beecher.html

Peeples, L. (2014, March 7). *U.S. Armed Forces Sickened After Fukushima Meltdown Get Help From Online Fundraising.* Retrieved from HuffPost: http://www.huffingtonpost.com/2014/03/07/fukushima-navy-radiation-fundraising_n_4916401.html

Penn Treaty . (n.d.). Retrieved March 10, 2015, from Peace Treaty Museum.org: http://penntreatymuseum.org/wordpress/history-2/peace-treaty/

Persson, J., & Lazic, N. (2015, March 30). *Pearson, ETS, Houghton Mifflin, and McGraw-Hill Lobby Big and Profit Bigger from School Tests.* Retrieved from PR Watch: http://www.prwatch.org/news/2015/03/12777/reporters-guide-how-pearson-ets-houghton-mifflin-and-mcgraw-hill-are-profiting

166

Phillips, D. (2013, May 19). *Disposable Surge in discharges includes wounded soldiers*. Retrieved from The Gazette: http://cdn.csgazette.biz/soldiers/day1.html

Phillips, D. (2015, April 22). *Few People Lost Jobs With V.A. in Scandal*. Retrieved from nytimes.com: http://www.nytimes.com/2015/04/23/us/few-people-lost-jobs-with-va-in-scandal.html

Pilger, J. (2003, Septmber 19). *Kissinger and Chile: In an Age of Vigilantes, There Is Cause for Optimism*. Retrieved from Truthout: http://www.truth-out.org/opinion/item/18933-in-an-age-of-realists-and-vigilantes-there-is-cause-for-optimism

Pilger, J. (2014, October 11). *From Pol Pot to ISIS: US Bombing Puts "Anything That Flies on Everything That Moves*. Retrieved from Truthout: http://www.truth-out.org/news/item/26738-from-pol-pot-to-isis-us-bombing-puts-anything-that-flies-on-everything-that-moves

Pilger, J. (2014, February 8). *The accessories to war crimes are those paid to keep the record straight*. Retrieved from johnpilger.com: http://johnpilger.com/articles/the-accessories-to-war-crimes-are-those-paid-to-keep-the-record-straight

Prins, N. (2014). *All the Presidents' Bankers: The Hidden Alliances that Drive American Power*. New York: Nation Books.

Protess, B., & Silver-Greenberg, J. (2014, March 4). *A Standoff of Lawyers Veils Madoff's Ties to JPMorgan Chase*. Retrieved from The New York Times: http://dealbook.nytimes.com/2014/03/04/standoff-of-lawyers-veils-madoffs-ties-to-jpmorgan-chase/

Pruszewicz, M. (2014, October 7). *The 1920s British air bombing campaign in Iraq*. Retrieved from BBC News Magazine: http://www.bbc.com/news/magazine-29441383

Raushenbush, P. (2013, December 15). *Don't Call Us Marxist Because We Critique Capitalism -- Call Us Christian*. Retrieved from HuffPost Religion: http://www.huffingtonpost.com/paul-raushenbush/pope-francis-unfettered-capitalism_b_4449643.html

Reich, R. (2015, January 6). *Why the Trans-Pacific Partnership Agreement Is a Pending Disaster*. Retrieved from HuffPost Politics: http://www.huffingtonpost.com/robert-reich/why-the-transpacific-part_b_6422088.html

RepresentUs. (n.d.). *One City. One Big Win. Now It's Your Turn*. Retrieved March 1, 2015, from represent.us: https://represent.us/action/tallahassee/

Roberts, J. (2004, June 1). *Enron Traders Caught on Tape*. Retrieved from CBS News.com: http://www.cbsnews.com/news/enron-traders-caught-on-tape/

Robles, F. (2014, September 30). *Kissinger Drew Up Plans to Attack Cuba, Records Show*. Retrieved from Nw York Times: http://www.nytimes.com/2014/10/01/world/americas/kissinger-drew-up-plans-to-attack-cuba-records-show.html

Rockwell Jr, L. H. (2007, April 23). *Sic Semper Tyrannis* . Retrieved from The American Coneservaive: http://www.theamericanconservative.com/articles/sic-semper-tyrannis/

Rogers, W. (2015, April 2). *Our Land, Up for Grabs*. Retrieved from nytimes.com: http://www.nytimes.com/2015/04/02/opinion/our-land-up-for-grabs.html?_r=0

Rohter, L. (1998, April 3). *4 Salvadorans Say They Killed U.S. Nuns on Orders of Military*. Retrieved from The New York Yimes: http://www.nytimes.com/1998/04/03/world/4-salvadorans-say-they-killed-us-nuns-on-orders-of-military.html

Salter, J. (2012, October 4). *Secret Cold War tests in St. Louis raise concerns*. Retrieved from Yahoo News [AP]: http://news.yahoo.com/secret-cold-war-tests-st-louis-raise-concerns-214608828.html

Sanders, B., & Weissman, R. (2015, January 21). *Five Years After Citizens United, Billionaires Are Buying Democracy*. Retrieved from Huffingtonpost.com: http://www.huffingtonpost.com/rep-bernie-sanders/five-years-after-citizens_b_6516246.html

Sara, S. (2014, March 25). *Facing the Past*. Retrieved from ABC: http://www.abc.net.au/foreign/content/2014/s3971320.htm

Scheer, R. (1965). *How the United States got Involved in Vietnam*. Santa Barbara, CA: The Fund for the Republic, Inc.

Scheer, R. (2013, August 20). *The Moment the U.S. Ended Iran's Brief Experiment in Democracy.* Retrieved from Truthdig: http://www.truthdig.com/report/item/the_moment_the_us_ended_irans_brief_experime nt_in_democracy_20130819

Schmidt, E., & Sanger, D. (2014, January 19). *Congressional Leaders Suggest Earlier Snowden Link to Russia.* Retrieved from The New York Times: http://www.nytimes.com/2014/01/20/us/politics/congressional-leaders-suggest-snowden-was-working-for-russia.html

Seidel, J. (2014, January 2). *Chilly MSU fans swarm returning Spartans with green gratitude.* Retrieved from Detroit Free Press: http://archive.freep.com/article/20140102/COL38/301020133/rose-bowl-michigan-state

Seldes, G. (1967). *The Great Quotations.* New York, New York, USA: Pocket Books.

Sharp, K. (2013, October 12). *Living the Orwellian Life* . Retrieved from Truthout: http://www.truth-out.org/opinion/item/19211-living-the-orwellian-life

Shen, A. (2012, August 4). *Private Prisons Spend $45 Million on Lobbying, Rake in $5.1 Billion for Immigrant Detention Alone.* Retrieved from TruthOut: http://truth-out.org/news/item/10688-private-prisons-spend-45-million-on-lobbying-rake-in-51-billion-for-immigrant-detention-alone#

Simkin, J. (n.d.). *The Palmer Raids.* Retrieved February 15, 2015, from Spartacus Educational: http://spartacus-educational.com/USApalmerR.htm

Singh, H. S. (2014, February 3). *Indian woman and baby burned alive for dowry, police say.* Retrieved from CNN: http://www.cnn.com/2014/02/02/world/asia/indian-burned-alive-dowry/index.html

Smale, W. (2015, April 19). *Gene Simmons from Kiss: 'I live to make more money'.* Retrieved from BBC News: http://www.bbc.com/news/business-32301157

Something rotten The hustlers and parasites who make up Washington's political establishment. (2013, August 24). Retrieved from The Economist: http://www.economist.com/news/books-and-arts/21583978-hustlers-and-parasites-who-make-up-washingtons-political-establishment-something

Speier, J. (2012, June 21). *Why rapists in military get away with it.* Retrieved from CNN: http://www.cnn.com/2012/06/21/opinion/speier-military-rape/index.html

Stone, I. (n.d.). *"Comparison to Walter Lippmann".* Retrieved February 6, 2015, from IF Stone: http://www.ifstone.org/

Strack, D. (1982, March). *Federal Government Assistance For The Building Of The Union Pacific Railway.* Retrieved April 6, 2015, from UtahRails.net: http://utahrails.net/articles/up-land-grants.php

Taibbi, M. (2014, November 6). *The $9 Billion Witness: Meet JPMorgan Chase's Worst Nightmare.* Retrieved from RollingStone.com: http://www.rollingstone.com/politics/news/the-9-billion-witness-20141106

Taibbi, M. (2014). *The Divide: American Justice in the Age of Wealth Gap.* New York: Spiegel & Grau.

Teachout, Z. (2015, January 26). *Legalized Bribery Zephyr Teachout on Sheldon Silver, Corruption and New York Politics.* Retrieved from The New York Times: http://www.bing.com/search?q=Legalized+Bribery&form=APMCS1

ThinkExist.com. (n.d.). *Hermann Goering Quotes.* Retrieved from http://thinkexist.com/quotation/naturally_the_common_people_don-t_want_war/339098.html

Tummarello, K. (2014, May 18). *Feinstein blasts critics of NSA phone program 382401.* Retrieved from The Hill: http://thehill.com/policy/technology/206434-a-surveillance-program-or-not

Uhlmann, D. M. (2013). *Deferred Prosecution and Non-Prosecution Agreements and the Erosion of Corporate Criminal Liability.* Retrieved February 16, 2015, from Maryland Law Review: http://digitalcommons.law.umaryland.edu/cgi/viewcontent.cgi?article=3578&context= mlr&sei-redir=1&referer=http%3A%2F%2Fwww.bing.com%2Fsearch%3Fq%3DDavid%2BM.%2 BUhlmann%2B%2522Deferred%2BProsecution%2Bmryland%2BLaw%2BReview%26fo rm%3DAPMCS1#search=%22David%20M.%20Uhlmann%20Deferred%20Prosecution%20mryland%20Law%20Review%22

University of College, Cork. (n.d.). *"Emancipation, Famine & Religion: Ireland under the Union, 1815–1870."*. Retrieved February 7, 2015, from Multitext Project in Irish History: http://multitext.ucc.ie/d/Famine

Vetlawyers.com. (2013, December 5). Retrieved from Bergmann & Moore Client Testifies Before Congress: http://www.vetlawyers.com/bergmann-moore-client-testifies-before-congress/

Wade, L. (2014, January 6). *You'd Be Shocked at What These Fashion Editors Are Editing Out of Their Photos*. Retrieved from HuffPost Style: http://www.huffingtonpost.com/lisa-wade/youd-be-shocked-at-what-these-fashion-editors-are-editing-out-of-their-photos_b_4542067.html

Wallace, K. (2015, April 11). *Parents all over U. S. 'opting out' of standardized student testing*. Retrieved from CNN News: http://www.cnn.com/2015/04/17/living/parents-movement-opt-out-of-testing-feat/index.html

Walsh, N. P. (2014, October 23). *Heads line streets of ISIS capital Source: CNN*. Retrieved from CNN: http://www.cnn.com/videos/world/2014/10/23/pkg-walsh-raqqa-syria-life-under-isis.cnn

WantToKnow. (n.d.). *Washington Post Owner Katharine Graham Advocates Secrecy in Press and Government*. Retrieved April 11, 2015, from WantToKnow.info: http://www.wanttoknow.info/secrecygraham.shtml

Wasserman, H. (2014, February 26). *Documents Say Navy Knew Fukushima Dangerously Contaminated the USS Reagan*. Retrieved from EcoWatch: http://ecowatch.com/2014/02/26/navy-knew-fukushima-contaminated-uss-reagan/

Watkins, T., & Mungin, L. (2012, December 28). *U.S. Navy sailors sue Japan over nuclear accident*. Retrieved from CNN News: http://www.cnn.com/2012/12/28/world/asia/japan-fukushima-lawsuit/index.html

Wedel, J. R. (2009). *Shadow Elite*. New York: Basic Books.

West Mick, A. (n.d.). *Context: "If people really knew, the war would be stopped tomorrow"*. Retrieved from Metabunk.org: https://www.metabunk.org/threads/context-if-people-really-knew-the-war-would-be-stopped-tomorrow.545/

Williams, T. (2015, March 30). *Steep Costs of Inmate Phone Calls Are Under Scrutiny*. Retrieved from nytimes.com: http://www.nytimes.com/2015/03/31/us/steep-costs-of-inmate-phone-calls-are-under-scrutiny.html

Wilson, R. (2014, May). *A Conversation with James Webb*. Retrieved from AARP Bulletin : http://www.aarp.org/politics-society/history/info-2014/james-webb-interview.html

Wolf, N. (2012, December 29). *Revealed: how the FBI coordinated the crackdown on Occupy*. Retrieved from The Guardian: http://www.theguardian.com/commentisfree/2012/dec/29/fbi-coordinated-crackdown-occupy

Wolff, L. (1960). *Little Brown Brother: America's Forgotten Bid for Empire Which Cost 250,000 Lives*. London: Longmans, Green and Co Ltd.

Wren, C. S. (1990, May 24). *Mandela Conciliatory in Talk to Business Leaders*. Retrieved from The New York Times: http://www.nytimes.com/1990/05/24/world/mandela-conciliatory-in-talk-to-business-leaders.html

WSVN TV. (2014, January 14). *Hollywood, Florida Police Discover Untested Rape Kits Dating Back To 2005: Report*. Retrieved from HuffPost Miami: http://www.huffingtonpost.com/2014/01/15/untested-rape-kits-florida_n_4602541.html

www.ingramcontent.com/pod-product-compliance
Lightning Source LLC
Chambersburg PA
CBHW060855280326
41934CB00007B/1052